In the Name of God
The Archbishop Who Armed the PLO

Translated and edited by Adel Beshara
Original interviewers
Sarkis Abouzeid and Antoine Francis

In the Name of God
The Archbishop Who Armed the PLO

Sarkis Abouzeid & Antoine Francis

Translated and edited by
Adel Beshara

First published in Arabic under the title
"Archbishop Hilarion Capucci: My Memories from Prison"
(Beirut: Dar Abaad, 2018).

Copyright © 2019 Black House Publishing Ltd

All rights reserved. No part of this book may be reproduced in any form by any electronic or mechanical means including photocopying, recording, or information storage and retrieval without permission in writing from the publisher.

ISBN-13: 978-1-912759-28-6

Black House Publishing Ltd
Kemp House
152 City Road
London
United Kingdom
EC1V 2NX

www.blackhousepublishing.com
Email: info@blackhousepublishing.com

Dedicated to the

'Children of the stones'

who keep Capucci's dream alive

Contents

Preface	7
Introduction	11
1 - An Orphan in Aleppo	19
2 - The Arrest	35
3 - The Interrogation	53
4 - The Trial	65
5 - Prison	85
6 - Reflections From a Rotten Prison Cell	105
7 - Letters from Prison	117
8 - Freedom	179
9 - In Exile	189
10 - Political Stances	205
11 - The Indefatigable Archbishop	227
12 - Death	243
Index	249

Preface

In 1974, Israel convicted a native of Aleppo, Syria, and a Melkite Greek Catholic archbishop in Jerusalem named Hilarion Capucci of using his diplomatic status to smuggle arms to Palestinian militants in the occupied West Bank. Capucci was given a 12-year jail term in December 1974, but he was released after serving three years of his sentence following a personal appeal from Pope Paul to Israeli President Ephraim Katzir. Vatican representatives began negotiating with Israeli officials shortly after Menachem Begin became premier. Informed sources said that Katzir agreed to free Capucci under four conditions:

1. He not be permitted to make anti-Israeli propaganda for the Palestine cause;
2. He be given a religious post far from the Middle East;
3. The Pope officially request the release; and
4. The Pope's letter not deny Capucci's guilt.

Soon after Capucci's release and transfer to Rome, two Lebanese journalists and close friends, Sarkis Abu Zeid and Antoine Francis, approached him in Rome for a biography of his exploits and remarkable courage. Capucci agreed, and in a series of taped interviews conducted in 1979 at his residence in the Monastery of Sisters of the Cross in Rome, he furnished them with the details of his life and ordeal as a prisoner in an Israeli jail. The Archbishop of Jerusalem opened up and recounted his personal experiences in a very frank and intimate way. He shared with the two journalists both his frustrations and triumphs without boasting or diatribes. He told his story as it was. His only condition to the interviewing journalists, which they fulfilled in a professional manner, was that he be allowed to look over the manuscript prior to publication.

In the Name of God

Toward the end of 1979, a French publishing company agreed to publish the book under the title L'Archevêque revolutionnaire (The Revolutionary Archbishop). However, just prior to publication, the Archbishop reversed his position and asked the two journalists to put the book on hold due to circumstances "beyond my control." Apparently, on learning of the book, the Vatican pressured Capucci to abandon the project lest it jeopardize its relations with Israel, as a book of such ambition and consequences was considered a potential breach of the agreement that led to Capucci's release. The Archbishop acceded to the Vatican's request, and in turn, the two journalists acquiesced to Capucci's request. Thus, the final manuscript was stored away "in an old wooden box" for 38 years.

Upon Capucci's passing on the first day of 2017, the two journalists retrieved the manuscript and organized its publication in Arabic in time for the Beirut International Book Fair the following December. In their introduction, they cite three reasons for publishing it after such a long interval:

1. Until now, no book has appeared dealing with Capucci's life or describing his tribulations in Israeli prisons.

2. A true fighter whose name and life struggle have become a symbol of Jerusalem (the city he loved and served with all his heart, mind and conscience to the very end) deserves tribute and recognition.

3. The memoirs contain some valuable and highly confidential details for scholars and laypersons alike, and these details should be disclosed for the sake of historical accuracy and authenticity.

I am deeply grateful to Sarkis Abu Zeid and Antoine Francis for giving me permission to render the book in English. This book is neither a history narrative nor a comprehensive autobiography. Rather, it is a biographical account of a very eventful and stormy

Preface

period told in the voice of its protagonist. The narrative travels through familiar social and political territory. Capucci takes the reader back to his childhood and explains how he joined the ecclesiastical hierarchy and why he became intimately involved with the Palestinian cause. In an "honest-to-God" trip into the dark side of Israeli occupation, he exposes its crimes and excesses before the world.

The actual events and plot of the narrative are as relevant today as they were four decades ago. Most importantly, the narrative reveals the mindset of a very determined and principled man of religion who was undaunted by fear and driven forward by faith and who risked his life for the sake of his people.

Because the recorded recollections end in 1979, two extra chapters are added here to complete the account. The first, entitled "The Indefatigable Archbishop", provides a concise reconstruction of Capucci's life struggles from 1979 to 2017, and the second deals with his death.

This book will make you consider many aspects of human life: courage, determination, faith, oppression, injustice, indifference, integrity, and the final goal of existence. It is a damning indictment not only of Israeli oppression, but also of the international community for allowing this oppression to continue while ignoring its brutality and rampant violations of the most basic human rights and humanitarian laws.

Given his relentless quest to promote the Palestine cause in the West, I am certain Archbishop Capucci would be delighted with the decision to render his narrative in English.

Introduction

God in Heaven and Palestine on Earth

"God and Palestine" are two powerful words that capture the spirit of the late Archbishop of Jerusalem, Hilarion Cappuci.[1] In a checkered career that is as well documented for its unprecedented accomplishments as it is for its decidedly endless affection for activism and sacrifice, Capucci served "God and Palestine" with gladness and singleness of heart. His devotion to them was absolute. It never wavered with time or dimmed with hardships. God strengthened Capucci's faith in Palestine, and Palestine brought him closer to God. The more devoted to God he became, the stronger his devotion to Palestine. The bond between God and Palestine in his heart and mind was so intense and total that it influenced and shaped his personality and outlook on life until the very end.

*****

In 1967, Jerusalem – the spiritual capital of the world – fell to the invading Israelis. The invasion turned into a permanent occupation and the occupation into a blood-soaked disaster. In the early days of the occupation, the people in Jerusalem were disillusioned. They did not know how to behave under the new conditions. The clergy, in particular, were uncertain and confused. Under the leadership of their respective institutions, they carried out a policy of cautious collaboration with the invading Israelis based on international law[2] for occupied nations. However, after

---

1   Capucci's love for Palestine was evident from the priestly name he adopted for himself. Hilarion was a Christian saint born in South Gaza in 32AD during the Byzantine era. Remnants of the St Hilarion Monastery, known in Arabic as Tell Umm Amer, stand today in the Gaza Strip as testimony to the fourth-century monk.

2   The Hague Convention of 1907

only a few weeks, it became apparent that the Israelis did not intend to withdraw or respect elementary human rights. Instead, they undermined international law and implemented a policy of the gradual Judaization of Jerusalem and the establishment of new Jewish settlements in and around it.

In this situation, the clergy had to choose whether to compromise with the occupants or join the upwelling resistance. Systematically, the resistance movement began to challenge the occupying power's lies, injustice, and arbitrary use of violence. The majority of the clergy reacted against the strong pressure exerted on their consciences by means of self-control and ideological ecclesiastical conformity. Some of them found the courage to speak out against the occupation, but their protests went unheeded. It was left to the Melkite Archbishop of Jerusalem, Hilarion Capucci, to step up and provide the leadership needed to drive and sustain the process of resistance.

Why Capucci? First, no organization, state, or individual tried to recruit Capucci or elicit his help. He was neither pressured nor persuaded to join the anti-occupation resistance. The decision was entirely his, but the implementation was in collaboration with others, specifically the Palestine Liberation Organization (PLO). Thus, the answer to "Why Capucci?" lies with Capucci himself. From his narrative, one can surmise three possible triggers:

1. A personality predisposed to rebelliousness and risk-taking. By his own admission, Capucci developed a defiant streak from an early age that was hard to suppress and continued to his manhood. The years of his training and preparation for an ecclesiastical life and his ordination into the priesthood gave him a new way of looking at the world, but it failed to curtail the defiant streak in his personality and thinking. Despite his appointment as Archbishop of Jerusalem, he continued to express his personal convictions and engage in nonconformist conduct spurred on by the urgency of the struggle against Zionist colonization.

Introduction

2. A progressive understanding of Christianity. Although Capucci belonged to the Melkite Catholic Church, which combines Catholic and Orthodox rites and remains under the authority of the Vatican, he also subscribed, knowingly or unknowingly, to the school of "liberation theology." He considered Christianity not a passive message of love and forgiveness, but an agenda for social and political activism concerned for the liberation of oppressed peoples. Like other liberation theologians, Capucci saw Jesus' life and ministry as both boldly progressive and revolutionary. Did Jesus not speak to centers of political power and challenge the religious authorities of the day? Did He not challenge the rich and powerful and place himself consistently on the side of the poor and oppressed? Did He not defy the Pharisees by nullifying a large section of the Levitical law and substituting a new principle in its place? The perception of Jesus as a revolutionary crusader against injustice and oppression provided Capucci with the theological legitimacy to translate the deep truths of the Christian faith into action with a clear conscience.

3. Attachment to Jerusalem. Capucci's deep local knowledge and love for Jerusalem influenced his attitude no less than theological and patriotic considerations. His attachment to Jerusalem was more than administrative and ephemeral. He regarded the city as the spiritual centre of "Christianity" in the full theological sense of the word and served it according to such a perception. Capucci did not deny the Jewish connection to Jerusalem, but he was deeply sentimental and protective of the city's Christian identity. When the city fell to the Israelis in 1967, it triggered deep feelings of rage in him and an indefinable urge to act, especially as organized Judaization began and Jewish settlements started to expand into Palestinian territories.

Capucci was an audacious leader with strategic capability, ecumenical experience, and persuasive power. His unique personality equipped him for new and difficult tasks. He combined spontaneity of heart with dauntless, firm leadership within his parish. However, his sense of immediacy and spontaneity sometimes brought him into unexpected difficulties. By 1974, he had received many stimulating and helpful commendations for his personal courage, church leadership, and theological thinking. Nonetheless, his weapons smuggling gamble took everyone by surprise, not the least his own Jerusalem parish and the Melkite Church. The Vatican, the Eastern Orthodox Church, and the Islamic world were stunned by the audacity of the act. Mostly, clergymen who engage in political activism let alone military activism tend to elicit opposition from two sources:

1. The laity through declining attendance and decreasing financial contributions

2. Higher church authorities through measures designed to punish the individual and prevent a repetition of the behavior and action.

In Capucci's case, opposition from neither source materialized. Despite the gravity of his act, both the laity and his ecclesiastical superiors stood by him. His Jerusalem parish remained fully loyal and snubbed any calls for his replacement. Its members demonstrated in the streets demanding his release, and both Moslems and other denominational Christians joined the chorus of disapproval of his arrest and conviction. Similarly, Capucci's superiors in the Melkite hierarchy refused to condemn his action or to sanction the Israeli response. They continued to recognize Capucci as Archbishop of Jerusalem and to seek his release urgently. The Vatican, too, bestowed a modicum of legitimacy on the act by endorsing the position of the Melkite Church.

This show of solidarity with Capucci was a measure of the love and respect he commanded. The nature and intent of his action was also crucial. Almost everyone felt that he acted purely out of religious and moral considerations rather than for personal gain

Introduction

or prestige. Furthermore, there was confidence that anti-Semitic feelings played no part in his decision. In his own mind and heart, Capucci believed he was doing the right thing. His objective was purely devotional (1) to his High God, Jesus, who stood for him as a paragon of struggle against injustice, and (2) to Palestine, the country he had come to regard as his own and served with grace and integrity. Indeed, Capucci's life and work rested on the two axioms "God and Palestine." Everything he did revolved entirely around them: a simple case of "God in Heaven and Palestine on Earth."

From this perspective, Capucci's action cannot be considered deviant or terroristic. It was an act of courage and wisdom motivated by benign intentions. On the one hand, it was a personal statement against the injustice inflicted on the Palestinian people, and on the other, it was an advocacy for the dignity of man and the necessity of truth and fairness. Beyond that, the act achieved several important objectives that Capucci may or may not have intended:

1. It attracted public attention and help to build an attitude of resistance among the people.

2. It gave impetus to a theology of activism that emphasized man's role as a partner with God in the fight against injustice.

3. It presented a theological and ecclesiastical basis for a deeper commitment to, and involvement in, struggles against foreign occupation.

4. It raised questions concerning Jerusalem's spiritual and political identity.

5. It belied western projection of Palestinian struggle as Islamic.

6. It created a renewed sense of solidarity between Christians and Muslims in the Arab world.

7. It jolted Christian supporters of Israel into an awkward position.

8. It embarrassed Israel before the world community by reviving memories of the pastors, priests, and bishops who willingly sacrificed their lives resisting the Nazi persecution of Jews in the name of divine justice.

Critics will almost certainly argue that Capucci went too far: that he crossed the red line and broke every rule in the book. Such a subjective assessment cannot be used credibly in this particular case because the moral duty to confront oppression, flagrant injustice, violence, and foreign occupation can sometimes be stronger than the obligation to use religious sanctioned means. As Weber once noted, "In numerous instances the attainment of "good" ends is bound to the fact that one must be willing to pay the price of using morally dubious means or at least dangerous ones." When "dubious means" are elicited to fight evil ends, the propagators of evil must be condemned and punished rather than those who stand up to them and risk everything to foil their evil plans. Where the evildoer is clearly visible and unrepentant, as in the present case, canonical guidelines take a backseat.

To condemn Capucci would be to condemn every clergyman and theologian in history who stood up to illegitimate tyranny, repression, foreign occupation, and state-sanctioned violence. Almost every one of them was compelled to resort to "dubious means" to achieve noble goals. We hail them as heroes today because they risked everything to make a difference. They risked their lives and some even paid the ultimate price to give us the freedom we enjoy today. Their efforts and sacrifices should not be forgotten or judged according to codified religious laws. It is the larger moral issues that matter: the meaning and purpose they added to make religion more relevant and humane.

Like them, Capucci was a hero because he used his clerical robe – or church-registered vehicle – to great effect. He saw no point

Introduction

in preaching brotherhood and love while ignoring the plight of his people. The church had to live its theology by matching its words with deeds, not by acquiescing in traditional loyalty and servility. Concern for others is a good indicator of religiousness and spirituality, not a negation of true faith. Christian love is best expressed through efforts to eliminate injustice, not through passive worshipping and torpid theology. Not only did Capucci understand Christianity in those terms, but he also practiced it in those terms. Hence his famous words: "Jesus Christ was the first fedayee. I am just following his example."

What Capucci did and how he did it is hardly important: it is the courage and dignity of his action that matter. His act vindicated the dynamic principle, long held and commonly accepted in the Christian faith, that service to God entails faithful service to one's country. Cardinal Francis Spellman once articulated this principle:

> Morale means courage, readiness to serve, high purpose. Morals is the sense of right and wrong, divinely taught, which makes a man strong in his duty to God, and morale makes him strong in his duty to country . . . Religion and patriotism support and strengthen each other.

Therefore, if we must condemn, we should not condemn Capucci. He set an outstanding example of coupling faith with patriotism. Instead, we should condemn the Israelis who forced him to do what he did through their own illegal and unjust actions. The aggressor should be shamed and punished, not the victims of aggression. Accordingly, the invading and oppressive Israelis should be shamed and punished, not the undeserved sufferers of their brutality. Furthermore, the Israeli violation of Palestinian human rights should be shamed and punished, not the casualties of the violation. Finally, the perpetrators of violence and repression should be shamed and punished, not the persecuted and recipient targets. This is what Capucci represented and stood for. He served as a voice not only for Palestinian rage and frustration, but also as a voice against the silence of the international community toward Israel on the one hand and against the indifference of the Christian world toward the systematic Judaization of Jerusalem on the other. What can possibly be more heroic and dignified than fighting for your country and faith simultaneously?

*****

In short, Capucci belonged to the unique breed of "clergymen" who take their religious beliefs very seriously, in words as well as deeds. They are the human angels of divine peace, the dynamic voice of the church, and the heavenly protagonists in the fight for dignity and justice. Their efforts might not always be appreciated or recognized, but their courage cannot be faulted. The work and sacrifices of this group of people give meaning and purpose to doctrinal belief and help to popularize religion as a "theology for life" rather than as a "life for theology."

Capucci's narrative captures all the aspects of this prophetic vocation. The aspects appear in different stages of his narrative and reinforce each other to form the foundations for a complete account. He discusses each aspect candidly and genuinely without regret or hesitation. He does not mince words or try to sugarcoat his story, but he tells it as it happened and is undaunted by how he might be judged or remembered. The honesty, transparency, and sense of contentment and joy he felt from describing the events of his life render the narrative both interesting and compelling.

*****

Capucci passed away on the first day of 2017. He rose to "God in Heaven" and left behind him a tattered "Palestine on Earth."

1 - An Orphan in Aleppo

"Destiny to some people is a preconceived notion as a design of blind faith, while in fact destiny is a constitution of endowed efforts in an attempt to steer toward a desired outcome. Create your destiny and reach for your dreams, you only live once."
— Husam Wafaei (Canadian Syrian Human Rights Advocate)

I

My mother ... the first influence in my life

I was born on March 2, 1925, in the Syrian city of Aleppo. My birth name was George Capucci, and I was the second of three siblings (the eldest Antoine and the youngest Rizqallah). My father, Bashir, passed away in the prime of his life when I was only five. Thus, my mother, Chafika, who was widowed at the age of 25, raised me. I still remember the face of my kind father whose death was a tremendous shock that cast a heavy shadow of grief over my childhood. It left me lonely, drifting, and vulnerable in a barren land.

My mother, God rest her soul, dedicated her entire life to her three sons. Her reply to whoever gave her advice to get married was, "A woman who has three men in her home does not need a fourth."

My father owned three taxicabs, which my mother sold after his death. We lived on a portion of the proceeds for a short time. Then she bought a sewing machine, placed it in a corner of our house, and started making clothes for the neighbors in addition to her house chores. She was a very ambitious woman who decided to enroll us in the best schools despite our humble circumstances. She worked very hard to secure our tuition fees, so we received our elementary education in the Collège des Frères Maristes (School of the Marist Brothers) in Aleppo.

Thanks to our mother, we never felt that we were deprived orphans, and our appearance was never inferior to our classmates at school. She worked diligently to give us a comfortable life and proper standing in society. We were the pivots of her life, and she vowed that life to us in every way without consideration to anything but our happiness. I do not recall ever returning home without finding her working at her sewing machine or preparing a meal for us. She embodied the spirit of sacrifice in the absence of our father.

My mother took the best care of us: assuming the roles of both father and mother. She gave of her effort and energy the way a father does while overwhelming us with the enormous affection and compassion of a mother. She was conscious of her double responsibility: thus combining firmness with compassion in the way she raised us. As compassionate as she was, she gave us a firm, solid upbringing. I hold her sacred, and I sense her powerful influence on my life. Her memory remains with me wherever I go.

I was a naughty child, constantly getting into brawls with the neighborhood children and fellow students. The principal used to say, "If there is trouble, then George Capucci must be behind it."

At home, I was never a quiet, silent child. I was always protesting. I would scream and object to my mother's firm decisions by saying, "No sooner than we leave the school bell behind we would face the home bell. We live in a constant state of alert."

My mother was very strict in disciplining me: beating me at times. Her painful slaps would bring me back to reality and force me to be a responsible person. I remember those sweet slaps and say to myself, "Perhaps if it weren't for my mum's slaps, that boy wouldn't have become this man today."

1 - An Orphan in Aleppo

Every time my mother reprimanded me, my maternal grandmother, who lived with us, would intervene. She would say to her daughter, "There is a limit to severity. It is impermissible to break the child and weaken his character; however, a light slap is necessary only to alert him so that he would not make the same mistake again." She would then take me in her arms, comfort me, and tell me a story or teach me a lesson from the pearls of wisdom, or she would narrate an anecdote that embodies the principles of honesty, morals, and respect of parents.

From my simple grandmother, I learned spontaneity. From her deep expressive stories, I learned the meaning of tolerating pain and misfortune. Many times, especially while in prison, I have remembered her stories and felt the lessons learned from her tales and proverbs.

One evening she said to us, "I love you so much my sons that I wish torment and pain for you." When she saw our astonished faces, she explained, "Laziness and lethargy are products of an easy comfortable life free of toil. Torment and pain, my sons, make men. The cruelty of life can only be overcome by the strong." Many times, she narrated to us real stories about people she had known personally so that we would learn a lesson from them and brace ourselves to face adversity and hardship. We would listen to her with childish joy and amazed eyes, but with the passage of time, I realized the great value of my grandmother's stories and that she was a second school for me.

In the Name of God

II

On the Path of Christ

In 1933, while I was still naughty and quarrelsome at home and school, my school announced that an optional religious test would be conducted for students. Whoever had the cultural and moral qualifications would be accepted to study at a seminary. Though I was only eight, I felt a strong desire to walk the path of the Lord, so I applied for the test.

Cardinal Coussa in Aleppo administered my test. At the time, he was a priest with administrative duties in the Congregation for Eastern Churches in Rome before he was later ordained archbishop and then cardinal. I passed the test and they summoned me to join the Basilian Aleppian School in Deir el-Chir Monastery near the city of Aley in Lebanon.

At first, my mother opposed me leaving Aleppo and moving to Lebanon. She wanted me to stay near her with my two brothers and she felt that my removal from her would be deadly, as if someone was ripping a vein off her heart. However, she yielded in the face of my insistence and stubbornness. For the rest of her life, my mother, may her soul rest in peace, would recall that day when I told her of my decision to join the seminary. After my release from prison, she narrated that incident to all those who came to congratulate her on my freedom. In her beautiful Aleppian dialect, she would say: "George was ten when clergymen came to his school in Aleppo in search of new priests. He came home and said to me, 'Mum, prepare my stuff. I wish to go with the clergymen and be a priest.' I said, 'No, my dear, you're not going anywhere.' But he went with them and became a priest."

I moved from our small Aleppian home to the boarding school, and a new phase in my life began. I was transformed from the rowdy George Capucci to the orderly George Capucci. I wished to become a priest rather than a physician or an engineer, because

1 - An Orphan in Aleppo

I believed a priest prepares men for society. In the world of priesthood, the roads are laid out for giving and exertion more than in any other field. The harvest on the Lord's path is plentiful but the harvesters are few. By nature, I love to serve people, and I find pleasure and joy in helping them.

I was a diligent student from the start: fully committed to performing my duties. However, I was a pioneer in anger and composure out of a dislike to be subservient. The rebellious boy inside me never calmed down. My rejection of all forms of oppression and tyranny and transgression on people's rights never subsided. The least violations would incite my anger, and they still do: propelling me to intervene spontaneously to fix whatever is fixable.

I received my preparatory and secondary education in the Basilian Aleppian School between 1933 and 1942. Then I moved to Saint Anne's Seminary in Jerusalem where I studied philosophy and theology for five years. Upon concluding my theological studies, I was ordained as a priest in 1947, and my name became Hilarion Capucci.

III

I witnessed the King David Hotel bombing

I fell in love with Palestine when I was a 17-year-old seminary student and moved to Jerusalem to be groomed for priesthood at Saint Anne's Seminary. Over the years, my relationship with Palestine took root, and my attachment to it, its people, and the Palestinian cause was established because I was a witness to its tragedy from the very beginning.

I became attached to this good land for two main reasons. First, it is part of the greater Arab world to which I belong with a mystic passion. It is a holy oasis and the meeting point of divine religions. The land of Palestine is a summary of our history and an embodiment of our beliefs, and it is our major cause. Second, Palestine was the target of evil ambitions that sought to devour it and turn its people homeless.

While I was studying in Jerusalem between 1942 and 1947, the hands of Zionist terrorism started to reach deep inside Palestine. International Zionist organizations worked to realize the dream of "the Kingdom of David" and turn the theory of "the Promised Land" into reality in order to create the Jewish Hebrew state on the ruins of the Arab land of Palestine. I felt from the beginning (and I still do) that my duty as a Christian priest and as a human being was to stand up to evil in all its forms and to fight it with all my power.

Inside the monastery, we were isolated from what was happening outside. However, news of the tragic events and the terrorist attacks of Zionist mobs would pass the high walls of the seminary with the breeze and reach us students like the rustling of leaves. We would shudder with pain and discuss the current events in secret during break times, because we were strictly forbidden from discussing politics. Although the spiritual fathers were sensitive to the painful events and reacted to them, they were cautious of their spread among us lest they weaken and distract us from our main goal of studying theology and philosophy.

On July 22, 1946, the Irgun Zionist organization, headed by Menachem Begin, blew up the King David Hotel in Jerusalem, which housed the headquarters of the British forces in Palestine. I was the only student who ventured outside the walls of Saint Anne's Seminary that day. Something stronger than me pulled me out, so I went to see the explosion site. I saw the destruction and the bodies of the 90 British and Arab victims and was overcome by immeasurable pain.

The scene of the horrendous explosion shook me deeply as I watched paramedics pull bodies out from under the debris.

1 - An Orphan in Aleppo

I envisioned the impending danger to Palestine from those criminals who targeted the headquarters of the ruling British authorities without mercy and as indifferent to the death of innocent victims. Their goal was to deal a brutal strike to the British to force them to withdraw as a first step to pave the way before the rise of the state of "Israel." Thus, they invented a new school of terrorism, which they continued to perfect throughout their long criminal history!

Upon my return to the Seminary, the Monastery principal reprimanded me strongly (perhaps because I wore my clerical uniform to the explosion site). He said, "You shouldn't have gone there. You are a clergyman and we are neutral." I answered, "But it is my land. They are blowing up my land. How can a person be neutral when his homeland is in danger?"

That painful day was imprinted in my memory and initiated my involvement in the Palestinian cause. For the first time, I personally witnessed the terrorism of the barbarians tearing up my homeland. Following that incident, I penned some diary entries about the accelerating Zionist terrorism, and I embraced the just cause of Palestine with my heart and soul.

After my ordainment as a priest, I left the seclusion of the monastery and joined public life. I became an activist in Jerusalem on all levels: societal and ecclesiastical. At the time, people were unaware of political affairs and the extent of the danger threatening their homeland, so I started urging them to unite and to sacrifice. I preached to them about Jesus Christ who was born, lived, and was crucified in Palestine. In my Sunday sermons, I emphasized that the Jews were the ones who crucified Jesus and they were the enemies of both Christianity (since its inception) and Palestine. Today, I say with absolute conviction that "Jesus Christ was the very first Palestinian fedayee (self-sacrificing patriot)."

In the Name of God

IV

I Lived Through the Nakba (Catastrophe) of 1948

On July 27, 1947, I moved from Jerusalem to Lebanon. I returned to the monastery at Deir el-Chir near the city of Aley where I had begun the path of priesthood 14 years earlier. I was appointed director of the National Nahda School affiliated to the monastery, and I transformed it within a few years from a preparatory school to a boarding secondary school.

In the first months of 1948, the Irgun, the Haganah, and other Zionist paramilitary mobs repeatedly attacked Palestinian villages. They forced people out of their homes and destroyed them to construct colonies to house the Jews arriving from Europe under the auspices of the International Zionist Organization. On June 15, 1948, war broke out between the Arab countries and the Zionist mobs when David Ben-Gurion announced the establishment of the state of "Israel" and the end of the British mandate over Palestine. Catastrophe struck.

The Zionists committed a series of atrocious massacres, especially in the villages close to Jerusalem and Haifa. The most notorious of those massacres were in Deir Yassin and Kafr Qasim. They carried out gory terrorist attacks that triggered a forced mass exodus of Arab inhabitants from their lands. The Palestinian refugees fled to neighboring countries and lived in dismal conditions in camps erected at city entrances. A large number sought refuge in Lebanon. Living in Deir el-Chir at the time, I witnessed the tragedy of that exodus up close. I was confronted again with the Palestinian misery with all its elements: starvation, poverty, homelessness, and humiliation. I felt the inhumane condition of the Palestinian individual and the depth of the Zionist crime committed against our homeless people. I helped Palestinian refugee families as much as I could, and I took a large number of Palestinian student refugees into the Nahda School. I also secured a bus to transport them from the camp near Beirut to the school campus in Aley.

1 - An Orphan in Aleppo

V

The era of Gamal Abdel Nasser and Abdel Hamid al-Sarraj

In 1952, I returned to my childhood homeland: settling there for almost ten years. My first stop was in Damascus where I was appointed assistant to His Eminent Beatitude, Patriarch Maximus Sayegh. I was his right hand and Patriarchal Secretary for the villages adjoining the capital. In accordance with my new duties, I established firm relations with Syrian statesmen, political leaders, and officials. Despite the constant change of Syrian officials because of the successive coups that Syria witnessed in that era, my relations with the different regimes were characterized by positivity and respect, since they were motivated by the desire to secure services for the citizens of different sects regardless of political inclinations and their repercussions.

Among my outstanding achievements in that phase of my life was my diligent effort and perseverance to consolidate the presence of our church congregation in their villages. To that end, I constructed a church, a school, and a rectory in most of the villages surrounding Damascus. However, my many ecclesiastical duties did not distract me from the Palestinian cause and the situation of the Palestinians. I tried in every way possible and in collaboration with all parties to extend help to the Palestinian refugees in Syria. I provided them with means of living, housing, medical treatment, and education out of my conviction that we were one family facing the same destiny.

Many events unfolded in succession in my beloved Syria over the ten years that I spent as Patriarchal Secretary in Damascus. Undoubtedly, the most prominent of these was the declaration of the Syrian-Egyptian Union, signed by Presidents Shukri al-Quwatli and Gamal Abdel Nasser in Cairo in 1958. On February 22, 1958, the "United Arab Republic" was born under the leadership of Egyptian President Gamal Abdel Nasser.

In the Name of God

I met President Nasser twice. The first time was in Cairo in 1959. I was in the company of His Eminent Beatitude Patriarch Maximus Sayegh. We had a long session with him discussing the general affairs of Syria. The second meeting was in Syria in 1960. It was a private intimate session wherein I became closely acquainted with the President's amicable charismatic personality. That session with the President of the United Arab Republic (UAR) took place in the home of the Syrian Minister of Interior, Abdel Hamid al-Sarraj, who later became Vice President. We were well-acquainted at the time given that I was the general supervisor over his children's school which was managed by our church in Damascus.

Abdel Hamid al-Sarraj was the strong man of Syria. He headed the intelligence agencies collectively along with his position as Vice President of the northern sector of the UAR. He regulated the law enforcement agencies and imposed on Syria a police system that terrorized everyone. Despite everything that people were saying about him and about his power – nicknaming him "the Red Sultan" – a good relationship developed between us that was marked by mutual respect.

I never asked Minister Sarraj for any personal favor. Instead, I used my acquaintance with him to serve people. Some individuals who were pursued by the authorities unjustly came to me for help. Some were suspected of conducting political activities hostile to the incumbent regime; others were ordinary citizens banned from leaving Syria for different reasons. I would take the just demands to Minister Sarraj and present the people's grievances to him. By virtue of our mentioned friendship, many services were rendered, and I helped all those I could.

One day, a weeping woman came to the Patriarchal headquarters. She told me that her husband had been in detention for a long time pending interrogation and that he was subjected to violent forms of torture. He was accused of distributing anti-regime fliers although he did not belong to any party and was not engaged in any political activity. I called Minister Sarraj and he expressed

1 - An Orphan in Aleppo

immediate concern. Investigation revealed that the man's charges were based on a fabricated rumor. The torture was meant to extract information he had no knowledge of. The detainee was immediately discharged and Sarraj asked me to apologize on his behalf to those concerned. He asked me to let him know of every fault that I learned of because he wished to do injustice to no one.

I once asked Minister Sarraj, who was very close to President Nasser, to arrange a meeting for me with the President. I held the President in high regard and had much respect for him, and I wished to get to know him more closely. A few days later, he sent his private car to take me to his house where President Nasser was having dinner. We held a long session and talked about many things. Most prominently, we discussed the consolidation of the Syria-Egypt union. We talked about how we could enhance it to attain full public support and how we could gain genuine support for it from Syrians versus mere acceptance. We also discussed regional sensitivity and the risk it posed for the union's endurance. I conveyed the opinion of the Syrian citizen who was starting to feel the overbearing pressure of Egypt over Syria.

Nasser was conscious of this matter, but he was convinced that it would evaporate after the establishment of union institutions and the development of national awareness. I realized that he was a sincere human being and an authentic Arab: however, a group of self-seeking opportunists surrounded him, presented fake reports, and gave him a false image of the situation in the country. Our meeting was quite delightful and had a profound impact on me. I praised his genuine sense of Arabism, his broad horizons, his charming simplicity, and his amazing modesty.

He was the man who transformed Pharaonic Egypt into an Arab center of gravity and gave pan-Arabism its status in the world. His ambition was to fuse the whole Arab world into one crucible ... but this broad ambition scattered his strengths, depleted his energies, and dispersed his efforts in various directions. It would have been more worthwhile had he focused his attention on the internal situation in Egypt and given priority to building a solid centralized state that presents a role model for all the states he sought to lure to the UAR. Had he succeeded in demonstrating the importance of unity by highlighting its beauty and power, he would have motivated the rest of the Arab states to join his grand pan-Arabian endeavor, which promised to achieve internal prosperity and external power for the entire region. Had he focused his efforts in this direction, he would have served his pan-Arabism in the most comprehensive manner. But, unfortunately, his ambitions were larger than reality, his concerns scattered in different directions, and his enemies many.

I met President Anwar Sadat twice when he was Vice President to Nasser and I was in the company of Patriarch Sayegh. The first time was in Damascus in 1960 and the second in Cairo in 1961.

VI

Superior General ... Archbishop of Jerusalem

In 1962, I was elected Superior General of the Basilian Aleppian Order and returned to its original headquarters in Deir el-Chir in Lebanon. I held that office for three years, during which I led a life of ascetic priesthood behind the monastery walls. I was almost secluded from the outside world: leaving the monastery only once a week. I tried to restore monastic life to its early beginnings when it embraced asceticism, total devotion to worship, carnal abstinence, pure spiritual giving for the sake of God, and complete submission to His teachings and will.

I believe in the necessity of the existence of covert soldiers serving society. They are worshipers who evoke the blessings of the Lord and His pleasure upon people through prayers and asceticism. It is impossible to dispense with those who devote themselves to prayer and piety just as a fighter devotes himself to revolution.

1 - An Orphan in Aleppo

Despite my seclusion in the monastery, I felt that I was in the heart of the world so long as the prayers that we raised to the Lord were intended to guide the world on the paths of goodness. We prayed that our Lord would bless people's minds, hearts, and consciences with guidance to righteousness and piety. We were striving through prayers: an endeavor that was of no less value than the efforts of any member of society. For each, there is a role and a function.

Despite my constant presence in the monastery, my relationship with the afflicted Palestinian people did not suffer. I used to visit refugee camps and assemblies regularly, and I tried to alleviate their pains and provide them with necessary aid.

Before completing my six-year term as Superior General, I was elected Archbishop of Jerusalem on August 22, 1965. My consecration ceremony was held on July 5, 1965, and I was simultaneously appointed Vice Patriarch for Roman Catholics in Jerusalem.

I arrived in Jerusalem on July 10, overjoyed to be back in the land that I had loved and cherished since my youth. I felt that Palestine was my destiny and that immense responsibilities awaited me there. I decided to carry them out in the best way possible and to work with all my might to serve the Palestinian people.

VII

I Buried 400 Martyrs in Jerusalem ... and the Course of My Life Changed

Catastrophe struck on June 5, 1967: a defeat that caused a serious change in my life. I witnessed the fall of beloved Jerusalem to barbaric Israeli occupation. I felt that a mighty will had drawn me to this holy city to be a witness to its wounds every time it bled ... which was indeed painful.

In the Name of God

I followed the military operations through binoculars from the Patriarchate's roof. The operation to occupy Jerusalem started on the evening of Monday, June 5, with the Israelis gradually advancing into its neighborhoods until they entered the Old City of Jerusalem on Thursday, June 8. The enemy forces reached the French Hospital on Friday, June 9, and the fighting ceased.

The Israelis imposed a curfew on the city. After several attempts, they gave us permission to go out, and I was the first person to go out of his home after the invasion. I wandered through the streets of the stricken city, witnessing its tragedy and trying to wipe away some of the agony from its forehead. The martyrs still lay on the streets covered in blood. Their bodies were scattered on the pavements everywhere: staring at the sky in wait of someone to return them to the dust. Not a single official was there to undertake the simplest of humane duties after the massacre. Therefore, I worked with the nuns and priests and some laymen to bury the martyrs in holes that we dug in different parts of the city.

Along with a Sheikh (Muslim clergyman), we simultaneously prayed for the souls of the martyrs before burying them. The blood of the Palestinians mixed with the soil of Palestine as if it were one single drop. Denominations and religions unified at the altar of martyrdom in the face of a savage enemy. At the time of disaster, one cannot differentiate between martyrs' denominations and religions.

The burial efforts went on for four days, during which we lowered not less than 400 martyrs into the ground without losing heart. After burying our dead, we turned to helping the homeless and needy. One week later, we established a charity organization for humane assistance in the city of Jerusalem. I was elected its president and received help from Archbishop Pellegrini and Fathers Rock, Julian, and Batih. We started with providing basic provisions, giving out financial assistance to needy families, repairing houses, and rebuilding the Islamic quarter (the Gate of Remission or Bab al-Huttah).

1 - An Orphan in Aleppo

Later, after I was appointed president of the global social services organization affiliated to the Catholic Church called Caritas, my activities expanded. We discarded the idea of extending financial assistance because we perceived it to be somewhat humiliating to the recipients. We replaced it with interest-free loans to help those who had lost small businesses. We established cooperative charity organizations such as the "Women's League" in some West Bank cities. We purchased sewing machines and employed women to provide for families afflicted by the occupation. To add a patriotic dimension to this effort, we brought in fabric from Lebanon and turned it into clothes and sheets that embodied Palestinian folklore in defiance of the enemy and in confirmation of the Arab identity of Palestine in the face of Judaization. I used to bring the fabric in my car, take the finished products to Beirut to be sold in Lebanese markets, and then return and distribute the revenues to those entitled to them.

Israel's plan was to dislodge people and force them to flee towards Jordan. Emigration accelerated in waves. The Israelis would prepare buses and shout at people: "Come on. Go to Amman."

My concern was the human beings first. Nevertheless, I did not neglect the stones. I worked hard to restore the Patriarchate headquarters that had suffered damage during the war. I repeatedly visited Lebanon and Syria and raised the funds necessary for the restoration efforts. I also developed the school and built a guesthouse that was more like a hostel to receive pilgrims to the Holy Land. It was popular among pilgrims from Europe because of its location in the center of the Old City.

However, the real struggle was in confronting the Israeli occupation that tightened around us relentlessly. The Israelis violated all sanctities and mocked our rituals and traditions insolently. I felt the nightmare of occupation from the first moment as we reached a state of humiliation and persecution beyond endurance. Three days after the occupation of Jerusalem, I was driving in the streets of the holy city wearing my clerical robes when an Israeli soldier approached me and spat on me. I got out of the car and pounded him with the cane until he fell to the ground. I realized that everything I did seemed very little in comparison to the brutality of the occupation. Silence was no longer possible. As far as I was concerned, neutrality was tantamount to collusion. Day after day, I became convinced that the invaders would not be deterred save by the whip. Violence is inevitable to crush them and crush their brutality.

They occupied our land and killed our young and old, but they did not destroy the spirit of resistance inside us.

2 - The Arrest

I

The bitter struggle between bishop and rebel

The 1967 war altered me deeply and changed the course of my life. I had never expected that I would wake up on the morning of June 5 to find Jerusalem and the West Bank no longer in Arab hands. They were now under the control of "Israel." Overnight, we were no longer part of the Hashemite Kingdom of Jordan; rather, we have become residents of the "Occupied West Bank." Jerusalem, the cradle of all divine religions, was now under Jewish control.

Military occupation changed the face of the city and altered its features. Its brutal fingers left painful scars in the hearts of its residents. I felt this new reality tearing at the veins in my heart, and I had to do something to combat the occupation.

That year I endured a long, bitter struggle. Every day I asked myself, "What should I do? I am a clergyman and the pastor of an eparchy in Jerusalem. I am the Archbishop of Jerusalem. What is my real role in a situation like this? Barbaric feet have trodden our lands and occupied our most sacred sites. They exert pressure on the citizens, on my sons, and terrorize them. Do we make peace with them? Do we remain silent? Or do I take the road of passivity?"

Many questions conflicted inside me in the first months after the occupation of Jerusalem. It was a time of push and pull between different attitudes, and I ultimately chose the toughest road: the road of struggle.

After the 1967 war, escalating fedayee operations were a thorn in the Israelis' side. The fedayees would come from outside the occupied bank. They would cross the Jordan River and walk long distances to execute military operations in the occupied Palestinian territories. The Israeli citizen felt threatened and voices grew loud demanding action to stop fedayee operations. The Israelis had to take security measures to prevent the fedayees from reaching their targets, so they placed barbed wire along the border and installed an electronic belt to prevent infiltration.

Over time, the occupation tightened its grip on the occupied bank and made it very difficult for a fedayee to reach his targets. If he tried to cross the barbed wire, the electronic devices would expose him. If he managed to get past the electronic devices, he faced minefields along the west bank of the river. If he were fortunate enough to survive those fields, he was chased by border police patrols, which were in a continuous state of alert. If he could evade those as well, he would fall into the hands of army patrols or be captured at the many barriers the Israelis had set up. They had taken extreme security precautions to prevent resistance forces from getting through. Hence, it was necessary to counter those measures with appropriate plans, and our primary goal was to secure cells that would cooperate with the resistance inside the occupied territory.

II

From my immune position, my relationship with the resistance began

In the early days of fedayee operations, young fedayees would come from outside, execute their operations, and then return to Jordan without any inside cell cooperating with them or extending help. However, over time, coordination between the occupied territory resistance and the brothers coming from outside became an extremely urgent necessity. Realizing this, I decided to partake

2 - The Arrest

in the resistance and offer what help I could from my immune position in the Archbishopric of Jerusalem.

The key figure in founding the resistance movement in the occupied territory was Mustafa Abu Firas, who had remained in Jerusalem after the occupation. He was the first activist against the Israeli presence in the holy city. When the Israelis arrested him for suspicious activities, they could not prove any charge against him. Despite the brutal methods they used in interrogation, they could not extract any confession from Abu Firas. He did not give any information, and they had no proof of his involvement in fedayee operations. Hence, they could not determine whether to put him in the so-called "administrative detention" or to release him for lack of sufficient evidence. They gave him the choice to be released and leave the occupied territory or to remain in prison. He chose to be released and leave for Jordan.

Upon his arrival in Jordan, I contacted him and we met in Amman. Our relationship developed quickly and we started coordinating our efforts. We realized from the very beginning that secrecy was the key to success. It was better that he did not know much about me or about those collaborating with me, and that I did not know much about him or his helpers. He had his group and I had mine, and we agreed that neither of us would interfere in the details of the other's activities.

I discovered that Abu Firas was a devoted freedom fighter with a glorious past. He was ardently protective of his people and filled with passion for the cause and every person who fought for it. I instantly felt close to him. Our relationship grew firmer continually. I was drawn to him by a solid bond that I felt deeply and intensely and by great trust. Any person who endures torture and harm for the sake of his homeland, who loves it, who fights for it, and who holds on to its soil to the point of martyrdom is a part of me. The land of Palestine was the bond between us.

As for "Abu Jihad," I met him a year later in Beirut. Upon my

In the Name of God

arrest, the Israeli authorities accused me of having a connection with the leader of the Black September Organization since they believed that Abu Jihad was the head of Black September.

At first, I worked alone inside the occupied territory without communicating with the Fatah movement. A group of fervent youth were with me who did not belong to any particular denomination or religion. They were all sons of Jerusalem who believed in the cause and chose to do something against the occupiers. We were not many at the outset: only a single active cell. It was a small simple organization with no name, no affiliation, and no objective save advocating an anti-occupation stance. We had no weapons and our initial activities were limited to distributing fliers and writing anti-occupation slogans on the city walls. I would leave Jerusalem every now and then to visit Arab countries, meet officials, and explain to them the situation in the occupied territory. In 1968, I met a large number of Jordanian, Syrian, and Lebanese officials.

III

My relationship with King Hussein... before "Black September"

At the start of the long journey, our relations with Jordan were firm despite the great difficulties the resistance members faced inside the Kingdom. I felt that the drowning man must hold on to "ropes of air." Throughout my meetings with Jordanian officials, I openly stressed that the West Bank residents resented the occupation and did not accept Israeli hegemony over them. I emphasized that we were an inseparable part of the Hashemite Kingdom of Jordan, that the only status we acknowledged and recognized was our former status, and that we wanted Jordan to become active at the international level to affirm our stance. We then drew up a document demanding unity of the two banks, had it signed by the dignitaries of the West Bank, and published it. This preceded the appalling massacres that took place in Jordan

2 - The Arrest

in September 1970 and their catastrophic consequences upon the Palestinian people. During that time, I used to meet with King Hussein and explain to him the real situation in occupied Palestine. We met several times. Whenever I went to Amman, I would phone him and head to the Palace to have a thorough talk with him. I would also meet with Prime Minister Bahjat Talhouni for the same purpose.

Among my Syrian contacts was Col. Ahmad Halawi, the intelligence officer who committed suicide with his wife after the 1973 war following the accusation of collusion in the Quneitra issue. I met repeatedly with him and relayed to him the information I had about the Israeli military forces and their locations and deployment. I used to receive such information from common citizens who had chosen to remain inside "Israel" in the occupied territory and outwardly showed cooperation with the occupation authorities. Some of us thought ill of them and accused them of melting into the Israeli society and of becoming Israeli, but this was not true. Remaining in their land was proof of their steadfastness. They lived under Israeli rule, yet their hearts remained with their sons and brethren in the diaspora. From these "collaborators," I received much information about military affairs, army deployment, location of bases "Israel" had constructed underground, and movements in the West Bank and inside Palestine. I would then relay this information to the Arab states concerned with the situation.

In Lebanon, I frequently met with President Charles Helou in the presidential palace, as well as some Lebanese army officers. I brought to President Helou's attention the hostile intentions of "Israel" against Lebanon because of fedayee operations launched from Lebanese territory. This was prior to the bombing of Middle East Airlines (MEA) aircraft at Beirut Airport.

In the Name of God

IV

Israeli enticements turn into terrorization

Since the first day of the West Bank occupation, I decided to strive to confront the occupier. I became active in different directions, whether through inside action or through collecting intelligence about the enemy that which I believed would help the neighboring states combat the occupation and restore usurped rights and pillaged lands. The first person I collaborated with since 1968 was Mustafa Abu Firas (as I mentioned earlier).

At first, our collaboration was limited to small-scale activity in the West Bank, especially Jerusalem. On June 5, 1968, the first anniversary of the occupation, we organized a huge protest that set out from the Hebron Gate and marched on to the cemetery at Gethsemane then to Zahra (Herod's) Gate. Thousands of Jerusalemites and West Bank residents participated. I walked at the forefront of the protestors beside the Grand Mufti of Jerusalem: thus symbolizing the spirit of unity. At the Zahra Gate, I gave a speech that was a shout from the deep. I strongly denounced the occupation authorities, demanded their departure from the sacred land, implored the citizens to hold on to the land, and urged them to persevere.

It was the first and grandest protest the occupying forces had seen and remained the largest, as it alerted the occupation authorities to the role of the West Bank residents. They started to forbid them from protesting or embarking on any action considered a defiance or rejection of Israeli existence. Moreover, the protest revealed my role to the Israeli authorities. They tried to be nice to me at first, but I was stubborn and refused to respond to them. My stubbornness amounted to collision and thus confrontation between us began. One day, the Secretary General of the Israeli Ministry of Religions visited me at the Archbishopric headquarters without a previous appointment. The purpose of the visit was to invite me to meet with Prime Minister Staff Yitzhak Rabin,

2 - The Arrest

but I refused to receive the Israeli government official. I sent my assistant, Father Peter Gregory, to meet him instead. Father Gregory said, "His Eminence the Archbishop does not see a reason for convening with you." The Secretary General left, angry and threatening, saying, "Tell Capucci this will cost him dearly."

The Israelis were unable to do anything against me personally in that period, because I was practicing my role as a Christian clergyman defending my existence in the holy city and conducting activities that are condoned by law and by the code of human rights. Therefore, they resorted to harming me in other ways, starting with oppressive practices against people who were close to me. The first such practice that affected me directly occurred in 1969 when they expelled my assistant, Father Naqoula Nasrallah, from Jerusalem suddenly and unjustifiably. They banished him from the West Bank because of his humanitarian efforts. On him, they found letters addressed to West Bank citizens whom they considered members of the Palestinian resistance. They thus considered him a link between the Palestine Liberation Organization (PLO) and the resistance in the occupied territory.

Actually, Father Naqoula was one of the most active freedom fighters and most hostile to the Israelis. His stances were not different from mine and of absolutely no less value. Since the first day of the occupation, he played a fundamental constructive role on the social, political, and anti-occupation levels. He would urge people to persevere and would distribute provisions, console the grieving, and extend every help possible. He would not let an occasion where he could denounce the occupation pass by without denouncing it. When he met a foreign journalist, he would express the resentment the Arabs inside "Israel" had for the occupation authorities. He did that many times: annoying the Israelis with his actions.

After banishing Father Naqoula, the Israelis kept threatening me with expulsion. They never asked me to cooperate with them. The most they asked of me was to be neutral (neither passive nor active) and to refrain from any activities opposed to their presence. Christian efforts annoyed them greatly because they found attentive ears in the West. Since the power of "Israel" was sustained by the moral halo that it was trying to gain abroad, it considered anyone who tried to tarnish its image a staunch enemy. The Israelis wanted me to be neutral because I was a clergyman and an opposition bishop on the inside who embarrassed them before western public opinion. When they failed to tame me and restrain my wild patriotic drive, in 1970 they asked Patriarch Hakim to remove me from my post in Jerusalem and send me outside the borders. Yet the Patriarch turned them down, and I remained steadfast and persevering in my solid stance. My cooperation with the resistance increased daily, and my anti-"Israel" stance grew sharper and fiercer.

V

I activated internal cells... so the Israelis decided to silence me

When it became difficult for the fedayees to cross the barbed wires, bringing operations to a standstill, we turned our focus to the internal cells. I held secret meetings and said to the youth, "We should not always seek external help and rely on a fedayee coming from Jordan to conduct operations in the occupied territory. A resistance movement must rise on the inside." I established the first inside cell in the city of Jerusalem and the meetings were held in the archbishopric.

The youth were determined and passionate, but they lacked arms. Initially, they manufactured simple local weapons, such as Molotov cocktails, which had low impact and exposed the fedayee to injury. Consequently, I decided to transport potent weapons from the outside to activate inside operations.

Since I had crossing privileges by virtue of my diplomatic

2 - The Arrest

passport and my car was not subject to inspection, I considered transporting the weapons myself and shared the idea with Abu Firas. He welcomed it. I went ahead and started transporting weapons and explosives across the Naqoura border crossing. The cell I had established carried out several operations before my arrest, and I was aware of them.

We had a guesthouse in Jerusalem, which was more like a hotel with the capacity to host 50-60 guests. Our visitors would come from all parts of the world and stay in the humble guesthouse because of its location at the heart of the Old City near the Church of the Holy Sepulcher. It was at the hub of all the activity, located in the midst of churches and religious landmarks. In addition to the family atmosphere that we provided to our guests who were mostly from Europe, I would sit with them and explain my stance towards the occupation authorities and my view of them and how they had usurped the rights of the Palestinian people. I would relate what the Arab citizen was suffering in terms of persecution and injustice at the hands of the occupation.

Everything I said reached the Israelis: infuriating them because they had no power to silence me. They started to be stricter with me: watching my every move and sending me more threats. I, in turn, increased my activities... until I fell into their snare.

They were extremely annoyed by the speech I gave at the Collège des Frères in Jerusalem on Mother's Day, March 21, 1974. Before thousands of people, I said:

> Our true mother is not the mother who gave birth to us; rather, our true mother is the land that we must love and hold on to and die for the sake of defending it... Jerusalem is Arab and will remain Arab even if under the yoke of Jewish occupation... We must not accept a non-Arab Jerusalem. "Israel" has desecrated the sanctities of Christians and Muslims and violated all human and ethical norms... Christians in Arab countries are citizens enjoying their

full rights just like Muslim citizens, whereas Christians in "Israel" are second- and third-degree citizens... Churches are desecrated, and our religious rituals are mocked and insulted... Jerusalem is Arab and will remain Arab. Verily, the Bank without its Jerusalem is like a human being without a heart; a mere corpse.

My speech drew a roaring wave of applause, and the audience carried me on their shoulders in a massive protest through the streets of the holy city. From that day forward, the Israelis held a grudge against me and decided to silence me.

I also printed fliers on the anniversary of the Balfour Declaration, denouncing the Israeli occupation of the holy land and calling upon resident Arabs to strive for the sake of God and country.

When Henry Kissinger, then US Secretary of State, visited Jerusalem, I called the dignitaries of the holy city to convene at the Patriarchate and addressed them saying:

> We must organize huge protests and go out to the streets holding black banners in objection to this visit... Israeli persecution of the Palestinian people will turn the moderate to an extremist and the extremist to a fedayee.

This meeting was quite disturbing to the Israelis. In its wake, I sensed a change in the way they treated me. The first such incident was at the Lebanese border in Naqoura. My car had a diplomatic license plate and the Vatican flag raised on the hood, so I was never bothered, especially when they were still trying to sway me in their favor or at least push me to be neutral. When I reached the border crossing, I would show my Vatican passport to the officer in charge and he would let me pass without any questioning or inspection. According to international law, they had no right to inspect me. However, after the Jerusalem convention, suspicion was obvious in their behavior and the way they treated me at the border.

2 - The Arrest

I arrived at the Naqoura checkpoint in the morning. Contrary to usual practice, the officer in charge asked me to open the trunk of the car. I refused, saying, "This is a diplomatic car. You do not have the right to inspect it." When the officer insisted, I said, "I will not enter" and turned and headed back to Beirut.

In Beirut, I called the Papal Consulate in Cyprus and related the border incident. The Consulate called Tel Aviv and objected to the way I was treated and the disrespect to my diplomatic persona.

The next day, I went back and crossed the border normally without inspection, but I did not let that incident pass in silence. Rather, I filed a complaint against the customs officer who wanted to open my car trunk. His superiors reprimanded him and deducted two days' pay from his salary.

When I was arrested months later and the weapons were confiscated from my car, this officer filed a lawsuit against his superiors. He demanded exoneration and financial compensation, claiming that he was right. He won the lawsuit.

I was treated differently at the Jordanian border as well. They often used to let me cross the bridge easily. It was sufficient that I showed my passport to enter the West Bank without questions, but they started to be stricter with me and to ask many questions before allowing me to enter.

I began to feel that I was being watched around the clock. I seriously thought about stopping at that point because I was targeted. However, at the same time, it was hard for me to do so because the Israelis had tightened their siege of the West Bank. It was no longer possible for fedayees to pass beyond the electronic strip because of heightened surveillance. The enemy had intensified the security belt at the borders, and a large number of youth were captured before executing their missions. Hence, the inside cells had to be activated. For these cells to become active and strong, they needed weapons ... How could I withdraw from battle while the cause was in dire need? Thus, I extended my hand to the cause and put my energy in the service of heroic young men who wished to stand up to a usurping occupation.

VI

Tardiness of the explosives expert led to my arrest by Israeli intelligence

Here, Archbishop Capucci falls silent and ceases to recount the details of weapon transportation in his car because of terms the Vatican had laid, which oblige him to remain silent about this topic. He is adamant on abiding by these terms to maintain his good relationship with the Holy See. The following details were related to us by a source very close to Archbishop Capucci who had knowledge of the innermost secrets of that interval. The source said:

Archbishop Capucci would make a telephone call from Amman to Beirut. "Abu Firas" would set the time for his arrival in Lebanon. Upon arriving in Beirut, he would immediately head to his mother's house in the Sodeco district in Achrafieh. As soon as he arrived there, Abu Firas would come to the house, drive the Archbishop's car to an unknown destination, and then return a few days later after packing the weapons in secret caches.

At the outset of the resistance efforts, when surveillance was light and Archbishop Capucci was able to cross the border without inspection, they placed the weapons in a suitcase in the car trunk. There was no caution at all. That was the case on the day the Archbishop turned back at the Lebanese border when the customs officer wanted to open the car trunk. Cappuci's composure enabled him to save the day, turn back, and call Cyprus to object to the treatment. The following day, he returned to the border with the weapons still in his trunk and crossed without inspection.

2 - The Arrest

When surveillance intensified, they started to hide the weapons inside the suitcases, so that if the surveillance officers opened the trunk, they would not find them easily. But the surveillance was not strict in the full sense of the word. Then came the third and final stage when Capucci sensed that the Israelis were following him and inspecting his car thoroughly. Abu Firas started to hide the weapons in different places in the car in a carefully planned, technical manner. They would be placed inside the front fenders, and then those fenders would be covered with metal plates (thus wedging the weapons in between). Alternatively, they would be placed on the engine hood and covered with metal plates or they would be placed inside the doors, which was the case that last time.

When the Archbishop crossed the border into Jerusalem, Abu Firas would send an expert to remove the weapons from the car and transport them to the fedayees. When Capucci was arrested and the weapons confiscated from his car, it was ten days after his arrival in Jerusalem. He was waiting for the expert to come and take the weapons out of their caches, but the expert was delayed and Archbishop Capucci fell into the hands of the Israelis.

VII

In the company of 30 kg of "TNT" in the July heat

Archbishop Capucci resumes recounting his memories of that time, saying:

I knew where the weapons were hidden, but I could not take them out as that task required an expert and he was late. I was driving the car in the peak of July heat in the streets of Jerusalem with a load of highly explosive TNT inside it. About 30 kg were hidden inside the car's hood, and there was an enormous risk that this substance would explode because of the heat from the engine. If it exploded, it would cause massive destruction, which was my worst fear. I was compelled to use that car so that everything would seem normal to Israeli surveillance. I did not want to attract their attention or give them reason to suspect me and wonder why I had switched my car immediately after my return from Lebanon.

The explosives expert was supposed to come two days after my return to Jerusalem. Ten days passed without him showing up, during which I felt that the surveillance of me was intensifying. I grew impatient and decided to head to Amman and make a phone call to Beirut to inquire about the issue. I left my car in Jerusalem and went to Amman in another car. There, I called Mustafa and we conversed in code. I said to him, "The patient needs the doctor, and no one understands his illness except this doctor. Why are you late in sending him? I'm on pins and needles." Abu Firas understood the message and replied, "The doctor has already gone to visit you."

I returned to Jerusalem on the evening of Tuesday, August 6. Upon arriving, I was told that the Israeli authorities had come looking for me. Then, I received a call from the papal ambassador who said to me, "Intelligence officers came looking for you here..." I realized then that something had happened and that the operation was compromised.

That evening, the expert arrived from Amman to dismantle the car and extract the weapons. He called me and said the password, but I told him to return whence he came. I told him in secret code that it was too dangerous. I said to him, "Your old father misses you greatly. It makes him cry how long you've been away from him. You must go to him immediately, no matter what the circumstances are. Go see him." He understood that the situation was dangerous and that he had to return. Hence, the next day, I alone fell into their snare and no one else was arrested with me. As to my arrest, it is a thrilling account.

2 - The Arrest

VIII

How the Israelis discovered the weapons cache in the car

It was the morning of Wednesday, August 7, 1974. As customary, I was on my way from my home to the Archbishopric in Old Jerusalem. I took the usual route, where I would cross police barriers without inspection by virtue of my diplomatic license plates and the papal flag raised on my vehicle.

Normally, I would not cross the barrier directly, since there would often be a long line of cars. Rather, I would pass them to cross from a side dust road outside the barrier without any obstruction. However, things looked different that morning. The number of soldiers at the barrier was multiplied and the side dust road that I used to take was blocked. A police officer stopped me and said in a firm voice in Arabic, "Get out."

I said, "I am Archbishop Capucci. I'm a diplomat and you have no right to stop me. Be polite when you speak to me." He answered in a fiercer tone, "We know who you are, so you'd better get out of the car willingly rather than by force."

I said, "Why do you want me to get out?" The Israeli officer looked at me with the ferociousness of a hungry wolf. With total confidence, he said, "You want to know why? Then look." With a violent move, he tore the leather cover of the car door, exposing the hidden weapons. He then said, "This is why. Are you convinced?!"

I was stunned. He knew exactly where the weapons were, as if someone had informed him or as if he had seen them being packed with his own eyes! Until this minute, this remains a mystery to me. Every day, I wonder, "How did the Israelis find out where the weapons were? Who told them? Did a spy give them this information? Did they eavesdrop on the phone call from Amman and decoded it? Was I under surveillance in Beirut and they noticed that my car was away from my home for days? Did they see me with Abu Firas when he returned with the car and I rode with him to a small road outside Beirut where he showed me where the weapons were hidden?" Even now, after my release from prison, I still do not have logical explanations for these questions.

The Israelis took me to the intelligence headquarters and the interrogation started. Immediately after my arrest, the Roman Catholic Patriarchate assigned the lawyer Aziz Shehadah to defend me. He was President of the Arab Bar Association in the West Bank. Two international lawyers from France also joined my defense counsel: (1) Roland Dumas who became French Foreign Minister ten years later in 1984, and (2) Christian Bourget, an international human rights advocate. To this day, I do not know who assigned these two to defend me or who paid their fees.

IX

My imprisonment was premeditated and predetermined

My imprisonment was neither accidental nor coincidental, nor was it the result of a series of events that intersected at a fateful point in time. Rather, it was premeditated and predetermined. I wrote a letter from prison with this meaning to my attorney, Aziz Shehadah. The highlight of that letter was the statement:

Before taking the first step and joining the ranks of the PLO, I fought a long psychological war with myself. I pondered over what I was embarking on. I contemplated the consequences of my actions. I was clearly aware that joining the ranks of the resistance and partaking directly in their work on the ground would have adverse consequences and a costly price, including prison. Nevertheless, I executed what I had planned, and I repeated it over and over again. Does that not mean that I walked to my destiny with open eyes and a conscious mind and with premeditation and predetermination?

2 - The Arrest

When I arrived at the Archbishopric in Jerusalem two years earlier, my first and foremost objective was to construct the premises and develop it, because I considered that my duty as a bishop. I did not receive sufficient earnings to secure daily expenses, pay the salaries of priests and teachers, cover the expenses of the schools and clubs, and start projects for new buildings. Nevertheless, I went ahead, and with the power of God, constructed a guesthouse that received pilgrims from all over the world and met modern standards. I also constructed one of the most beautiful churches in Jerusalem and built a private house for the archbishop, which cost me much effort, fatigue, and sleeplessness. I was about to finish the construction when I joined the fedayee efforts and everything came to a stop.

Before resolving to collaborate with the resistance, I went through a difficult struggle with myself. I was hesitant and confused. I asked myself many questions, thought deeply, and contemplated for a long time. I used to say to myself every moment, "What should I do? What is the right decision to make?"

On one hand, the bitter reality on the ground, my great love for Palestine, and my attachment to Jerusalem with its historical religious value and its legal status and global role were all urging me to commit myself to the brethren of freedom fighters and to share with them the honor of defending the sacred cause that I believed in. On the other hand, I did not wish to get involved to the extent of personal participation in the fight as long as I was perfectly doing my duty as an archbishop. I raised my voice every day, in every occasion, encouraging, inciting, guiding, denouncing, demanding, and helping, and I was active in social work through Caritas, which I presided over in Palestine for a long time. I was thus doing my full duty. Why then would I take this dangerous step that would entirely change the course of my life?

Ultimately, my conscience overpowered my reason and humanness, and I made my decision without regret because my conscience is the voice of God inside me. I went to prison by my own will, not by force, propelled by God through the voice of conscience.

In the Name of God

I did not randomly end up in prison. Rather, it was the work of a profound will that the mind cannot fathom. This was something I knew very well and was quite aware of. I knew where it would take me and what would happen. Therefore, I was not at all surprised when I was captured. I anticipated my imprisonment, and I wished to make of my prison cell a platform for the truth in the face of falsehood.

3 - The Interrogation

"His cross was ... his sword – he never carried a weapon in his life. He was a great man and lived by his convictions despite the tremendous amount of psychological and physical pressure that he was subjected to by the Israelis." – Suha Arafat

I

Seclusion Between Two Arrests

The first arrest, which took place on August 8, 1974, lasted only 17 hours. At 2 a.m., the Israelis released me to go home. They confiscated the weapons, and a Polish officer ordered me to be photographed next to them. I refused, because I realized the consequences of the picture if the international press circulated it. He threatened to beat me up if I did not comply. I saw evil gleaming in his eyes and realized that he meant what he had said, so I complied. They retained the car and a military police vehicle carried me to the Archbishopric.

My arrest relieved me. Before the arrest, I was living in a state of anxiety. The weapons were packed in my car along with a large quantity of explosives, and I awaited the expert to come and extract them but he did not arrive. They said to me: "Today, tomorrow... today, tomorrow..." until I fell into the Israeli trap. At that moment, the anxiety caused by the waiting and wondering ended and a new phase dictated by human nature began, because when a person is expecting something to happen, he lives in a state of confusion and doubt until the event happens. In a crucial moment, everything ends and life seems to restart. Thus, when I was detained at the barrier, I breathed a sigh of relief and said, "Finally, the crucial moment has come. My mission now is to face the new phase because it has become my new goal."

In the Name of God

I knew that my release a few hours after my arrest was a ploy or police tactic on the part of the Israeli occupation authorities. They wanted me to return to daily life so that they could watch my every move and tap my phone more thoroughly perchance they could uncover and arrest the members of the cell I was collaborating with.

I knew their goals and the purpose of my release. Hence, when I returned home, I cut every connection I had with the outside world and secluded myself in my room, refusing to receive anyone, regardless who it was, or to answer the phone. My assistant, Father Peter Gregory, gave the same reply to anyone who inquired about me: "The Archbishop is ill and cannot talk to anyone." My seclusion lasted for ten days, during which I frustrated the hopes of the Israelis. Despite round-the-clock surveillance, they discovered nothing. They could not identify any of my collaborators. Therefore, I remained the sole suspect in the case.

When the Israelis arrested someone in the West Bank, it was their customary practice to subject the detainee to intense beating and brutal torture leading to his collapse under their savage hammer, so that he revealed the names of his friends. I knew that, and I knew of many cases where low-ranking activists collapsed and revealed the names of senior members: thus unintentionally causing tremendous harm to the cause. Consequently, I exerted every possible effort to spare anyone else from falling into the trap of Israeli intelligence in which I had become both bait and prey. I went into total seclusion and adhered to silence to realize a superior benefit that dictated secrecy, for I possessed a godly resolve and a strength of faith that enabled me to persevere no matter how painful the torture. But I feared that one of my co-activists would contact me only to be later arrested by the Israelis. He would then collapse under torture and reveal information. Therefore, I cut every contact with the outside world and foiled the Israeli plan. They could not arrest anyone.

Between the first and second arrests, I broke the silence protocol

3 - The Interrogation

only once. I called one person, the Apostolic Delegate William Carew, and I visited him at the premises of the Apostolic Delegation in Jerusalem. I recounted to him everything that had happened to me and imparted to him the truth, saying, "The Israeli authorities found weapons inside my car. I denied having knowledge of their existence, but, given the way they arrested me, I believe that they have information about the case that I do not know of." I asked His Eminence to take the appropriate stance, so he said to me, "I have to consult with my superiors." I do not know what he did after I left him, because I went home and resumed my seclusion for a short time. When the Israelis realized that they would not achieve any result by continuing to watch me, they arrested me again.

II

Brutal interrogation in the "City of the Sun"

At dawn on August 18, 1974, an Israeli military group knocked at the Archbishopric's door in Jerusalem. They dashed in barbarically without even saying "good morning." The minute they saw me, they arrested me and handcuffed me without questions and then searched my quarters. They inspected the furniture piece by piece, but did not find anything of interest. I knew they would come sooner or later and therefore I had destroyed all the papers and documents that might incriminate me or tie me to any resistance brother. After concluding their search, they led me handcuffed to the prison in Beit Shemesh: a biblical city west of Jerusalem whose name translates to "City of the Sun." In 1950, "Israel" constructed a Jewish settlement there. This prison was notorious for being the site where military intelligence conducts its brutal interrogations with detainees who are considered a threat to the security of "Israel." In the prison, they put me in a narrow two-meter by two-meter cell with a damp floor, leaking walls and no window or any opening to let the sun in. I had to stay in darkness all day, which made it very difficult to move around. There was no bed in that room: only a straw mattress that reeked of something rotten.

This was intentional on their part to humiliate me and break my resolve. They wanted me to collapse at the threshold of my interrogation and divulge the names of my local collaborators. I knew that ... and I decided to stand my ground. From my first moments in the cell, I refused to sleep on the mattress and preferred to sleep on the floor. I held on to my clerical robe, which they wanted to replace with the prison uniform, but I categorically refused. When I grew tired of standing, I would lie down on the cold floor: choosing to expose my body to the narrow room's dampness rather than the foul stink of the mattress.

There was no book, table, or chair in the room. The food was not food in the true sense of the word: it was a mix of disgusting substances that was not even suitable for a dog's consumption. I was aware that my detention in the prison was a careful plan designed by the Israeli terrorist organization to humiliate me and push me to break down. They wanted to destroy my resolve, and they thought they were achieving their goal by inflicting physical fatigue on me, imposing psychological siege over me, and forbidding me contact with the outside world.

Their psychological war reached the peak of savagery when they banned me from keeping my prayer book: an action that violates all laws and international codes. I am a clergyman, and it is obligatory for me to recite my daily prayers. Jewish clerics are the most abiding by this religious right. Nevertheless, the Israelis refused to let me have a prayer book. This was a prelude to destroy my morale and weaken me psychologically and physically into a state of exhaustion and fatigue that would facilitate their interrogation task.

They used to take me to interrogation sessions abruptly and at different times (sometimes at midnight). I never knew when the heavy iron door would be opened and the soldiers would walk

3 - The Interrogation

in to take me to the interrogation room. It was a narrow dull room that resembled a concrete box. More than five military personnel would interrogate me at once. The sessions were long and continuous without the chance to rest or without a moment of silence. Their questions would pour on my head nonstop like a pounding hammer: clear concise questions revolving around the activities of the resistance cells inside the occupied Palestinian territories at all levels and focusing principally on the smuggling of arms.

They tried to determine how the smuggling operations were conducted, who my collaborators were, to whom I delivered the weapons, where the meetings took place, who distributed the communiqués, and who wrote the slogans on city walls. They tried different methods to force me to give them details about my local collaborators, but they did not extract a single word. Despite their brutality, I stood fast to the end. My faith and my resolve were stronger than their schemes and their savagery. Despite their barbaric methods, they could not arrest any person other than me in this case.

III

I refused to be released on condition of leaving Jerusalem

Four days after my arrest, a delegation arrived in Jerusalem from the Roman Catholic Synod that was held in Ain Traz in Lebanon. It consisted of the Archbishop of Latakia, Boulos al-Ashqar; Superior General of the Aleppian Order, Archimandrite Bartholamus Samaan; and Superior General of the St. Paul Order, Archimandrite Habib Pasha. They asked to convene with me, but the Israeli authorities refused to give them permission to meet privately with me. After intervention from the Vatican, the meeting was held on August 26 in the presence of the Papal Delegate in Jerusalem, Monsignor William Carew, and a large number of guards and Israeli intelligence officers.

In the Name of God

Though the meeting was under intense surveillance, one of the delegation members was able to whisper to me: "Deny all charges." As to the Papal Emissary, he addressed me reproachfully during the meeting saying: "How could you as an Archbishop and as the Archbishop of Jerusalem do what you did and smuggle weapons?" I answered firmly:

> I did it and I would do even more! I didn't do anything that the Israelis themselves haven't done before. What I did is something that they've already done before me. They started a school that I learnt from. They exceeded all human laws and conventions to take what they have no right to take and usurp the rights of others. If I take the same road to restore my usurped right, then what I do is not wrong; rather, it is a sacred duty.
>
> If the Israelis denounce their actions then, I, in turn, will denounce what I did. But they do not denounce their actions. They consider what they did as their duty. I, in turn, did not do more than try to restore my usurped right. Therefore, I am more right than they are.

The meeting with the Synod delegation lasted about half an hour. During it, the distinguished Fathers tried to make me understand implicitly that the Vatican was concerned with my case, and that the most appropriate way to close this case satisfactorily was to deny the charges.

I was still under interrogation when I received a second visit from a member of the Synod committee, Archbishop Boulos al-Ashqar. He came alone after the two Superior Generals, Samaan and Pasha, had returned to Lebanon and His Eminence remained in Jerusalem to follow the case. The Israelis permitted him to meet me in private, so he relayed an oral message from the Israeli authorities summarized as:

> On account of the Vatican's intervention, the Israeli

3 - The Interrogation

government will agree to release you on one condition; that you leave Jerusalem permanently and vow never to return to it for the rest of your life.

My immediate reply was:

I'd rather stay in prison and die in it than leave it to any place outside Jerusalem. I refuse even to go to any Arab country. I want to go back to my congregation, to my flock. Staying in prison among my children is more morally pleasing to me and more beneficial to my children.

I rejected the offer in preference for imprisonment in Jerusalem to freedom outside its sacred walls... but what would later happen, after years of imprisonment, was out of my control. Nay, it was, rather, against my will.

IV

I transported the Katyusha rockets that targeted Henry Kissinger

The brutal interrogation lasted a few days. Its second focus, after the smuggled weapons confiscated from the car, was the Katyusha rockets that were found in the woods opposite the King David Hotel during the meeting of the US Secretary of State, Henry Kissinger, with Israeli officials in Jerusalem. The two rockets failed to explode because of a technical error.

Arab young men had positioned those rockets in a wooded area facing the hotel with one of them targeting the Wailing Wall. But they installed them in a hurry and saw a man coming on the back of a donkey before finishing the job. So they rushed the installation process and left in a hurry: resulting in the failure of the rockets to explode.

After discovering the rockets, Israeli authorities arrested two Arab young men. They were brothers from the Malaabi family. In the woods, they found two leather suitcases that were used to transport those rockets. When the Malaabi brothers were confronted with those two suitcases, they were forced under torture and beating to confess that they had obtained them from the College des Frères in Jerusalem: the school affiliated to the Archbishopric.

After my arrest, the Israeli authorities considered me responsible for smuggling the Katyusha rockets which, had they exploded, would have caused an international crisis and a catastrophe in "Israel." They brought the suitcases and asked me: "Do you recognize these suitcases?" I could have answered in the negative, but I said: "Yes, I recognize them." In fact, I smuggled the Katyushas into Jerusalem, and I had mixed feelings during the interrogation. On one hand, I was compelled by the Vatican's request to deny all charges against me. On the other hand, I was wondering: Why should I deny these charges as long as I do not feel any guilt? What I did was a right established by all laws, especially ecclesiastical laws. It is the right to self-defense. Therefore, I did not deny what I did because I was convinced that I had done my duty. I did not set up Katyushas at the offices of El Al Airlines in Paris or in Munich; rather, it was in Jerusalem, inside the territory that "Israel" usurped. I consider my action to be a warranted right and a legitimate deed, intended for self-defense...Thus, I felt that I should not deny what I did.

During the interrogation, I believed that I was the Archbishop of Jerusalem, and that the Archbishop is a father to his congregation whose duty is to defend his children. I would wonder: "Is defending myself a mistake?" The answer would come screaming out loud: "No, it's quite the contrary."

"Is resisting the occupation inside the occupied territory a mistake and a crime?"

"No, it's quite the contrary."

3 - The Interrogation

The law gave me the right me to defend myself, and I did nothing but practice my warranted right. I could have denied and refused to admit the charges, but I said to them: "Yes, these suitcases are mine." At that moment, I felt that the heavy burden on my shoulders would not get any heavier if they added a new charge to it.

The kind of questions they asked me made me realize that the Israeli authorities had been watching me for a long time, that they had a lot of information that they would use to indict me, and that all their techniques with me were based on lying, deceit, and cheap promises that would lead them to nothing but a dead end. Since the first interrogation session, the interrogator said, "Your arrest is temporary. We will release you as soon as your interrogation is over, so it is better for you to admit the charges against you as soon as possible to make our job easier and your detention shorter."

I never believed the interrogator's claims. I was certain that his words were a mere allurement and a part of the psychological war they were launching against me to obtain the information they wanted. Accordingly, I laughed and said to myself, "They do not know what they're doing or the kind of man they're dealing with." When the technique of cheap promises failed, they resorted to exerting different types of pressure on me and then they threatened to kill me to force me to admit all the charges against me. I once mentioned their threats to kill me in a trial session and spoke about their brutal interrogation techniques.

I decided to respond to their psychological war by admitting to the charges, stating what I had actually done, and bearing the responsibility alone. I confessed! I said: "Yes, I smuggled the weapons..." But I did not give them any information. I did not divulge the names of the young men who were collaborating with me, which was their main goal. Thus, they utterly failed.

A word of truth that I say now for history's sake: the real reason I confessed stemmed from an inner conviction rooted deep inside me in which I had absolute faith ever since the moment of my arrest at the barrier. I had absolute conviction that what I did was a good deed. I felt proud because what I did was a sacred duty that every human being must do. If I was proud of my deed and I cherished it, why then would I deny it before the interrogators? On the other hand, I doubted the Israeli promises of releasing me soon although the human being inside me longed for the sun of freedom.

V

Israeli inmates insulted me and spat at me

I spent ten days in the Beit Shemesh prison. They felt more like ten years. Everything in that prison was intended to break me down: malnourishment, lack of sleep, terrible hygiene... My health deteriorated, I lost weight, and I looked pale and emaciated. That was part of their psychological and media scheme.

They wanted me to reach court while on the verge of perishing. They pushed me to collapse with all the means they had. If I collapsed, I would undoubtedly speak and divulge to them what they wanted to know. However, I remained steadfast, maintained my composure, and resorted to complete silence. I confessed, but then became an expert at silence. When they failed to obtain the names of my local collaborators and expose the outside cells, they started humiliating me and tarnishing my image in the eyes of my congregation and friends.

One day, they transferred me from the interrogation center in Beit Shemesh to Kfar Yuna prison in the east. On the road, we stopped for one night at the prison in the Beit Lid colony in the west of Tulkarm Governorate. I will never forget that night. The cell in Beit Lid was a mere 140 cm wide and two meters long, with the ceiling almost hitting my head. I found it impossible to stand

3 - The Interrogation

on my feet, walk, or turn, so I had to sit motionless on the floor all night. I could neither sleep nor rest until morning. There was no bed or mattress or even a small chair. It was pitch dark without a window or any light. Fortunately, I only stayed in that chicken coop of a room for one night, after which they transferred me to another prison in Kfar Yuna.

The atmosphere in Kfar Yuna was charged with grudge and malice against me. That prison was dedicated to a special category of detainees awaiting trial. It was dominated by bigoted prejudice, as it comprised two sections: Arab prisoners and Jewish prisoners.

As soon as I arrived, the Jewish inmates showed hostility towards me. They hurled verbal insults, spat at me, and shouted and insulted me all night to deprive me of sleep. Jewish detainees would often spend one night at this prison on their way to trial in Jerusalem. When they learned that I was there, they would mimic the rest of the inmates and shout all night: directing verbal insults and foul words at me.

Another disgraceful irritation that I faced in Kfar Yuna was that, every time I left my dingy cell to go to court or to meet my lawyers, the inmates would emerge from their cells, throw filth at me, and spit at my face. This kept me stressed and exhausted. After nights without sleep, I looked like I would collapse.

But what exhausted me the most and pushed me to the verge of insanity was the continuous feeling of total isolation from the outside world: no newspapers, radio, or news. I was totally cut off from the life outside, without any knowledge of what was happening inside or outside the occupied territories. Even visits were strictly forbidden. Throughout the duration of my detention for interrogation, I met no one except the Synod delegation and the lawyers assigned to defend me. The isolation affected me and resulted in a state of depression, grief, and desolation. Simultaneously, I was aware that I was under constant surveillance day and night. But I never gave up, and I never lost my resolve.

Rather, my principles were taking deeper roots and my faith in God and the cause was becoming stronger.

The cell had no door. Rather, a mere set of iron bars surrounded me. Two guards sat outside facing the iron bars. They would stare at me and follow my every move all day and all night. If an official passed and found one of them standing or sitting slightly out of place, he would reprimand him. I could not move or sleep... I was not allowed to even conduct simple life activities without being watched. There was no bathroom or toilet: only a hole inside the cell that I had to use in plain sight of the guards without the least respect for my clerical robes.

I do not wish to speak about the food in the Kfar Yuna prison because I cannot call what was offered to me "food." Dogs would refuse to eat it. As for the water, it was boiling hot while we were in the dead heat of summer. There was no bed in the room: only a simple plank (which we colloquially call "jahsh," which means "base") covered with a simple straw mattress. I could not sleep on it because of the horrible stench, so I preferred to lie on the floor.

I met my defending lawyers several times during my detention and devised the defense strategy in the courtroom. Our meetings were constantly watched by two guards. They stood a few steps away and never left the room lest the lawyer slip a paper to me or some other item without their knowledge. Despite the intense surveillance, we drew up a strategy to turn the trial of Hilarion Capucci into a trial of Israel.

4 - The Trial

> When I speak of Archbishop Hilarion Capucci I feel proud to have this struggler priest in the ranks of the Palestinian revolution. It shows how sound, profound and deeply rooted is the revolution's line in the ranks of our people. – Yasser Arafat, al-Nahar, Beirut, December 31, 1974

I

I gestured "V" for victory, and the magic rebounded on the magician

The trial started on September 20, 1974. They took me early in the day from the Kfar Yuna prison to Jerusalem in a National Security vehicle accompanied by a heavy guard: a military truck with many border police and two civilian cars carrying intelligence personnel.

All the roads on the way to Jerusalem were blocked with military checkpoints. The motorcade took crooked zigzagging roads instead of the often-trodden road in case a commando operation to free me was planned.

At the entrance to the courthouse, a multitude of Arab citizens gathered, along with a number of journalists who were given permission to take pictures but not to ask questions. The outer courtyard was packed with Jerusalemites.

I was not handcuffed. Rather, I got out of the car with absolute freedom of movement, although I was surrounded by policemen. They wanted me to appear before the audience, after ten days of detention, with a face other than my real face, that which the people of Jerusalem knew. The face with which they were familiar, especially those who belonged to my congregation, was that of the strong Archbishop: the face of a leader, preacher, and rescuer in whose strength the weak found support and in whose resolve the strong found a role model. In all honesty, I was physically exhausted and looked pale after having lost ten kilograms of weight. But I realized the purpose of that Israeli scheme and decided to foil it. As I stepped out of the car with all the cameras focused on me, and before anyone noticed my pale face, I raised my fingers with the victory sign. The roles were thus reversed, and the magic rebounded on the magician! Instead of an image of a collapsed, weak, pale Archbishop, the people saw the sign of victory and the signal of defiance and perseverance.

This image had an immense effect on the residents of the West Bank and the occupied territories. They found in it an incentive to go on. It was proof of an obstinacy and steadfastness that I drew from the depths of my soul, so it made people oblivious to my weak body and pale face.

My gesture had the opposite effect on the Israeli soldiers. They interpreted it as a challenge to their authority and their repressive methods. One of the officers approached and said sarcastically, "What do you think you are doing with this sign? It is a childish sign that children use." I shouted at him: "Shut up! I know what I'm doing."

Although I was exhausted and drained, I walked into the courtroom with my head high and a broad smile on my face which I "feigned" after premeditation. My resolve was restored in full the minute I walked through the courtroom door and saw the faces waiting for me inside. The room was packed with Arab citizens of all social groups and religions. I recognized many faces, but did not recognize many others who came to support me. As soon as I crossed the threshold, the crowd burst out in chants of support and rapturous applause: giving me more confidence, faith, resolve, and strength to face that crucial moment of my life.

4 - The Trial

As I stepped into the defendants' cage, I had a recollection of the image of Jesus Christ when he stood for trial in the court of Pontius Pilate. With a profound faith and a resolve that even the gates of hell could not overpower, I looked at the tribunal. The presiding judge was Miriam Ben-Porat, and the representative of the state of "Israel" was State Attorney Gabriel Bach.

II

Three charges supported by documents and witnesses

The session started with the State Attorney reading out the three charges against me:

1. Maintaining contact with a foreign agent, as per Article 34 of the Penal Law of 1957.

2. Carrying and possession of an illegal weapon, as per Article 66 of the Criminal Law of 1936.

3. Conducting activities for an "unlawful organization" and contacting terrorist organizations, as per Article 85 of the Emergency Regulations of 1945.

From day one of the trial, I drew a plan with my defense attorneys, the Arab Aziz Shehadah, and the Frenchmen Christian Bourget and Roland Dumas to confront the court and prove its incompetency to conduct the trial and to prove the incompetency of the Israeli judiciary system to put me on trial.

I had already admitted, during interrogation, all the charges the state attorney had raised against me, so our real goal was not to prove my innocence. Rather, it was to turn the trial from a personal trial of the Archbishop of Jerusalem, who was accused of smuggling weapons to the fedayees and collaborating with Fatah, to a political trial wherein Israel would be indicted before the world public opinion, which was following the trial in the press and media.

Therefore, on the first day of the trial, I said in my first statement: "I do not acknowledge the legitimacy of this court to consider my case." I decided to abide by complete silence. I would not take part in the discussion, and I would not comment on the court proceedings. Thus, the trial proceeded in my presence, but without any participation on my part from beginning to end.

The trial was conducted in Hebrew with interpreters translating into Arabic. My lawyer Aziz Shehadah was the only one entitled to speak inside the courtroom, because Israeli law does not permit a non-Israeli citizen to address an Israeli court. Accordingly, the French lawyers, Dumas and Bourget, did not address the court and their role was only consultative. We would coordinate with each other, and the court allowed me to speak freely to the lawyers.

III

The sons of Jerusalem enraged the judges ... and gave me joy

The court hearings were a chance for me to return to life after having been cut off from the world. I seized the opportunity of my presence in the courthouse to reconnect with people. I would smile at one person or shake the hand of another, and I felt great joy when I met people I knew. They were friends with whom I had lived and whom I loved, but I could no longer be in their midst except for the brief duration of the hearing. I took advantage of my trial to return to freedom, albeit for a few hours. I would find this freedom in the faces of friends and sons that I loved. A human being, no matter how much power and resolve he possesses, remains a human being. The one confined behind prison bars and deprived of the simplest of human emotions is overcome by deprivation and nostalgia. His heart is ripped by his yearning for the cool breeze, the sunrays, the faces of people, and

4 - The Trial

the simple ordinary life. Meeting people used to restore me to myself, to my nature, and to my episcopal reality, so I would feel, in that moment, that I was indeed pastor of the parish.

Because the prison atmosphere was charged with malice against me, and because the guards, just like the inmates, treated me with cruelty, harshness, and contempt, I would regain my resolve and high morale the moment I walked into the courtroom. The people's love and support made me forget the hardship and humiliation of prison and gave me an overwhelming sense of happiness. My true solace in that tough prison phase was their love. Their faces reflected a comprehensive Arab solidarity with my case. Despite the curfew, people would gather in front of the court to support me and cheer me on. The citizens of Jerusalem organized a protest to challenge the Israeli authorities and demand my release. Every time I stepped into the courtroom, a wave of loud applause and cheering would ensue: giving me a refreshing feeling of euphoria. I would think of myself as going into a courtroom to pass judgment, not to be judged! Truth was on my side, and justice is more powerful than oppression. This was how I felt: that I was stronger because I was advocating the truth and the Israelis were wrongful because they usurped the land and committed horrific massacres. I would thus walk into the courtroom cheerful, comforted, and holding my head high.

Although I held the court incompetent to consider my case and decided not to take part in the hearings, leaving all the pleading and objection to the defense lawyer, I would often stand up and start speaking without permission. I would shout at the judge and say what I wished to say. My goal was to defy the court and hold it in contempt, especially as the Israeli authorities thought that my arrest would make the Vatican angry at me and they would abandon me and that the citizens of the West Bank would gloat at my misfortune. However, the opposite transpired when we changed the course of the case and decided to prove the incompetency of the court, and we turned a personal issue into a national cause.

In the Name of God

IV

A trial of Hilarion Capucci or of "Israel"?

At the trial, we spoke out about the injustices of "Israel" and its oppressive policies, and we described to the world how the Arab citizen inside the occupied territories suffered at the hands of the repressive occupation authorities. We exposed before international public opinion the policy of the Judaization of Jerusalem; and not just Jerusalem but, rather, the entire occupied territories.

The defense built its case on clear specific points with the following statement as its pivot:

> Annexing Jerusalem to the Israeli state is an illegitimate action that is unjustified by any international law. Accordingly, a civil Israeli court established in Jerusalem has no right to try any Arab citizen because it is affiliated to an occupation authority.

The lawyer presented proof that this action contradicted international laws, UN resolutions, and the Geneva Convention.

As to the Judaization of Jerusalem and the West Bank, we confronted the court with the reality of what the occupation authorities were doing; that Judaization is not just a military occupation; rather, it had started with naturalization of things and places in different fields, be them cultural or social or otherwise, especially in Jerusalem which the Israelis placed under a security siege to isolate it from the rest of the West Bank. I would stand in the courtroom and shout: "The sacred nature of Jerusalem, its sacred face, and the religious character of the holy city have been lost under the occupation. Jerusalem has turned, at the hands of the Zionists, into a tourist city, swarming with groups that come to vacation. It is no longer the meeting point of pilgrims and worshipers. The air of piety and prayer has left its streets, replaced by manifestations of trade and tourist entertainment."

4 - The Trial

We explained how the Arab citizen was suffering suppression and persecution and how his freedom was non-existent. He did not have the right to express an opinion, hold a group meeting, or say a word. He was burdened with exorbitant taxes imposed by the Israelis. We explained that the repressive policy had its origin in the Israeli mindset and Israeli characteristics, which are at the foundation of Nazi characteristics. We explained that the ultimate purpose of this repressive policy and of Judaization techniques was clear and had precise goals. They wanted the Arab citizens to leave (to abandon their lands and go to another place), whereupon the Israelis would have liberty to build their settlements. We actually changed the course of one court hearing into an attack on the settlement policy and the construction of Israeli settlements on occupied Arab land. That day, we brought up the story of Deir al-Ahmar: an Arab village on the Jericho road where the Israelis were planning to build an industrial city. They were exerting pressure on its residents to force them to leave their homes so that they would possess this land after seizing ownership from its rightful owners.

In another hearing, we spoke about freedom. We presented proof that, though the Israeli authorities claimed that their press was free, it was a fake one devoid of the slightest semblance of freedom. We stated that the Israeli authorities monitored our newspapers and forbade them from publishing news or articles that exposed the pressures the Zionist occupier was subjecting us to.

My diplomatic status was among the matters that my lawyer tried to base his defense on to prove the illegality of the court to consider my case, since I was carrying a diplomatic passport issued by the Vatican State. After pleading my innocence on the grounds of international laws and UN charter to prove the validity of his defense, he invoked an exceptional historical law of the city of Jerusalem, issued by an Ottoman decree in 1806 regarding diplomatic immunity in Jerusalem. That law stripped the Israeli court of any authority to try me, and it was still effective because no later law was issued to revoke it. However, the court declined to admit the validity of the document he presented.

In the Name of God

V

Suhail Malaabi and the Katyusha rockets

While the defense team was focusing on political issues and exposing the crimes of "Israel" against Arab citizens, the State Attorney was trying to prove the charges against me and produce evidence to incriminate me. He called 16 witnesses to testify against me in court and submitted a big stack of documents to the judges to prove that I was caught red-handed while smuggling a stash of weapons in my car. He also presented another bundle of documents to indicate my collaboration with the fedayees. In his presentation, the State Attorney said, "Capucci confessed during interrogation that he was transporting weapons in his car. Logic dictates that someone provided him with these weapons. Since the weapons came from Lebanon, then the two men who sent the weapons are Abu Firas and Abu Jihad."

The Israelis had nothing save the names Abu Firas and Abu Jihad. To them, everything that was happening inside the occupied territories was, without doubt, initiated by either of these two Palestinian leaders who lived in Beirut. Therefore, the State Attorney tried to prove my connection with Abu Firas and stated that I should be considered one of the planners of fedayee operations inside the occupied territories.

The Israeli authorities obtained the names of Abu Firas and Abu Jihad from the confessions of captured fedayees. They also obtained some information from their network of spies who had detected the role of these two leaders in the heart of the occupied territories. For this reason, the Israelis considered that either Abu Firas or Abu Jihad planned every operation conducted inside the territories.

As to the major charge they were trying to pin on me, it was the story of the Katyusha rockets that were found erected opposite the King David Hotel while the US Secretary of State, Henry

4 - The Trial

Kissinger, was meeting with Israeli officials in May 1974. They confronted me during the interrogation with the suitcases they had found at the rockets site, and I identified them as I have mentioned earlier. Accordingly, they called the prisoner Suhail Malaabi to court to testify in the case.

I later found out that, when they had arrested Suhail in the wake of the rockets incident, he confessed during interrogation that he was the one who transported them to the wooded area, but he did not inform them where he had obtained them. Despite extreme torture, he refused to admit that he had received the suitcases at the College de Frères. He insisted that he had brought them from another place, even while receiving brutal torture.

His Beatitude Patriarch Maximus V once recounted in a press interview the brutal torture that Suhail Malaabi had undergone to force him to say that Archbishop Capucci had given him the suitcases. He said:

> Despite the beating, insults, and threats, Suhail Malaabi who was a Muslim from Naples, insisted on denying any relation between Archbishop Capucci and the story of the suitcases. But finally, the Israelis brought Suhail's mother and stripped her of her clothes in front of him, threatening to rape her before his eyes if he did not say that Capucci was the one who gave him the suitcases... Faced with this horrid scene, Suhail broke down and his human emotions overwhelmed him. He said to them, "I'm willing to sign anything you want on condition that you release my mother."

Then they forced him to sign a fake confession.

On this basis, they brought Suhail Malaabi to the courtroom, believing that he would testify against me and repeat to the judges what he had said during interrogation under duress. However, instead of doing what they wanted him to do, he turned against them and said to the court, "I have no connection with Capucci.

In the Name of God

I did not bring the suitcases from the College des Frères. It was from another place." He described before the attendees and journalists what the Israelis had done to him and how they seized his confessions forcibly. This story stirred a lot of discussion and commentaries in the Israeli press, which accused us of mocking the court and holding it in contempt.

In addition to smuggling weapons and anti-Israel activities, another charge that the State Attorney tried to pin on me was representing Fatah inside the occupied territory and running their operations and planning for them. He accused me of being the liaison officer between the fedayees in the West Bank and the outside resistance. They called several witnesses to the stand to prove this charge.

At the outset of the hearings, the State Attorney asked me, "How is it your right, while you are a clergyman, to work in politics and engage in political activities?" I replied, "Clergymen, too, belong to the homeland, and they have to defend their homeland." While the defense lawyer was pleading about the weapons smuggling and dealing with a "terrorist organization" (trying to prove my innocence of these charges by bringing up the subject of Israeli terrorism), I would interrupt him, as pre-coordinated between us, by standing up without permission every time he mentioned a sensitive point. I would start speaking despite the judge's objection and the angry taps of her gavel. The defense lawyer was once speaking about terrorism when I sprang up and yelled at the judges:

> You taught us terrorism. You did Deir Yassin, Kafr Qasim, and the King David Hotel bombing. In comparison to you and your terrorism, we are but pupils. You used methods of destruction and ruin to usurp our rights. If we have taken the same road to restore those usurped rights, then we have done nothing but what you taught us to do, with the difference that you worked for falsehood and we work for truth.

4 - The Trial

At this point, the presiding judge was enraged, ordered me to be silent, and asked the defense lawyer to keep me quiet. The lawyer came near me and said, "Your Grace, be patient and I will say everything that you wish to say." I answered, "You say what you wish and I, in turn, will say what I wish."

There were often such clashes between me and the judges or the State Attorney. The courtroom atmosphere was confrontational from day one: marked by aggressiveness and loud voices. I was deliberately confrontational: I would always create reasons to quarrel with the Israelis. I did not want a single session to pass without an uproar. My plan was to make the most possible noise during the trial, because news about commotion in the courtroom would be wired to the world via the press, and it would have a positive effect on the citizens inside the occupied territories.

The means I used to reach that end was simple: I would stand up, speak up, and say what I wanted to say. If the judges refused to listen to me and ordered me to be silent, I would confront them in a way that could not be legally counteracted. I would make a single statement: "I dismiss the defense counsel." Such dismissal would force the judge to adjourn the hearing, because it is impermissible that the trial proceeds without a defense lawyer. Using this simple method, I forced them either to grant my request or adjourn the hearing.

Once, about four hours into the hearing, I felt tired. So I stood up and said to the judge, "I want to get out to rest." But the judge denied my request, so I dismissed the defense counsel and the court was adjourned.

VI

The Vatican did not abandon me despite the pressures

Once again, and this time it was the most significant, I stood up and started shouting at the State Attorney in objection to his statements. A military person tried to stop me by force, so I raised my hand at his face: threatening to hit him. I felt empowered by the presence of a large number of Arabs in the courtroom. It was inconceivable that the Israelis would treat me with brutality in such a setting.

Two young men from the West Bank once attended a hearing. One of them tried to pass a slip of paper to me, but it fell into the hand of an Israeli soldier. So they arrested the two young men and took them outside the courtroom. I sprang up and started yelling and demanding their release from the judge. A soldier approached me, trying to silence me, but I threatened to hit him if he got any closer. Thus I found strength through the people surrounding me, and the motivation to stand my ground. I addressed the judge, saying, "I will not continue to attend this hearing unless the two young men are released immediately."

When she denied my request, I dismissed the defense counsel again so the court was adjourned for two hours after which the Israelis realized that the two young men were innocent and released them.

I erupted at the judge and the State Attorney many times, directed accusations at them, and attacked the occupation authorities. One of the most prominent of those times was the notebook incident. I had a small notebook where I wrote down my notes. I wrote some simple matters connected to the arms smuggling operation. During my detention, the guards took advantage of my hunger strike and consequent ill health. They stole that notebook and delivered it to the State Attorney: distorting some of my writings in the process.

In the courtroom, the State Attorney wished to use the contents of my notebook as evidence against me and asked to incriminate me based on information in the notebook that they had tampered with. I sprang up objecting to the use of those writings

4 - The Trial

as incriminating evidence against me, because they had stolen it from me and distorted its contents. I attacked the State Attorney and accused him of theft and forgery.

I would devise incidents to interrupt the court hearing with the persistent goal to ridicule the court and mock the occupation authorities. For example, I would stand up suddenly in the middle of court proceedings and say out loud, "It's been many hours. I'm tired and hungry. Bring me some sandwiches." It was forbidden to bring food or coffee inside the courtroom, so they had to either adjourn or grant me my request. When the judge refused to adjourn the court, I would resort to my usual technique: dismissing the defense counsel without whose presence the hearing could not proceed. The hearings were interrupted many times. On one of those times, the presiding judge ordered that coffee be brought inside the courtroom because she wanted to wrap up the case as soon as possible. Her decision caused uproar in "Israel," and the newspapers that came out the following morning carried editorials that attacked me: "Archbishop Capucci mocks the Israeli judiciary."

One of the most violent court clashes occurred when the State Attorney addressed me, saying, "You are a criminal. You are accused of smuggling weapons and explosives into "Israel."" I retorted, "I'm neither a criminal nor a killer. I have a right that we lost at your hands so we rose to restore our right from you." Here, the judge interfered and scorned me saying, "Silence, killer..." I immediately remarked in a stern tone, "I do not kill except those who killed our people and usurped our land and desecrated our temples." Enraged, she asked, "Who gave you the right to speak in the name of this nation?!" To everyone's surprise, a young man from the attendees, not past thirty years of age, rose from his seat (I later learned that his name was Salim Safawi). He shouted in the midst of the courtroom, "We the entire nation gave Archbishop Capucci the right to speak in our name."

Uproar erupted in the court in support of his stance, and the heated atmosphere was transferred outside the courtroom and support chants soared in the street. The citizens who had gathered outside the courthouse started chanting support for my case and denunciation of the Israeli authorities. When the chants were heard inside the courtroom, the presiding judge stood up and said in obvious agitation, "It is no longer possible that the hearings proceed in this terrorist atmosphere." She adjourned the court and postponed the hearing to the following day.

I felt I was doing my duty and exposing the Israeli enemy through my trial. The more I exhausted myself, the happier I became. I was able to sacrifice without tiredness or fear, because to me, sacrifice meant happiness. Deep down I was composed and reassured with a clear conscience and inner harmony from start to finish after having done my duty towards my case and towards Palestine. Above all, I felt that God was pleased with my deeds, as I was totally surrounded by support and solidarity during the trial. As long as the people I was serving still supported me and believed in my cause, I believed this meant that God was pleased with me... Verily, the voice of the people is the voice of God and the voice of Truth. The people of Jerusalem openly supported me and my cause, which lifted my morale and encouraged me to defy the oppressive authorities with a louder voice.

VII

The cost of my pleading... four years in prison

When the court sentence was passed, I was not upset. I was living in a world different from that of law and judges: in a different psychological state far removed from the labyrinth of prosecution statements and pleadings. This state resembled spiritual detachment from the tangible perceptible realm. I was living in seclusion, as if I was in the midst of my beloved city of Jerusalem; living in darkness, as if I was basking in the splendor of light; and sleeping in a cell worse than a cave, as if I was residing in a palace

4 - The Trial

more beautiful than the Iwan of Khosrow. I created my own state of mind and made a world outside the perceptible realm. It is hard for any human being to understand this world or realize the size of the invincible fence that I had erected inside me which isolated me from my trial. I took myself out, by virtue of a divine power, from that hellish Israeli state.

I no longer cared for the cruelty of the sentence or the number of years I would spend behind bars. The only thing I wanted was for the trial to end so that I would proceed to confront the enemy in a new way.

My lawyer, Aziz Shehadah, visited me in prison a few days before the last court hearing. He told me that he expected an eight-year prison sentence for me, and he showed me his closing arguments in which he would plead for my innocence. His argument was based on private reasons and the court's jurisdiction, without accommodating the Palestinian national dimension which I sought. So, I said to him, "I've decided to make a statement at the end of the hearing and I've spent the past days preparing it."

When I read to him what I had written, his face turned pale and he was strongly averse to it, saying, "Your Grace, I believe it is better that you remain silent and listen to the judgment only. This statement of yours will upset the tribunal and they will issue the maximum prison sentence, which is 12 years. I have deliberated with the State Attorney's office and I expect a reduced sentence of eight years. So why do you want to speak and spend an extra four years in prison? Your statement will provoke the judges and cost you dearly. Four extra years in prison, your Grace! Think about it well." I said to him, "Then let it be!"

I was overwhelmed by a great power inside me; a strange power that made me utter with perfect composure, "Four more years... four less years... there is no difference. More important than the sentence that day is that I say the word of Truth, and I will say it no matter the cost." Deep inside, I was hearing the voice of that old priest who taught us in our prime of life in the preparatory years of the Clerical school. He used to say, "My children, since you have pursued this vocation, then behave as if you will never leave it. Try to adapt, and once you have adapted, you would feel that everything is normal."

I have embraced the whole experience. I lived through what happened to me as it is, and I realized that I was a prisoner and what it means that the Archbishop of Jerusalem becomes a prisoner and why. I truly believed that the charge that put me behind bars was an honor. I considered it a medal on my chest, so I no longer asked myself confusing questions that lead to doubt and hesitation: "Had you done such and such...! Had you behaved as such...!"

Therefore, when the lawyer warned me that the sentence would increase to 12 years if I made the statement that I had prepared, I was indifferent to the consequences. I made my statement as if I was announcing to the world the triumph of the Palestinian cause. I felt that my destiny had led me to that historical moment to stand before the world and prove to the nations that our cause is a cause of truth, humanity, and justice. I felt that the provocation I stirred and the irritation I caused to the tribunal was massive and it was as if I was delivering a speech after the liberation of Palestine inside a freed Jerusalem. With such vigor and with such spirit and strength, my voice was raised. It was not the pleading of a prisoner; rather, it was the performance of a prayer emanating from my heart that believed in a just cause. It was an echoing scream in the face of oppression. I was not delivering a speech; I was praying a real true prayer that cost me four years of prison! I did not care! I came out of the courtroom with a smile of pride and honor.

4 - The Trial

VIII

I addressed myself to Jesus Christ, screaming: "Shame and disgrace be upon those who desecrated your holy land"

When we entered the courtroom the following day, and after the State Attorney had presented his summation, my lawyer Aziz Shehadah stood up. Before starting his pleading, he approached the bench and said, "My client, His Eminence Archbishop Hilarion Capucci, Archbishop of Jerusalem for the Melkite Greek Catholics, wishes to represent himself."

After deliberating with the counselors, the presiding judge categorically refused to grant me permission to speak and asked the lawyer to resume presenting the statement of the defense. I immediately sprang up and said, "I have the right to represent myself, and I will say what I wish to say. No one has the authority to forbid me."

The judge ordered me to sit and be silent, saying, "You do not have the right to speak if I do not grant you permission to speak. We are no longer in a trial hearing. The trial is over. This session is assigned to pass judgment."

I said to her, "I wish to speak, and this court had better listen to what I have to say."

But the judge insisted on forbidding me from representing myself. Thereupon, I resorted to my usual tactic of obstructing the session to get what I want. I yelled at the top of my voice, "I dismiss the defense counsel!" After lengthy deliberation, the presiding judge reversed her position and granted me permission to speak. I delivered a speech that had an astounding impact on the audience. My lawyer, Shehadah, distributed the text of my speech to the Arabic newspapers which published it the next morning. The Al-Quds newspaper wrote: "This is the text of Archbishop Capucci's statement before his court sentence was

In the Name of God

passed. Any person with an atom of conscience and morals must inevitably support what he says." I do not recall now what I said in detail, but I remember that I addressed our Lord Jesus Christ:

> I will not address you with my statement; rather, I will address it to my teacher Jesus Christ in Heaven who is weeping for what has come upon the holy city, the cradle of Christianity and Islam; a city desecrated by invaders and its sanctities are violated.
>
> O my Lord, Jesus Christ,
>
> If you are looking at this holy city (Jerusalem) now, you would see your children imprisoned and you would weep... but this city will remain sacred forever, and its sacredness will trample on its rulers because your way and your work are stronger than the oppression of rulers. I hold peace sacred, and I believe in love, and I will follow your steps and hold our land sacred, this land that You love which is called Palestine.
>
> O my teacher and my lord Jesus, you are the light to the world and they are the darkness... May those who disfigured Jerusalem be disgraced!
>
> I am held captive by invaders and barbarians... I will convey to the court tribunal what is in my heart at the end of a long torment... from the top of the Mount of Olives you looked, O Jesus, at Jerusalem and said, "A day will come when you will be besieged from all directions, and they will destroy you and destroy your sons." If you look now from heaven, you will find your land that you loved, and you will find Jerusalem exactly as you had wept for it. And you will find your true son tied in chains, and you will weep.
>
> And here I am, prisoner to the conquerors and victim to the power of rulers. O Jesus, all of us humans are destined

4 - The Trial

to leave this life to another, but your land is eternal and it will remain stronger than the power of conquerors and their laws.

You taught us to love the land that is yours and ours and to defend it. We have done so in obedience to your will because we are your soldiers, and Jerusalem, the cradle of Christianity, will remain free forever despite their deeds.

You are love, O Lord and Master Jesus, and they are injustice. You are light and they are darkness. Your banner, O Master, is the symbol of love and freedom, and it will remain raised and fluttering.

Shame and disgrace be upon those who desecrate the holy land.

O Master Jesus, I hold our land sacred; our beloved land that is called Palestine.

The audience interrupted me several times with roaring applause: aggravating the judges even more.

After a trial that lasted 108 days, the Israelis sentenced me to 12 years in prison.

5 - Prison

"Capucci will be remembered in the ranks of Castro, Mandela and other revolutionaries." – Al Gafoor, *The Argus*; Cape Town 9 Jan 2017

I

The Israelis tore up my clerical robe

In the Kfar Yuna prison, I was isolated in a solitary cell that was empty except for a stinking straw mattress. A group of Jewish inmates accused of different crimes surrounded me. Thus, I dwelt among murderers, thieves, and people who are the most capable of committing evil. The Israeli authorities put me there to humiliate me and break my resolve. They did not consider me a political prisoner because that prison was assigned to hardened criminals.

I suffered in the Kfar Yuna prison. Ill-treatment, daily insults, and contempt were reflected in the simplest of daily matters. All the inmates, without exception, directed verbal abuse and profanities at me. The prison administration treated me with unspeakable contempt and hatred. They singled me out by giving me the worst food. My meals were limited to a bowl of soup and a loaf of bread. The soup was water mixed with tomato pulp to change its color and nothing more. They used to bring it cold and on a wooden plate. The guard did not open the door and come into the cell to serve the food. Rather, he threw the plate violently on the ground and pushed it with his foot under the cell bars. The "soup" would mix with the bread and water and become inedible. He used to make sure that I could see his foot pushing the plate.

The guard keenest on throwing my food on the ground was a

In the Name of God

Jew of Arab origin from Yemen called Abboudi. He would look at me with malice and say in Arabic, "You are more inferior than any common prisoner, and your clerical robe does not do you any good." I realized they were humiliating me because I was a clergyman and that staying among those criminals was a threat to my life, so I resolved to leave the prison at any cost. I declared a hunger strike and demanded transfer to another place.

Among the humiliation methods that they used in prison, which disturbed me tremendously, was contemptuous treatment. They would call me by my bare name, not by my clerical title, which is the core of my life. They would scream with contempt "Capucci!" instead of "Archbishop Capucci." They did this on purpose to enrage and insult me. I refused to answer if my name was not preceded with "Archbishop".

One day, a soldier came and called me by my name and I did not answer. When he repeated the call, I jumped at him, saying, "You know that I am an Archbishop, and you must respect my rank as a clergyman." I wanted to hit him but the guards restrained me and took me inside. I decided not to bear any more insults and contempt and declared a hunger strike until I was removed from that disgraceful prison and its humiliating atmosphere.

A few days into my fast, the police chief offered to transfer me to Ramleh prison located 15 kilometers northeast of Ramallah. I immediately agreed. I stopped my fasting, so they transferred me to Ramleh at the end of February 1975. I had spent six months in Kfar Yuna.

II

A hero in Ramleh Prison

The atmosphere was very different in Ramleh Prison due to a large group of Arab inmates there: mostly political prisoners

5 - Prison

accused of carrying out fedayee operations or joining Palestinian organizations. I was enormously relieved by the move from the hostile Jewish environment to the supportive Palestinian climate. I wanted to be among them, live with them, and be a brother to them. I was delighted to be removed from the psychological war the Jewish inmates in Kfar Yuna were waging on me.

Upon my arrival at Ramleh, they took all of my belongings, my papers, my watch, and my cane. They wanted to take my clerical robe and make me wear the prison uniform, but I refused and hung on to it. I shouted, "This is my sacred right. This is my life. If you take the clerical robe off me, you tear my soul apart from me." The prison warden reversed his position and led me to my cell himself. After passing through a long corridor, we stopped at a small damp room with water leaking from its walls. It measured no more than two meters long by 140 cm wide with a toilet bowl in one corner.

When I laid eyes on that disgusting cell, I looked at the warden and said sarcastically, "But I did not bring the dog along." I had a German Shepherd in my Archbishopric in Jerusalem. The warden did not understand and gave me a perplexed, wandering look. So, I said, "My dog would refuse to sleep in this room. How do I expect me to?"

He said, "This is your cell, and it is your problem not ours. Would you rather go back to Kfar Yuna?" At that moment, I realized that this was my destiny and my road to Calvary, so I decided to carry my cross and continue no matter how hard and painful it was. I lived in that infested cell for three and a half years.

Over time, I discovered that the beautiful atmosphere of spiritual bonding between the Arab inmates in the Ramleh prison somewhat compensated for the state of the cell. I felt that we were one family even if I were isolated from them in solitary confinement. A bond pulled us together. This brotherly solidarity among the prisoners gave me some inner comfort that belied my situation as an imprisoned bishop. Despite living behind bars in seclusion from the world, I felt I was among my brethren and surrounded by a family that loved me. Despite the cruelty of prison and the bitterness of being away from the struggle-oriented church life that I vowed myself to, a strange feeling of joy overwhelmed me, because there were people with me behind the walls who knew who I was and my image to them had not been altered. I felt that the love and respect my sons had for me as the Archbishop of Jerusalem had multiplied when I became the prisoner Archbishop. To them, I was not just another prisoner: I was the prisoner of the Palestinian cause. That love was reflected in the simple daily life affairs.

The most beautiful example of this love involved L&M cigarettes. I used to smoke L&M cigarettes before going to prison. Inside prison, a cigarette is a very valuable and rare item. Remarkably, when the young men in the Ramleh prison learned that I smoked L&Ms, they asked their families to bring them L&Ms for me.

Prison regulations forbade the prisoner from taking cigarettes into his cell, and he was only allowed one cigarette after each visit. But during the visit, he could have as many cigarette packs as he wished on condition that he took only one cigarette inside the cell. Prisoners were subjected to meticulous inspection before returning to their cells. In my case, I never ran out of L&Ms throughout my prison stay, and I used to smoke an average of three cigarettes a day.

This incident was simple in itself but great in terms of what it symbolized: the extent of the Arab prisoners' solidarity with me and love they surrounded me with during my time in prison. Cigarettes in prison are quite important. The prisoner would often cut one cigarette into three to satisfy his dire need to smoke.

5 - Prison

III

Holy Mass inside the cell

The second incident that showed me the extent of the Arab prisoners' solidarity with me and sympathy for my case involved my clerical robe. When my 12-year prison sentence was passed and I returned to the Ramleh prison, the prison warden insisted that I take off my clerical robe and don the regular inmate uniform. He considered that I was no longer entitled to the privileges I had while on trial. He said that I was an inmate just like all the other inmates and he wanted to apply the prison regulations that imposed a uniform on sentenced prisoners. I refused to remove my robe, and the warden avoided using force to remove it in fear of the reaction of the other inmates.

I later discovered that the warden had a plan to achieve his goal without causing a commotion. One night, after I had undressed and gone to sleep, the guards came and replaced my robe with the prison uniform. When I woke up the next morning, I found myself forced to wear a stinking transparent prison uniform that resembled tissue paper. I was quite upset by this, because I was always overcome by a strange feeling if someone touched my clerical being or offended it even with a glance. It would cause an explosion of rage deep inside me. In the cell, I was forced to suppress my rage, so the anger turned into immense grief that was difficult to screen from people's eyes.

When the inmates noticed how upset I was, they sewed a new robe for me in the prison workshop while the Israelis were not looking and managed to send it to my cell. My delight with it was indescribable. Their gesture represented ultimate compassion and love, and it healed my morale to a great extent. Prior to that incident, I thought that prison had taken everything from me including my clerical robe, which is the moral symbol of my role on this earth. Then fellow prisoners took the initiative and returned it to me with spontaneity and love. It was as if they returned to me the dearest of my possessions. I realized that I was not alone and started feeling that I was living with my brothers, my compatriots, and the sons of Jerusalem. I wore the robe they made the day I was released and stepped out into freedom, and I still keep it as a precious treasure.

Depriving me of my clerical robe was but part of the integrated oppressive scheme that the Israelis were executing against me from the beginning. I was not allowed to celebrate the Holy Offering (Eucharist), which is a daily ordinance and obligation on me as a priest. They did not permit me to keep any book of prayer or any ecclesiastical items necessary for holding mass. In vain I raised my voice and demanded them. The church authorities intervened, but the Israeli prison warden categorically refused to comply with this demand, which is inscribed in the Geneva Convention and grants the prisoner the right to practice religious rituals.

When I failed to get my holy right through legal channels, I decided to get it through sacrifice, so I declared a hunger strike. News of my strike and the reason for it soon became public: stirring an uproar that moved the ecclesiastical circles. Thus, the Israeli again retracted his oppressive decisions and allowed me to pray in my cell. They gave me prayer books and brought the Holy Communion to my cell. After mass, I would keep the consecrated meal inside the cell.

A relationship of closeness and affection grew between God and I in prison. Despite all the hardship I went through, my faith in the Lord and my closeness to Him increased. I would address him from my seclusion and converse with him day and night. As a clergyman, God was not an illusion to me. I regarded him as a living being and drew from Him the power of my existence. I relied on Him to persevere. I saw in Him the image of a father merciful to his children, a friend stretching his arm to me when I needed it, and a brother who shared with me the tragedy, sympathized with me in my grief, soothed my wounds, and alleviated my pains.

5 - Prison

Thus, I talked to God and implored Him through prayer. He was my hope and the source of my strength. He lived with me night and day when I was cut off from the world without a friend, companion, or consoler. God alone was my friend, my companion, and my strength in my solitude. By virtue of prayer and closeness to the Lord, I no longer felt psychologically alone. I no longer cared for my situation or thought about what would happen to me. Our Master Jesus Christ said in his Sermon on the Mount:

> Look at the birds of the air; they do not sow or reap or store away in barns, and yet your heavenly Father feeds them... See how the flowers of the field grow. They do not labor or spin. Yet I tell you that not even Solomon in all his splendor was dressed like one of these. [Mathews 6:26-29]

I would recall the words of the Lord and joy would flow inside me like a breeze. Although there was not even a small window in the cell, I no longer saw it as pitch dark. I no longer saw its physical reality because God was with me. Because it pleased Him to be with me in this cell, I started to feel it overflowing with light like the Bethlehem Cave. In my eyes, it seemed like the most magnificent palace on earth. By virtue of faith and closeness to God, I felt inner comfort in that place and said, "This is what God willed for me, and His will be done."

IV

Gold smuggling... and hunger strike

Among the bitterest and hardest memories of prison were the hunger strikes. Resorting to a hunger strike was the only way to get the occupation authorities to answer a demand. I went into strike several times. None of my demands were answered without going on a hunger strike, and it was also my ticket out of prison.

In the Name of God

A hunger strike is grueling, exhausting, painful, and hard. But I was able to endure it by virtue of an internal conviction that I constantly had in the cell and that never left me. It was the conviction that I was imprisoned for principles that I believed in. The days of my hunger strikes throughout my imprisonment amounted to seven or eight months. In the wake of these, I had lost 32 kg of my weight and become as pale and skinny as a stick.

The first time I declared a hunger strike was during my detention at the Kfar Yuna prison before my trial started. I went on strike in protest of the rumors the Israeli authorities circulated against me during my interrogation period and in objection to the statements that the Israelis made and leaked to the press: claiming that they were the results of the initial interrogation with me and the summary of confessions that I made to the interrogators.

This incident was the subject of a news report circulated by the Agence France-Presse (AFP) on August 19, 1974:

> The Israeli authorities tried to fabricate some disgraceful charges against His Holiness Archbishop Capucci in what they announced as the initial results of interrogation. Among those charges is that the Archbishop was illegally smuggling drugs, alcohol, gold, and foreign currency into "Israel". The same sources mentioned that a girl of ill repute was arrested at the Bishop's quarters during the interrogation.
>
> The Israeli police sources also tried to pin another charge on Archbishop Capucci; that he had a connection with two Arabs accused of murder. Those sources claimed that the two Arabs accused of killing a cab driver in Jerusalem a few months ago and setting up Katyusha rocket launchers in areas of central Jerusalem were in contact with the Archbishop.

When I learned of these fabricated reports intended to tarnish my image as a Christian clergyman and my struggle and sacrifices

5 - Prison

for the cause, I decided to announce a hunger strike in protest of the abusive treatment I was receiving at Kfar Yuna. I demanded transfer to another place and to be treated as a political prisoner (not as a criminal accused of smuggling weapons).

I was imprisoned for the sake of convictions that were deep-rooted inside me, and I was capable of enduring all sorts of torture in defense of these convictions and in protection of my dignity. They wanted to tarnish my image before my congregation and church. I decided to confront them with pride and perseverance. Whenever the psychological war escalated against me, I perceived the pain as simple regardless of its intensity. Whenever my pain intensified and my torture increased, I felt the magnitude of the challenge and was motivated to persevere even more.

I was no longer terrified of the torture, and I became capable of doing anything. I had reached a level of detachment from my physical being that made me insensitive to pain. Rather, whenever I saw myself melting, I felt happier; and whenever I realized that my body was collapsing, I became more resolved and joyous because I was in a war of defiance with my enemies and I had to win that war at any cost. By virtue of this internal strength, I triumphed over my warden at the Kfar Yuna prison and was transferred to Ramleh.

V

They tortured me and made me drink milk forcibly

The hunger strike system at the Ramleh prison allowed inmates who abstained from eating as a form of protest to not consume anything other than water for the first five days. Starting on day five of fasting, the prisoner was given half a liter of milk before noon and half a liter mixed with an egg in the afternoon to keep him alive. Because I refused to drink the milk and would not open my mouth, they poured it down my throat through a plastic tube inserted in my nose. It was very painful.

In the Name of God

The Israelis were deeply annoyed by my fasting, especially because I received a supportive reaction inside the occupied territories. Therefore, they poured the milk into my stomach in a violent, brutal manner. They would then withdraw the tube from my nose with speed and violence, which felt as if one of my veins was being pulled out. The objective of this barbaric method was to force the prisoner to end his hunger strike without having his demand answered.

I once declared a hunger strike in demand of some basic life matters, such as permission to leave the cell once a day to breathe fresh air and the right to join the rest of the prisoners and talk to them during the break. At the time, I was isolated inside in a solitary cell inaccessible to sunshine. A hunger strike was my only means of protest.

Forty-eight days passed without the Israelis responding to my demands. The milk they poured through my nose kept me alive and kept them insistent, so I decided to stop it. I said to the guards, "From now on, I do not want milk. It's either death or having my demands met. More than a month and a half of my strike has passed without you doing anything. I will no longer be patient."

They called the prison warden who came and said to me, "You must have the milk."

I said, "I will not." He said, "If you do not have it willingly, you will have it forcibly." He gave me the afternoon to think about it and then returned with his assistant. I did not change my mind, so he said to me, "If you do not yield to the law, we will use force with you." I answered, "Then use force."

The assistant warden left for a few minutes and returned with five strong policemen. When all seven were inside my cell, they sounded the siren and locked all the inmates in their cells lest a mutiny erupt. They feared that the Arab prisoners might attack them to defend me.

5 - Prison

When all the inmates were settled behind bars, four policemen grabbed my legs and arms. I was wearing my clerical robe that the prisoners had sewn for me. I had taken it out from under the mattress where I had hidden it and put it on that day, saying to myself, "Perhaps they would have respect for my robe." But they did not.

One of the guards seized me by the shoulder and lifted me off the mattress violently: tearing my robe in the process. I still have that torn robe, and I wore it the day I was released from prison as I mentioned earlier. They carried me by force to a neighboring room that was sealed from all sides. After forcing me onto a chair, they said, "Think about it well; perhaps you will change your mind." I said, "No need to think. I will not change my mind."

Thereupon, two guards held my shoulders and two held my legs. They pinned me to the chair, and then a fifth guard dug his nails into my mouth and inserted his fingers inside my throat while a sixth guard stepped with his foot on my toes to force me to scream and open my mouth. The minute I said "Ahhhh," they forced the tube and the milk into my throat. When they returned me to my cell, there was blood on my hands, neck, and toes. My socks were soaked in blood and the inside of my throat was injured. They carried me like a sack of wheat, threw me on the cell floor, and locked the iron door. They left me there without any care, and I bled through the night.

The Arab prisoners did not know about my ordeal in the torture room until the next morning. They immediately announced a mass hunger strike in solidarity with me.

That day, I wrote a letter to Patriarch Maximus Hakim describing the incident in detail. His Beatitude moved in several directions and contacted the Apostolic Delegate, who denounced the brutal treatment I had received.

VI

The streets of Old Jerusalem resonated with the chant: "O Archbishop, we would die for you!"

Flyers in my support were distributed during my trial, and the slogan "O Archbishop, we would die for you" was written on the walls in the streets of Old Jerusalem despite Israeli round-the-clock surveillance. The walls were covered with flyers, images, and writings. The Israelis could not stop them because they were the fruit of organized action. Organization unites people, and when the citizen feels the presence of a conscious leadership that works with efficiency and has concern for him, he sacrifices for the sake of the cause. Those who moved inside the occupied territories using all possible means to release me were the inside cells. They were groups of young men working under my direction. I was the link between them and the leadership outside. Those young men remained active after my arrest and launched several operations to release me. I will not speak about these, because those who undertook them are still free and living in the occupied territories and I do not wish to expose them to danger. Their attempts assured me that I lived in their consciences just as they lived in my heart.

The resistance did not neglect any means to free me from captivity. They tried diplomatic channels and international pressure. Some fellow freedom fighters even used force... The last fedayee operation I heard of while in prison was the hijacking of the Air France plane to Entebbe Airport in Uganda on June 27, 1976. The fedayees demanded the release of captives in Israeli prisons. My name was at the top of the list.

A year before (June 15, 1975), a group of four fedayees infiltrated the Kfar Yuval colony in Galilee, took hostages, and demanded the release of detainees in Israeli prisons starting with me. But, unfortunately, they engaged with the Israeli army and all were martyred.

5 - Prison

The news used to reach us through some Israeli newspapers: particularly through Al-Anbaa', an Israeli newspaper in Arabic that they allowed into the prison. I used to say to them, "This newspaper is called Al-Anbaa' [literally 'news'], but there is no news in it. It is only published to speak about 'Israel' and carry to us the Israeli point of view." I read an article in that newspaper about the "Entebbe Operation" whose purpose was to glorify Israeli power and honor the (Israeli) Commando team who executed the operation. Following that daring Kfar Yuval operation, I sent a letter to Abu Ammar:

> I feel that my duty has multiplied manifolds now that there are brothers of mine whose blood has been spilt for the sake of my release. The martyrdom of those heroes pushes me to feel more and more responsible towards my people, to commit to the cause with greater faith, and to sacrifice for the sake of Palestine until martyrdom.

I asked him to relay to the families of those martyrs that "I am with them, offering my condolences, sharing their grief, and praying for them... and wishing I were in Beirut to visit them in their homes and squeeze their hands."

VII

The last hunger strike almost killed me

My last hunger strike started at the end of January 1977 and lasted four and a half months. It left me looking like a ghost. Anyone who saw me thought that I was dying. I looked collapsed, weak, exhausted, pale-faced, and emaciated: having lost 32 kg of my weight.

When I reached a state near total collapse, or more correctly, when I was on the verge of death, the prison warden walked into my cell and tried to dissuade me from fasting. He cited my health condition. When he failed to express in words my terrible condition, he brought a mirror and placed it before me, saying, "Look at your face. Do you not see that you are on the verge of death?" He was expecting me to tremble at the sight of my pale face, sunken eyes, and skinny figure. However, I said to him with firmness and resolve, "You do not know that we are like rockets, because our real take off starts with countdown. When we reach the zero, it is then that we really take off. I'm not yet at the zero. When I reach it, my resolve will be regenerated and I will take off more powerfully."

From the depth of my suffering, I received the voice of hope in salvation. I heard a clear merciful deep voice saying to me, "Rely on God. Hold on to faith." That voice never left me throughout my time in prison, and I used to hear it louder and clearer during difficult times of torture. I knew that it had its source in my faith in God and His omnipotence, because the reason for my suffering was my faith in a just cause. I used to rejoice with that voice. When I heard it, I would see the face of Jerusalem. Then my mother's face would shine and I would see her sitting behind her sewing machine staring at the door awaiting my return. My pain would vanish and I would smile.

I was ready to face death, and I did not stop the hunger strike until I received a clear and explicit promise from the Vatican that my release from prison was imminent. I learned that it was only a matter of days and that only legal and logistic arrangements remained to be completed after the Israeli government had agreed in principle to release me.

VIII

His Holiness the Pope intervened for my release

When I reached the threshold of collapse, the Apostolic Delegate in Jerusalem, Monsignor William Carew, visited me on June 9 and informed me that His Holiness Pope Paul VI had personally intervened and asked the Israeli authorities to release me. He said to me, "We do not want you to die in prison. You must end the hunger strike and regain some strength before you return to freedom." I rejoiced at the Vatican message and believed that my suffering and sacrifice had borne fruit. I believed I would regain my freedom, return to my church and congregation, resume my role, and practice my usual activities in my beloved Jerusalem. However, my calculations did not match reality, as my detention continued for a few months.

During those months, lengthy negotiations were underway between the Vatican Secretary of State, Cardinal Agostino Casaroli, and his assistant Monsignor Monterezzi on one hand and representatives of the Israeli government on the other. The latter would visit Rome and relay the Israeli demands and place tough conditions for my release. Their conditions and demands changed constantly. I was waiting for the glad tidings to reach me at any minute. When I yielded to the Vatican's will and ended my hunger strike, I was expecting to be released within a few days or weeks to accommodate the legal procedures. However, my release occurred five months later.

At first, the Israelis procrastinated in making the legal arrangements necessary for my release. Then they stipulated harsh conditions regarding my place of residence after my discharge. When they had reached an agreement with the Vatican regarding my stay in exile, they demanded measures that would limit my freedom and prevent me from engaging in any political activity related to the Palestinian cause.

The purpose of that initial procrastination was to win time for me to recover a little and regain my physical strength, because my collapsed appearance in the wake of a hunger strike that lasted more than three months was bound to tarnish the image of "Israel" before the world given that it was claiming to be a democratic state that respected international covenants and defended human rights. If my image with my pale face and sunken eyes was not much different from the images of the children escaping the Biafra famine and was circulated in global media, it would become a worldwide symbol of the injustice of "Israel" and its oppressive treatment of prisoners: political prisoners and clergymen included. Rather than democratic "Israel," it would become Nazi "Israel".

IX

The corpse of Eli Cohen... for barter

Another critical matter of extreme importance delayed my release. The Apostolic Delegate in Jerusalem visited me and said, "The Israelis stipulated a new condition for your release which they did not mention when negotiations started." I was expecting release any day, so I wondered, "What is this new condition?" Ambassador Carew said, "They want the Syrian authorities to hand over the body of Eli Cohen to 'Israel,' and this condition must be met before they release you."

I was dumbfounded and screamed, "What?! Have those Israelis gone mad? I refused to be traded with live detainees, so they want to trade me with a corpse? And whose corpse? A criminal Israeli spy who conspired against my homeland Syria? Impossible! I'd rather die behind bars than be released in return for a corpse! I'm worth much more than that! What kind of a despicable end is that?!"

Even worse, they wanted my written consent to the exchange

5 - Prison

to use it in negotiating with the Syrian government and taking advantage of the Syrian people's sympathy for my case. But I refused and threatened to resume my hunger strike unless the promise of release was fulfilled as soon as possible.

I then sent a message to President Hafez al-Assad stating my objection to release from prison if it included this condition. I asked him not to agree to it, so the Syrian authorities refused to consider the matter. Thereupon, "Israel" forfeited this demand after it had delayed my release an extra few weeks.

Finally, on November 5, Monsignor Carew came to the prison and told me, "We have finalized all the procedures and you will be released tomorrow." I was thrilled and said to His Grace, "I cannot wait to return to my congregation. We've been separated for too long." The Ambassador smiled and said, "Unfortunately, 'Israel' has stipulated harsh conditions on us before agreeing to release you."

I wondered, "What are these conditions? I would like to return to Jerusalem." The Apostolic Delegate replied, "The first condition the Israelis stipulated was that you leave the land of Palestine forever. You are forbidden from returning here even on a passing visit. The second condition is that you are forbidden from living in any Arab country."

His words shocked me like an electric current. I interrupted him screaming, "Impossible! This is ultimate oppression! Where do you want me to go? I cannot breathe except the air of Palestine. I cannot survive except under the sky of Palestine." He said with a somewhat distressed voice, "What is done is done. You will leave the prison, head directly to Rome, and stay there until further notice." I responded:

> When Israeli police arrested me four years ago, you came to visit me with His Grace Archbishop Boulos Al-Ashqar, and you offered me release from prison to any Arab country

without any terms or conditions. That day, my answer to your offer was: "No! I refuse to leave Palestine even to an Arab country. I will not leave. I'd rather remain in prison." Here, I feel I'm among my brothers and sons. When I look at the sky over this prison, I say to myself: "This is the same sky that covers Jerusalem, Bethlehem, Haifa, and Jaffa. The people of Palestine and me live under one roof. Therefore, I do not wish to get out of prison except to return to my congregation and my archbishopric in Jerusalem."

Why do you want me now to get out upon conditions that I have refused four years ago? My stance has not changed. I do not wish to leave prison except to return to Jerusalem, and I am capable of remaining steadfast. Please send a message to His Holiness the Pope and relay to him my thankfulness and gratitude for his fatherly initiative towards me. But if His Holiness considers that he is rescuing me by removing me from prison, then I consider it the opposite. My real prison is leaving Palestine to any place other than it! I feel that staying here inside this cell is an honor! Remaining in prison gives me inner peace and relieves my conscience a thousand times more than freedom in exile. I hope that His Holiness would understand that I do not want to go against his wish but would prefer to remain in prison.

The Apostolic Delegate replied, "These are the orders of His Holiness the Pope. The Holy See has exerted strenuous efforts to reach this agreement with 'Israel' and we will not go back on it."

I answered, "I cannot go against the orders of His Holiness the Supreme Pontiff. He is the head of the church, and he is my superior and I will never mutiny against the orders of my superior. His will be done, not mine." However, for this reason, I said in my first statement after my release, "I came out of the small prison only to enter a bigger prison."

5 - Prison

X

A Farewell Note from My Mother

I dreamed that my mother would be the first face I would see after leaving prison. She was still alive the day they released me, but I was forbidden from going to Lebanon to see her compassionate face and kiss the hand that continued to wipe the sweat off my forehead and console me while I was behind the bars of the Israeli prison cell.

My aging mother was living in her house in al-Ashrafiyya, Lebanon, with my brother Rizqallah. She never left it throughout the war years. Although she was yearning to see my face and was worried sick about me, she sent me encouraging words urging me to be patient and to persevere. She would say that she was waiting for me and that she would not leave this world before my release from prison and before she embraced me at least one more time. My mother was my source of consolation in prison. She used to be a cheerful person, full of joy, but my imprisonment ripped the happiness from her heart, the cheerfulness from her eyes, and the peace from her mind. She was anxious to share all my grief and pains. Since the moment of my arrest, she supported everything I did and believed in my cause just as I believed in it or even more. When I learned while in prison that she was ill and that her eyesight was fading, I feared I would never see her again and my longing for her intensified. A mother always holds a special place in her children's hearts: what then is the place of a mother who had sacrificed everything she had for us and was both mother and father?

The last message I received from my mother was verbal and delivered to me by a Lebanese nun from the Rosary Sisters of Jordan. The nun obtained permission to visit me and came to the prison in the West Bank to whisper my mother's words in my ear: giving me great consolation. My mother said:

I know how much torture and pain you are suffering. My heart is always with you and I pray for you from dawn to dusk. But I want you to know that your imprisonment is but a temporary phase and that you will soon see the light. A day will come when our Lord will put an end to your suffering, and when you think then about your time in prison, your suffering will seem to you to be mere memories. Hold on to faith because you will soon see the sun of freedom. That is my advice to you.

My mother's prophecy came true, but I was prevented from visiting her. Thus, despite her illness, she travelled to Rome to see me after my release, and I basked in the brightness of her face.

My mother, may her soul rest in peace, insisted on remaining in her house in the thick of war in Lebanon amid the bombardment and whizzing bullets. She refused to leave it for a safe place and would say to those who asked her to move to save her life, "I wish to stay here where I feel I'm sharing with my son some of his pains." She was forced to leave her house, which was close to demarcation lines, when she fell and broke her leg. They took her to the hospital. Later on, she became blind and passed away in 1979 after my release from prison to exile in Latin America.

I remember now her words; may she rest in peace. Yes, indeed, the prison phase seems like mere dark memories, but they are memories that taught me many things. The most important lesson I learned was to see that everything in this existence is beautiful. I am now happy with simple things such as light, breeze, and the chirping of birds. They are all sources of joy and reasons to thank God for His blessings.

In prison, material things lost their meanings. I discovered new kinds of happiness created by my imagination and interwoven with laughs from my memories...the fondest of which were in Jerusalem and Lebanon.

6 - Reflections From a Rotten Prison Cell

"The life and works of Hilarion Capucci, his commitment to Palestine above all, for which he paid a heavy price, are a testament to how Arab Christians have always identified themselves with their Arab homeland. Today, as many Christians are forced into exile, leaving their homes in Iraq, Syria, and Palestine, Capucci's life offers a valuable lesson to all, for although circumstances may force many to leave their homeland, distance will never transform into forgetfulness." – Fadi Esber, the editor of the peer-reviewed historical journal *Dimashq*

I

I escaped from my prison every day

Ever since I first stepped on the Jerusalem soil, I felt that it was my spiritual land. My spiritual birth was there, just as my physical birth was in Aleppo. I grew attached to Jerusalem, the soil of Jerusalem, and the essence of Jerusalem more than my attachment to life. Jerusalem is the holy city of which I was given the honor to be bishop. An unspeakable love and yearning drew me to it.

Throughout my time in prison, I used to pass in my imagination - as in the song of Fairuz - through the ancient streets of Jerusalem. I would go into temples and churches and pray. I would run away from prison and roam around the alleys, visit friends, and spend my day in memories among family and loved ones. Then, I would return to myself and realize that my time in prison would inevitably end.

When that gloomy dark feeling used to come over me, and when the grief of isolation and estrangement away from my loved ones ate at me, I would say to myself: "Come on, let's go on a trip to Syria." I would take the road to Syria and walk, in my mind's eye, among the orchards and then wander around the old markets. I would enter the houses of friends and have tea with them. I would continue my imaginary trip to my birthplace, Aleppo, or go to Beirut to reminisce on its beloved mountain about youth and the taste of my beautiful days. My story with Lebanon is a long one: a chronic love story. I fell in love with the beautiful Mount Lebanon, the green pine hills, the shimmering fresh water, and the unique breeze of freedom. I used to feel that breeze across my face as I lay on the straw mattress in the dingy Israeli cell which the sunrays never visited. Prison life is hard no matter how tough the prisoner is.

II

A gift of olive trees for Yasser Arafat

A prisoner lives cut off from the world. Time stops and loses its value. In normal life, time is a tangible reality that we live moment by moment all day because we divide time into minutes and hours that we distribute according to our schedule. In prison, there is no schedule or division of the passage of time; therefore, time becomes an eternity. It does not pass. It freezes, and the prisoner lives isolated behind iron bars that block freedom from him. Consequently, he sends his thoughts in all directions in search of a role to play that enables him to divide time as in normal life. I used to focus my thoughts on my fellow inmates: how to help my brothers and how to lift the oppressive shackles and the harsh system imposed on us.

I was not allowed to mix with the other inmates or for any of them to approach me. However, the need to communicate would overcome this strict prohibition. I would exchange a few words with them on my way to meet a visitor who managed to obtain a

6 - Reflections From a Rotten Prison Cell

permit to visit me, on my way to the pharmacy, or when I went out in the fresh air for a short break (half an hour a day). Despite the constant presence of guards at my side, I would manage to communicate a few words to the other inmates. They were only a few words, yet often sufficient to deliver the intended message. I used to prepare what I wanted to say, and while some of the young men distracted the guards, I would communicate with the intended person and pass my message, which often reached its address.

Among those who requested to meet me was a Jewish prisoner named David Kelly. I met him three times. He was an Israeli citizen and an expert on manufacturing weapons. I had mentioned him earlier, as he was accused of leaking information abroad.

My encounters with the prisoners would often take place in front of the door to the sawmill where they spent time making artifacts and wood sculptures. The most prominent of their sculptures were the olive trees, which I used to send as small gifts to those dear to me outside prison. Their importance lay in the fact that olive tree wood would be smuggled in from outside the prison, and we would sculpt it and re-smuggle it to our people as a symbol of our adherence to the land and the cause. I sent an olive tree sculpture as a gift to Yasser Arafat. He placed it on his desk and it never left him. On the sculpture, the cross and the crescent embraced on the olive wood next to the inscription "Allahu Akbar."

III

Strength makes victory

You ask if I had moments of hesitation or regret in prison. No! As for suffering, yes. I lived through many days of suffering and I experienced different kinds of pain. I am a normal human being: I feel happy and sad, I cry and I laugh. By nature, I do not like suffering; rather I love life. I am no Zarathustra. In prison, I faced many situations that hurt me deeply and caused me immense pain. Foremost were the times I was insulted, humiliated, and treated with contempt by the warden and Jewish inmates. It started in the early days of my detention in the Kfar Yuna prison and never stopped throughout four years of incarceration!

I cannot describe the extent of my grief and pain when I woke up in the morning and did not find my clerical robe, and I was forced to wear the inmate uniform. I felt that I was walking around naked. I was overwhelmed by a feeling of shame and humiliation that turned into an excruciating pain that has never left me. I suffer every time I remember that despicable incident.

I accepted life in prison, and I was content with what God willed, based on my inner convictions and patriotic principles. But on the human level, it was totally different. As a human being, I did not want this for myself, and therefore, I suffered intense agony: agony of prison, agony of loneliness, agony of contemptuous treatment, and agony of separation from my loved ones.

Physical pain does not differentiate between people. They are equal before the pains of the body. Christ suffered pain: it made him scream from deep within and he asked his Father to let the bitter cup be taken away from him. The difference is the ability of each person to endure agony.

A very painful incident happened to me in Iran. I was getting out of the car to enter the InterContinental Hotel to attend a reception held in my honor by the various Christian denominations in Iran. Suddenly, the car door slammed on my hand and my finger was squeezed. My nail was detached from the flesh and I felt acute pain, as if my soul was leaving my body. Nevertheless, I did not scream. The heads of denominations were standing at the door to receive me, so it was a critical moment without any room for weakness. I got out of the car as if nothing had happened and shook hands with everyone. I sat for two hours listening to speeches and gave a half-hour speech while the pain drilled through me like nails. I felt that my finger was being plucked off my hand. When I arrived at my hotel, sweat was pouring from my forehead and I almost fainted because of the excruciating pain. A physician came and bandaged the wound. He injected me with morphine and said, "This is strange! How come you did not lose consciousness? You will definitely lose your fingernail and you will have to bear a lot of pain for quite some time."

IV

Christ speaks with my tongue

When I recall the memories of my trial, think of the statements I made during the hearings, and remember how I used to spring up from my seat to protest with full strength and competence ... and when I remember my dismal physical condition at the time, I ask myself: "From where did I draw that strength? How did my exhausted mind shine with such brilliant thought? From where did all this energy to speak with such eloquence come at a time that I was weak and physically exhausted? How did I say what I said?" I cannot understand myself or the source of my strength except through profound faith deep-rootedness in the words of Christ. Thus, I say that it was God speaking through me. A divine strength descends upon us and grants us the ability to speak, as our Lord Jesus Christ says in the Bible:

> When you are brought before synagogues, rulers and authorities, do not worry about how you will defend yourselves or what you will say, for the Holy Spirit will teach you at that time what you should say. (Luke 12:11-12)

I felt deep down that Christ was speaking with my tongue in that court!

In the Name of God

V

Death in prison... or freedom!

Deep down, I felt that I would not stay in prison for 12 years. As far as the Israeli law was concerned, I was sentenced and had to serve my entire sentence. But I felt that I would leave prison when the clock strikes, and that I would be able to smash the wall or make a gap in it to break the lock and open the door.

I was making plans from the very beginning. I never did anything without calculating every step. Everything I did since my arrest was oriented toward the principal goal, which was to expose the brutality of "Israel" and get out of prison. I studied each decision beforehand and thought it over. I made my decisions based on prior planning and predetermination. Since the first minute, I knew that I had two choices: either I die in prison, or I force them to release me before the 12 years had passed.

VI

Hunger strikes are a platform against "Israel"

The purpose of my recurrent hunger strikes was not to make personal gains or improve the wretched conditions and the worst kinds of suffering I was experiencing. In fact, I adapted to the pain over time and no longer wished anything for myself. So, I sought to turn my imprisonment into a media platform to fight "Israel" and to make my trial an alarm bell that sounds in people's consciences and makes them wonder: "Why are they putting that Archbishop on trial? He is a clergyman who devoted himself to God and to doing good: it is not possible that he would do evil. So why then did he get himself involved in working with fedayees and smuggled weapons and explosives for them?"

I wanted the world to pose difficult questions in order to

6 - Reflections From a Rotten Prison Cell

understand the reason for fedayee action and realize that military operations were launched not because fedayees love blood; rather, because they had a cause that the world had forgotten about despite its horrible tragedy. No one hears anymore that there existed a Palestinian people with a cause! The Nakbah (catastrophe) of 1948 has faded, and the aftermath of the 1967 defeat has settled. The world - with the Arab states at the forefront - has returned to normal life as if nothing had happened. No one knows what it means to confront that state of indifference. I wanted to scream from my depth: "We are here! We have a cause. We are homeless. We have lost our land. Understand!"

Military action was a means to rouse consciences, but the enemy was able to cripple military operations and eradicate them on the inside. Now, they are almost non-existent.

Since my goal was to turn my imprisonment into a platform to confront "Israel," I had to do whatever was possible to draw the world's attention to my existence in prison and shed light on the reasons for my imprisonment, which were patriotic, not criminal, as the enemy wished to depict them to the world. I asked myself: What makes noise in the world? A hunger strike! A hunger strike is the most powerful weapon a prisoner can use.

A one or two-day strike would not achieve any goal, but when it continues for a month and a half and the prisoner loses 35 kg of his weight, people will be concerned. They will move and talk about the possibility of the Archbishop's dying in prison. Then more questions will follow such as "Why is he going on a hunger strike?" So, they will search for answers that would be a slap to Israel. To achieve that end, I used to contrive reasons to go on a hunger strike without consideration for the negative effects it would have on me personally. I was seeking repercussions in the media abroad.

One of my earliest plans was to work towards the day that I would start a hunger strike, lose much of my weight, and see my health collapse until I was near death. I wanted to force the Israelis to choose between two options: either let me die in prison or release me!

We all know that the fabricated reputation of "Israel" is all that it has and that everything that affects its reputation abroad affects the credibility of its existence, given that it is a usurping entity. Therefore, it is as keen on its reputation as it is on its very existence. The death of an archbishop in an Israeli prison would strike at its reputation like a cross-continental missile landing at the center of Tel Aviv.

I said to myself: "If the enemy is given the choice between letting me die in prison and releasing me, they will choose the lesser of the two evils, which is releasing me." Although I was certain that they would yield to the embarrassing situation I put them in and release me, I was prepared to die in prison. I would repeat to myself: it is better that one person dies for a nation than an entire nation. My demise in prison would deal a painful strike to the reputation of "Israel" and shed light on the inhumane, unethical, or rather brutal way in which it treats its prisoners. This is a positive factor that would be of benefit to the cause. With this in mind, I knew with certainty that I would never spend 12 years in prison and that the date of my release was not in the hands of "Israel"; rather, it was in my own hands because it was me who drew the start line and who would draw the finish line. This is exactly what happened.

When I went on the last hunger strike that lasted for three months, and after losing 35 kg of my weight, global broadcast media reported news of my imprisonment, hunger strike, and health deterioration. The news reached His Holiness Pope Paul VI whom I had met more than once and talked to at length about Jerusalem. I also wrote to him from prison explaining the circumstances of my arrest and what I was suffering behind bars. I received a written reply from His Holiness, which upon reading it, imparted to me the feeling that he was a father, a brother, and a

6 - Reflections From a Rotten Prison Cell

source of inspiration and guidance. When he became acquainted with my dismal situation and realized that my life was in danger, he hastened to rescue me and extended his hand to Israel, which was a major concession on the part of the Vatican.

In fact, the initiative of His Holiness the Pope was a rescue operation for the Israelis from a serious dilemma. They had no choice whatsoever. I was ready to continue the hunger strike until the end, and I insisted on it: either I die or they release me. There was no third choice. The papal initiative saved the Israelis and served many purposes.

Instead of caving in and releasing me reluctantly, they let me out of prison upon conditions and made their decision look like a service rendered to all Christians around the world. Instead of stepping out with my head high and the freedom of movement to go wherever I want and live wherever I choose, they imposed their own conditions on the Vatican. The Vatican officials, in good faith and out of their love for me, took the initiative to make a request to "Israel." Thus, "Israel" won.

I do not wish to say that that papal initiative offended me, but I can say that it "harmed" me when it provided the way out of the dilemma that the Israeli was looking for. I am certain that "Israel" would never have allowed me to die in prison. It had to release me. Someone might think that what I am saying is "inappropriate" or a denial of a favor, but I had confidence in my plan. I am a stubborn person, and when I insist on a matter, I must make it happen regardless the circumstances.

I do not insist on a matter except after lengthy contemplation, and when I give my word, I never go back on it. When I insisted on the long hunger strike after spending those years in prison, I chose the right time and was certain of the validity and seriousness of my decision as well as its feasibility. The Israelis knew how indefatigable I was. They knew when I said "I am going to the very end" that I really meant it and that they had to release me before I reached the end point that I had my eyes fixed on. From the start, I drew a plan to end the battle of my arrest and imprisonment. I knew that it would end either with my death or my unconditional release, and that my release would not be by virtue of their noble manners: no, it would be me forcing them to do it. But, unfortunately, the Vatican's love and will were stronger than my decision.

VII

My morale was the secret of my strength

The toll that prison took on me had a more decisive impact on my morale than on my health and physical wellbeing. Despite all my suffering behind bars, I came out of prison physically intact. I suffered torment and distress, and I went on a hunger strike and lost 32 kg. However, in spite of it, I did not take a single pill, visit a physician, or stay in a hospital. Even here in exile, I have not visited a medical clinic. It is true that I am physically weak, but I am in good health. I was not suffering any chronic disease, and I did not have any digestive pain, dizziness, or ulcer. I endured all the agonies of prison and felt I had the energy to endure more. I felt I had enough energy, strength, and "prowess" equal to the whole world. The reason? High morale. Morale is everything. My body remained unharmed, praise be to God, because my morale was high.

I received letters of support from all over the world. Letters arrived from young children who wrote to me: "We love you." I received words of support from America, England, Australia, France, and other places. They came from all corners of the world and said in one voice: "You are in our thoughts. We love you. We follow your news. We pray for you..." Such genuine spontaneous solidarity warmed my heart and made me stronger, firmer, and more determined to continue the struggle until the last breath.

VIII

The ultimate victory is in death

Under all circumstances, if you ask me what is my joy in this life or what I worship after God, I will say "work." Work to me is like water to a fish. If you deprive it of water it dies, and I die without work. The value of a person is measured by the volume of his output. If he produces ten, his value is ten, and if he produces zero, his value is zero. Based on this principle, I never stopped working for a single day in my life. Even in prison, I did not recoil or slow down. The hunger strikes that cost me dearly, the messages I wrote and sent in all directions, the uproar I sought to stir abroad... all of this was work. However, it was not the sort of work I wished for.

My death was the real work that I sought to achieve! My death for the cause would have been the biggest achievement for me, because I had an unshakable inner conviction that my death would not pass unnoticed. I told myself that my death would cause an international reaction, and I wanted to open the eyes and rouse the consciences. I wanted to be useful. My death would be the strongest way to achieve that goal. If the hunger strike had the explosive force of 20 kg, then death had a force many times as large. I wanted to score the ultimate victory when I took my last breath behind bars...but God did not will that.

7 - Letters from Prison

"He was a rare man, one of those who looks you in the eye because he knows he has nothing to hide, and much to teach." – Alberto Palladino, Italian journalist

I

The Dove

From behind the bars of my rotten cell inside the Ramleh prison, I sent out many letters, which I proudly regard as an act of defiance of my jailers. I used to communicate with fellow prisoners through short messages that I wrote on small paper clippings. For the letters I sent outside prison, I used to look for writing paper through every possible means. The letters were often written on "shabby" paper: wide, large, small, or wrinkled. I would write mostly at night on a small wooden table. I would be overjoyed with any paper that I obtained through fellow inmates who had their ways of bribing the guards. The Jew worships money, and he will do anything for its sake. We knew that, and we took advantage of this weakness whenever we could.

One of the most interesting anecdotes regarding these letters was when one of them reached an Arabic newspaper (either Al-Quds or An-Nahar). When the paper published the letter, it sparked an outcry everywhere and forced the prison warden to launch an investigation. He came to my cell and asked me, "Are these letters published in the papers authentic? Did you write them yourself?"

I answered, "Since they are published in international newspapers, then they must be authentic."

In the Name of God

He said, "Did you send them in a legal way?"

I said, "Did they pass by you? Did you read them?"

He said, "No, they did not pass by me. I would like to know how they got out of this prison."

I said, "Grant me protection and swear that you will not take any measures against the one smuggling the letters, and I will tell you who it is."

He said, "You are granted protection."

I said, "Listen. We, Christians, believe in the Holy Trinity: the Father, the Son, and the Holy Spirit. In the Bible, the Holy Spirit is embodied in the shape of a dove. Every day, before sunrise, a dove lands on the cell window and asks me what I want, so I ask it to carry my letters to the outside."

Outraged, he said, "Are you mocking me? Do you think I am a fool to believe your story?"

I answered him sarcastically, "And am I fool to tell you how I smuggle my letters to the outside?" Despite ordering stricter surveillance of my cell, he never discovered the way we used.

II

My Letters

The following are a sample of the many letters I wrote from prison:

His Beatitude Maximos V Hakim, the Honored, Patriarch of Antioch and All the East, of Alexandria and Jerusalem
Ramleh Prison, May 1976

7 - Letters from Prison

Your Beatitude,

I have tried many times to write to Your Beatitude to inform you fully of my situation, but I have not succeeded. God knows how I long to see and talk to you, but though I may be far from you in body, concealed in the darkness of prison, I am closer to you than ever before in my thoughts, my heart, and my prayers. God is content with me and my conscience is at rest, so my morale is high and I am supremely happy. In the depths of my heart, I enjoy peace and tranquility. I find myself in prison at the guidance of divine inspiration (commanding me not to oppose God who desired that I should be led as a lamb to the slaughter), from a desire to achieve peace, and from obedience to the dictates of my conscience which compelled me to be of service to the dearest of lands, our beloved Palestine, and to love the most holy of cities, our beloved Jerusalem.

The religious leader is a man of peace who builds and does not destroy, joins and does not divide, reconciles and does not set apart. I desire that my imprisonment, which I sought, should be the road to tribulation, the price of peace, and a beacon that will focus light for the world on our cruel affliction and our unrelenting problem, which has ruined our life and made it a hell. I pray daily that, with God's help and protection, all may unite in their efforts to ensure that the doors of our great prison, the Middle East, are flung open wide, so that its people may emerge from darkness into light and from the prison of their differences to the freedom of the children of God. I pray that they may come together in brotherly harmony and love one another: mobilizing all their resources not for war and bloodshed but for felicity, welfare, and prosperity in all fields; so that they may enjoy a just and permanent peace which will safeguard the rights of all, transform the area from a gloomy prison into a luxuriant garden, and turn the lives of those who dwell in it from a hell into a heaven.

But inasmuch as the religious leader also embodies the truth, because he represents Almighty God Who is the very truth, it is incumbent on him to combat falsehood, succor the truth, and defend the rights of peoples and individuals, especially in vital matters affecting the destiny of nations. If he fails, he is devoid of manhood and religion knows him not. Accordingly, the religious leader must be a strong bulwark against injustice: he must support those who are oppressed and have suffered injustice. He must feel with them, share their sentiments, and respond to their righteous and legitimate demands. In other words, he must be the shield, the support, and the refuge of all. This is what God and conscience require of every religious leader, and since God is entitled to obedience from man, I have done my duty. It is all the more required of me inasmuch as, within the limits of the Patriarchate of Jerusalem, stretching from the Gaza Strip through the West Bank, to Caesarea of Palestine, of which I am the Titular Archbishop, and lying at the gates of Haifa, I am responsible for a land in which right has been obliterated. In this land, the usurper is trying, with all the means at his disposal and in all fields, to make slaves of those whose rights he has usurped. All of these and their land are a sacred trust reposed in me. The Lord will call me to temporal account for them, and my fate on the Day of Judgement will depend on how faithfully I have served them. "Come unto me.... Inasmuch as you have done it unto one of the least of my brethren, ye have done it unto me," says Christ to the elect on the Day of Judgement.

I have loved our dear Palestine and its people. I have loved my Jerusalem, the capital of this usurped land. I have loved it and sung of it to the world as the Song of Songs, because it is the throbbing heart of the children of Jesus and the people of Muhammad. I have loved it because it is the country of my Master, Christ, and the cradle of my religion, Christianity and its land contain relics that are holy to me. I have loved it because it is the city of the Haram al-Sharif and the Aqsa Mosque, the first Qibla, and the third most sacred Haram. So when I saw it sorrowful and stricken, afflicted and humiliated, and garbed in black, I decided that I would follow in the footsteps of my Master who bore the cross to redeem humanity. I decided I would bear the cross to redeem the land of the cross and publish its tragedy, which is our

7 - Letters from Prison

tragedy, to the world: making my prison the pulpit from which I spread these tidings.

The most precious thing in the teachings of my Master is love. This was his last precept. Therefore, I believe in love and hold sacred brotherhood and friendship with all people, without distinction, and I respect all religions and their holy places as deeply as I do my own religion and its holy places. I have been grieved heart and soul and shocked to the very depths by the violation and desecration of the holy places that I have witnessed personally.

I shall never forget what I have experienced and what I have seen. Along with hundreds of my fellow citizens, I have witnessed terrible things in the Church of the Holy Sepulcher in Jerusalem! We have seen dogs in it and people strolling inside it smoking cigarettes, as if they were in a museum! How we have wept from grief and pain! The statue of the Virgin Mary on Calvary, in the Church of the Holy Sepulcher, was desecrated and her crown stolen. This was a criminal act repugnant to religion and morality. The place where Christ was born, in the court of the Church of the Nativity in Bethlehem, was spattered with colored paints and the Star of David was drawn on it. This provocative act aroused the resentment of all who believe in the holy places. A picture of Christ was hung in a Tel Aviv showroom surrounded by pictures of film actresses and Parisian beauties. This criminal act shocked everyone who had an atom of conscience and honor. The attempt to burn the Aqsa Mosque under the pretense that the man who made it was mad gave rise to interminable discord and strife. The continued excavations around the wall of the Aqsa Mosque threaten the cynosure of the whole Arab world with collapse. The contempt shown to us, religious leaders and Christians, the mockery of our appearance, and the scornful words and gestures which accompany our customary processions (for example, of the Via Dolorosa on Fridays) foster confessional tendencies and lead to grave discord with undesirable consequences. All this, unfortunately, has happened. Our precious land has been desecrated, and we have shuddered with repulsion.

Holy places derive their sanctity and dignity from the faithful. What would the Church of the Holy Sepulcher or the Aqsa Mosque be worth if there were no Christians living near the church and no Muslims around the mosque? Worshippers are to their holy places what the soul is to the body: they are their throbbing heart and life. Without them, they are no more than stones. Thus, my grief, dismay, and alarm are redoubled by the torrent of emigration on the part of Christians and Muslims alike.

I have seen my flock and my people, the protectors of Nazareth, Bethlehem, and the Church of the Holy Sepulcher, and all who live around the Via Dolorosa from the beginning to their departure. Since the declaration of the establishment of the state of Israel, the number of Christians in these places has fallen from 150,000 to 45,000. Since the occupation of the West Bank in 1967, the number of Christians has diminished from 55,000 to 45,000. Today, the total number of Christians in Palestine is only 90,000. What will happen if this emigration continues? The Christians in the Holy Land will die out within half a century, while the holy places will become mere museums bewailed and lamented by those to whom they are holy.

Has not all this broken my heart? Has it not evoked my tears? It has indeed. Have I not called on God to preserve the Church of the Nativity, the Church of the Holy Sepulcher, and the Via Dolorosa for His people? I have indeed. But when I was overcome by despair at the tragedy, I resolved to cry out to the world, from my heart, from here, from my prison, so that all who have ears to hear may hear my cry. "Come, rescue the children of Christ, rescue those who believe in Him. Come rescue the Muslims, His people, His friends and His neighbors. Come, the torrent of our tribulation has burst its banks."

The Jewish people suffered coercion, maltreatment, and torture in Europe. With all my heart, I deplore this persecution and abhor those who carried it out because I am the enemy of every usurper, criminal, and torturer. But I did not expect the victim to

7 - Letters from Prison

turn into the avenger. I did not expect that those who had been subjected to the horrors of terror should come to God's Holy Land, to the land of love and peace, to practice terror against my country, my people, my brethren, and my flock: employing a policy of aggression designed to empty the land of its people.

You, if anyone, Your Beatitude, who were in charge of the diocese of Acre, Haifa, Nazareth, and all Galilee for more than 25 years, are aware of the tragedy of this exodus and of its roots, which lie in racial discrimination: the disregard of rights in all fields, and maltreatment. Nevertheless, the Arabs in Israel, in the eyes of its rulers and because of their decisions, are second-class citizens.

In the West Bank, where Christ was born to free us from the yoke of slavery, we live in repression and terror. We are unable to exercise our liberties even in the simplest tasks of our life. Meetings are forbidden. Protests are forbidden. Strikes of all kinds, expression of opinion, and peaceful demonstrations are forbidden. Israel's concern is to stop all mouths, crush all revolt, and persuade the world that life in the West Bank has returned to normal and its people have become oblivious to their cause: nay, that they have been fused in the Israeli crucible. The intention of this concern is to use this fabricated propaganda as a cover and a pretext for perpetuating the occupation and liquidating the problem. Therefore, anyone who has tried to rebel against the interdict, to exercise his freedom to deny these artificial manifestations, to refute these claims, and to expose these expansionist intentions is expelled from his land and severed from his family, which is left destitute. Or else he is sent away to prison without trial and without being charged until he either dies or is released after being mutilated by torture. "Too much pressure causes an explosion," says the proverb. The bloody explosion that spread throughout the West Bank some months ago was engendered by this constant strangling pressure. The tumultuous demonstrations and the widespread disturbances that spread throughout the towns of the West Bank occurred in protest against the occupation and are clear proof that my description of it is true.

In the Name of God

This indignant uprising has made it clear to the world that the people of the West Bank were, in the most cruel and difficult circumstances, expressing their unanimous determination to recover their Palestinian identity and to decide their own future. As the voice of the people is the voice of God, the voice of truth has pierced the barrier: reaching the conscience of the world and the heart of the United Nations, which endorsed it despite Israel's determination to plug the world's ears so that it might not hear.

Shall I also tell of the Arab villages that have been blown up to the last house and been completely devastated, like Amwas, Yalu, and Beit Nuba? Shall I tell of the tragedy of the houses that have been demolished in their hundreds by order of the Military Governor in reprisal, intimidation, and punishment? Shall I tell of the many settlements that have been established in various places in the West Bank in conformity with the policy of the fait accompli and expansion? Shall I tell of the Judaization of Jerusalem? Of the thousands of dunums of land that have been confiscated around Jerusalem on which fortified buildings have been grafted: disfiguring the peace of Jerusalem and its character, complexion, and serenity and changing it into an American city, as if no Apostle had lived in it and no Prophet made his Night Journey to it?

If this dark picture is a true representation of the bitter situation the people of the West Bank are living in at present, what future can they expect if the occupation weighs on them for long? As long as it continues, their horizons will be dark, their hopes no more than a mirage in the desert, and all their wishes frustrated, so that all that will remain for them is to emigrate.

Shall I tell of the thousands of pilgrims and tourists I have met when giving lectures on the Palestine problem or on many other occasions who showed by the questions they asked me and the discussions following the lectures that the greater part of them were replete with Zionist ideas to the point of fanaticism, while the remainder knew nothing of our cause?

7 - Letters from Prison

It was for these bitter reasons and others that I was prompted to rise up so as to make world public opinion aware of the facts, to open eyes, ears, and minds, and to arouse consciences. "It is far better that one man should die for the people and that the whole nation perish not."

I am very happy in my mind inasmuch as my imprisonment was not imposed on me, but I chose it myself. Rather, God imposed it on me. I spend my days, which pass quickly, in prayer and reading. Thus, I am happy, especially as the feeling that possesses me here is that I am not wasting my time – I, who love work as a fish loves water. I am working for peace, firstly by prayers, because every true gift and genuine talent descends from on high, from Thee, the Lord of Lights. Peace is a boon from the Lord of Peace, and except that the Lord build the house, I labor in vain. Secondly, I am working for peace by my sufferings. Peace is above all price and the best currency with which to buy it is suffering, whose value is infinite. If it does not die, a grain of wheat remains but one, but if it dies, it brings forth fruit a hundredfold.

This does not mean the conditions of my detention are not very harsh. I am isolated from all other prisoners in a cell that never sees the sun and measures three meters long by one and a half meters wide. I cannot rest in it day or night because of the noise and uproar, the oaths, curses, and obscene language, and the fighting between the prisoners. In a word, I am being badly treated, for they are constantly waging against me a cold war of nerves, threats, provocation, and reprisal to destroy my self-respect and break my nerve. I reply to them with a smile of scorn, because God is with me. "He, God is with us, know ye nations and be vanquished, for God is with us."

Their disgraceful conduct I accept most willingly. What I cannot accept is that I should be expelled from this land. I insist on staying in my homeland, even as a prisoner. I have lived here, loving and loyal to my country, sharing in its construction, and trying to alleviate the tragedies of its peoples. Thus, I want to stay with it and in it. To be expelled and parted from my homeland, my holy places, my flock, my people, and my brethren is the punishment that I refuse, for it would deprive me of all meaning, pleasure, and purpose in life.

Finally, my heart and prayers turn towards the millions of Arabs of Palestine, some of whom have been dispersed all over the earth while others are suffering here in their homeland. All of them are strangers. All of them in the eyes of right and truth are martyrs for the recovery of their self-respect and their homeland.

My heart and my prayers turn towards all our honorable Arab rulers, their aides, and their armies in the hope that the Lord may support them in every right action. Towards His Holiness Pope Paul VI, our father and spiritual head, who has encompassed me with his paternal sympathy in my trial. Towards Your Beatitude and those for whom you are responsible, praying that the Lord may preserve you as a treasured possession of our Melkite Church: its priests and its people. Towards my brother bishops and their beloved dioceses.

In conclusion, I thank Your Beatitude for your insistent paternal efforts to achieve my release, and I apologize for the trouble you have been caused. May the Lord recompense you for what you have done for me with abundant grace and blessings and keep you in health and well-being. May I request Your Beatitude to do all you can to comfort my dear mother. This, indeed, is my only care, for I have been informed that despair has almost cost her life. This is the nature of mothers: they are governed by compassion, especially at her age.

Include me, Your Beatitude, in your blessings and your paternal supplications so that I may surrender to the will of God so that He may do with me what He wills. "Not my will but Thine be done, O Lord."

*****

7 - Letters from Prison

Your Beatitude Maximos V Hakim,
the Honored, Patriarch of Antioch and All the East,
of Alexandria and Jerusalem

Ramleh Prison, 21/01/1976

I take this opportunity of the glorious Christmas with the New Year and the feast of St. Maximos, your patron, to convey my heartfelt love and to send you, despite intense censorship, my warmest felicitations and best wishes. Many happy returns of the season for many years with abundant blessings. May God the Most High guard you with His vigilant eyes and fulfill your hopes, for His glory, to the best of the Church and our community, and for the service of our dear Arab countries. Your patron, who was displaced twice and died in defense of his faith as an exile, is my role model and source of consolation. As you, Your Beatitude, stood by my side in my tribulation as supporter and protector, a brother, a faithful friend, and a believing Arab, you established my determination and rooted my feet. I am deeply grateful and appreciative to you, with my sincere affiliation and earnest respect.

Behind the iron bars, I celebrate a second glorious Christmas. Those who dwell in darkness have seen the Christmas light with Christ in the prison, His grace, and His blessing. Christ stipulated the spiritual birth as a requirement to enter the kingdom of God. Christmas in prison is wondrous: the feast is a blessing. It is the appearance of the star, the radiance of the light, the sign of the beginning of our joy, and the beginning of our liberation from slavery. This occurs through the Savior who broke the chains, shattered the shackles, opened the kingdom, restored our lost dignity (the stolen paradise), and reconciled us having made Himself nothing through incarnation, deprivation, and redemption.

On Christmas Eve in my cold narrow cell (which is similar to the Savior's manger in terms of pettiness and to the Savior's tomb in terms of darkness and guards), I found myself, like Him, at night and in solitude. I was away in my body from my heavenly kingdom, my big family, my nation, my people, my children, and my Church. Like Him, I was in a distant place: stripped of my priestly garments with no place to rest my head other than a manger! I returned to my seclusion and my humbleness and felt myself shivering surrounded by deep sorrow. A dense cloud, woven by memories with longing pain, obscured the sky of my cell. It landed on my chest and left me in a state of grief.

I burst into tears. The murky atmosphere soon dissipated when I heard angels singing, "Glory to God in the highest heaven, and on earth peace to those on whom His favor rests.." I listened carefully to this song of hope, which was originally sung from our land: from Bethlehem and from Palestine. It echoed throughout the prison proclaiming the great joy and the glorious salvation and calling for peace and love. When I understood it and grasped it, I glorified God. Joy overwhelmed me, and my heart was filled with reassurance. The shining light defeated the darkness of my cell, and the Messenger of Peace filled it with his joy. Suddenly it turned into a heaven. My manger turned into a pulpit. I felt the warmth of His grace flowing into my heart and the heat of His love overwhelming the depths of my spirit. I found myself very close to Him, for He is Emmanuel, God with us. I saw myself in my thoughts, in my heart, in the midst of all my people, in my kingdom, and with all my dear ones. I knelt down, praying with the shepherds rather than the Magi, for who am I now compared to their greatness and richness? I prostrated to the Savior Child. I gave Him all my gifts: all that I owned, my faith in Him, my hope in Him, and my love for Him. I believed in Him as a new Child. "The Word became flesh and made His dwelling among us."

I believed in the incarnation of the Word and in the manhood of love as a path to us for our salvation. I believed that the word of God is effective, because His word is life: "My Father is always at His work to this very day, and I too am working." I believed that, if I did not represent my belief in Him and in His love in my deeds, if my belief was not practical, it would be dead. I am in darkness,

7 - Letters from Prison

in death, and in the separation of the spirit and the body. Life is in the incarnation of the Word, and the word is love.

Therefore, I believed that Christianity is not a doctrine to sing for, nor the Church an institution to be proud of. "Show me your faith without deeds, and I will show you my faith by my deeds." So, Christianity is life: it is action. The Church is light and guidance, because Christ is the head of the Church. He is the way, the truth, and the life. He sacrificed Himself to sanctify her.

So, I believed that the Church, represented by her people, is a revolution: the authentic revolution of truth. It follows Christ who drove all money-changers and sellers from the temple. He overturned their tables, scattered their coins, and drove them out with a whip. They had desecrated the sanctity of the temple and robbed Him of His rights and dignity. The Church is a revolution in all fields: a revolution against injustice, falsehood, and backwardness. The Church has to reflect the hopes and aspirations of mankind because she is the center of radiation and conscience in the world: thus we define the Church. This is her mission.

Based on my belief, the Palestinian cause with its dilemmas tests the essence of the Church. It questions the meaning of the Church, the extent of my commitment to social issues, the extent of my effectiveness and human interaction, my faith in the highness of my religion, and my destiny. The end time depends on the extent of my contribution to human services. "Come... for... I needed clothes and you clothed Me... I was in prison and you came to visit Me."

Palestine is inside of me in my heart. Its cause springs from my conscience. My struggle for it is merely an embodiment of my faith in the love of God who was incarnated to redeem and save what had been lost. My love for it is my expression of appreciation of the Church - the secret body of Christ - and of the message of the Church. My conscription in the service of Palestine is only a sign, a testimony, until martyrdom and redemption.

In the Name of God

In a fervent prayer, I asked God Incarnate that His Church may fulfill the hopes placed on her and stand out in the service of fellow humans, as mother and educator, as a little yeast that works through the whole batch of dough, so His name may be glorified, the earth full of peace, and the people be pleased. However, my hope "Glory to God, peace, favor"– the echo of what the angels sang on the Nativity Eve – became void words and statements. In the twentieth century, man combined contradictions into a combination of light and darkness. It is the generation of light in terms of science and the generation of darkness in terms of religion and values. Man's mind progressed so that he invaded the moon, yet he fell down to the depths. Man descended morally and humanely. The development of his mind can only be equal to his mental retardation. His original image was distorted, and he was likened more to animals, not to God.

Where is God? Where is His glory? Materialism is the human idol: it has overwhelmed the spirit and choked it! Is there peace while nations and individuals adopt power, violence, and selfishness as a slogan? As long as instincts and fancies, antagonism, aversion, and hatred remain, favor is just an illusion. Therefore, by excluding God from the hearts, and excluding principles and values from the society, few are the places where peace reigns and where people are blessed with favor.

There are wars: racial ones, class conflict, and social crises. From every corner, there are stenches: the stench of fighting, destruction, and devastation. All are covered with dim clouds of loneliness, sorrow, pain, and the specter of death.

The first thing to remember in this gloomy picture is two dear Arab countries: Palestine and Lebanon. Yes, Palestine, the earthly Paradise, the cradle of the heavenly religions. In Palestine, the prophets' calls for love and brotherhood were echoed and angelic peace was chanted. Palestine, the place where divine revelation descended, is torn today as a country and as a people. It is crying for her people: the residents and the displaced. Palestine, the land

7 - Letters from Prison

of peace, which was swept away and destroyed by four wars, is a volcano on the verge of its fifth eruption. The people of Palestine, the present and the absent, had their rights violated and their dignity dishonored. They are all strangers and martyrs.

The fighting in Palestine has achieved what imposes it and what sanctifies it. A tyrannous elusive enemy robbed us of our homes by perching on our chests. This enemy took arrogance as a slogan, intransigence as a technique, and force as an approach, so the only way for liberation and return is strife. In Lebanon, does the escalating massacre logically explain anything to our conscience? Why is this blind fighting? What is meant by the destruction of Lebanon? Lebanon, the safe Arab country, the oasis, the haven? O Lebanon, a civilized country, a place of admiration, a site of hopes, a green country which is a piece of heaven . . . why did you, with your people and territories, turn into hell? Why have you become deserted? Why have you become darkened that your enemies are gloating over you? What has beset you that you took the path of suicide? Why do you bleed? Why are you full of pain? The guideposts of brotherhood in you were obliterated and became food to the wolves. The slogans of love that I used to raise and adopt have gone with the wind: they evaporated and vanished. The last word is no longer left to God: conscience, reason, values, or to the Lebanese and Arab interests. You have been wrapped in selfishness, hatred, and power, and there is no conversation in you except the buzz of gunfire and the hum of bullets.

O Lebanon, a desperate, depressed country, I am the Arab citizen lying far away in the darkness of prison. The tragic shameful news coming from you increase the darkness of my prison and add bitterness to my sorrow. The bullets fired among your people are bruising my heart. The pounding of guns leaves me restless. Your ruin hurts me. Your people - children, orphans, widows, and the mutilated - are wailing. Smoke rising from your territories (mixed with blood and full of misery, terror, and hatred) has leaked to my cell: increasing its darkness and engulfing the depths of my spirit.

In the Name of God

Lord! How long will Your face turn away from the beloved Lebanon? How long will it cause grief in my heart? My soul is overwhelmed with sorrow to the point of death for this escalating massacre among Your children. The tragedy of Lebanon made my enemies humiliate me, disdain me, and hurt my dignity even more. I have become their laughingstock! Lord, have mercy on me. The torment I suffer day and night is almost unbearable. Do not let me carry what I cannot bear. I have offered You my torture, pains, and life as a sacrifice so that Lebanon may live. What else may I do, O merciful Lord? Have mercy on Lebanon so You may have mercy on me and relieve my distress. Set Lebanon free from the traps set for it. Do not make it an easy target, but rather a nail in the mouth of its enemies. Break all conspiracies against its rock. Lift up its immortal cedar trees over the bodies of those who kindled the fire of sedition... let it avoid the disaster of division. Do not divide Lebanon: unite the Lebanese people. O You, the One in love, in three Persons, unify in love the hearts of Muslims, Christians, and Palestinians, so they may believe and live in an independent and free Lebanon. In our present fateful national circumstances, the unity of Lebanon and the Lebanese people and the unification of the hearts of all those who are covered by the skies of Lebanon are victory for our nation, a guarantee for the safety of our shared supreme Arab interests, and the first stretch on the road to save Jerusalem and liberate Palestine. Victory comes with love, and power comes with union.

At the beginning of the New Year, I did not ask God to release me. I asked Him for the safety of Lebanon, the victory of the truth in Palestine, and peace for the whole world. A prisoner, Your Beatitude, is sensitive: more sensitive than a barometer. Each sign has its bearing on a prisoner. A prisoner is constantly prone to psychological fluctuations. So, my pen is unable to express my fears and concerns: the pain that is afflicting me or my weary soul. A buried prisoner needs fresh air, but I breathe nothing but toxic gases. I smell corpses, fire, smoke, the dust rising from under the rubble, and the stink of grudges! A person lost in the darkness of prison delights in good news that releases their distress, but I hear

7 - Letters from Prison

only what stimulates anguish and discourages resolve: the whining of the wounded, the screaming of children and old people, the wailing of widows and orphans, voices calling for separation, and the sound of explosions! My permanent question is, "Is it not time for this dark night to disappear?" I am perplexed. Where are the Lebanese thinkers? Where are the dignitaries of Lebanon and the leaders? Why are they not calling upon each other: gathering and joining efforts to encircle the fire of the consuming war, cut off its complications, and eliminate its dimensions? A friend in need is a friend indeed: is it not so? Is Lebanon a milking cow from which we enjoyed fruits and drew blood, and when it fell down with ailment, many butchers were around? Have we become thus negligent and failed to do ourselves justice?

While I am confused about the causes of the fighting due to their ambiguity, I am sure of the following. First, history will starkly condemn all the parties of the conflict without exception. Those who were right in their demand were certainly mistaken in their approach. Violence breeds nothing but violence, and kindness among brethren is more efficient, not to mention that Israel, the mastermind of sedition, is the only winner. Second, Lebanon is burning, melting, and facing the most serious plight in its history that might destroy it, God forbid. Third, this fierce war must end immediately, whatever the obstacles. This is obvious to me. In the future, there must be an open brotherly discussion about its causes in light of the bitter lessons we have learned. The discussion should be held to come up with fair, logical, and realistic solutions that will eradicate the disease from its roots and eliminate strife without return. Then those who will proclaim victory will be neither Muslims nor Christians, neither the right nor the left, neither the classes nor the parties, but the people. Then the last word will be left to conscience, reason, love, and to the public interest, and victory will be to Lebanon.

Proverbs are the extract of the experience of generations throughout history. A proverb goes, "No construction come unless after ruin, and no friend is made unless after fight."

In the Name of God

We did not destroy this country except to build it. We did not separate except to meet again, more resolutely and more sincerely, to overwhelm this beloved country with hearts full of faith in one God, one Lebanon, one Lebanese interest, and one Arab destiny. May we, with the unity of heart and class, and with mutual trust, construct our new Lebanon. This atmosphere is the only one that is favorable to the constructive dialogue: the only one that is encouraging us to "Give back to Caesar what is Caesar's and to God what is God's.." We and Lebanon would thus be safe.

Now that I have poured out the pain and hope in my heart into your big heart, Your Beatitude, I feel some comfort. I ask God that peace prevail over the entire world, that we see on the glorious Christmas and New Year a new Lebanon where joy and reassurance fill all hearts. I hope that we move from the exhausting disuniting destructive side battles to our national battle, so we may devote ourselves fully to mobilize our powers and intensify our energies to the paths of return... to Jerusalem and to Palestine. To achieve this goal, I do not cease daily prayers for our honored Arab rulers, their helpers, and their armies to unite the Arabs and the ranks of the two sisters: Egypt and Syria. Before and after the Ramadan War in 1973, we experienced the good coordination in their close ties. We saw the extent of its usefulness and we reaped its tasty fruits, so we want more!

My prayers for you, Your Beatitude, are incessant. May the Most High guide your steps and fill your heart with His joys. I asked Him today, in the divine sacrifice, to grant you all that you had requested at the feast of your patron of benedictions and blessings. Please convey to His Holiness the Pope, our father, my most sincere feelings of sonship. My tongue is speechless at his patriarchal attitude towards me. I always remember him in my prayers. Please convey to the eminent bishops, my brothers, my warm greetings and love. I pray for each of them continually, for their respected priests, and for their people, that they may attain success and abundant blessings. I pray for our great monastic orders, for the clergy, and for the monastic and priestly vocations.

7 - Letters from Prison

In conclusion, remember me, Your Beatitude, in your blessing and fatherly prayer. I urgently need your prayer. My health has deteriorated with the escalation of the Lebanese crisis and its repercussions on our Arab interests. My sadness is deep, and my morale is dwindling. My headache, chest pain, and back pain are continuous. Pray to God so He may bless me with patience so I may bear my psychological and physical pains for His glory and so He may fill hearts with His peace throughout the world, in the bereaved Palestine, and in the grieving Lebanon. May Your angels, O God, rejoice in the birth of a new Lebanon, with the glory of Your name, so Lebanon may continue its genuine, avant-garde message nationally and on the Arab and international levels. May the people of Lebanon and all sincere people be blessed with favor.

Sincerely,

Hilarion

Titular Archbishop of Caesarea, Palestine

Patriarchal Vicar of the Greek Catholics in Jerusalem

*****

His Beatitude Maximos V Hakim, the Honored, Patriarch of Antioch and All the East, of Alexandria and Jerusalem

Ramleh Prison, 20/02/1976

Your Beatitude,

It is my heart writing this letter to you, not my pen. However, the simple language of the heart is eloquent in its sense because it is a replica of the abstract truth. The total exhaustion that afflicts me may not enable me to coordinate my thoughts: so please excuse me in advance and accept my letter.

In the Name of God

As of January 28th, I have not consumed anything but water. I am on a complete hunger strike, which I will continue to the end. I have had enough of the enemy's extreme insolence and mistreatment, blatant psychological warfare, and provocation against me. If only I were personally the sole target of their disgraceful behavior, I would not have cared, for the reasons that I will explain, and I would have forgiven them with my whole heart according to the will of my Teacher. "Love your enemies and pray for those who persecute you." However, the purpose of their vile harassments and tightened restrictions against me is the humiliation of the dignity of the Church and of my nation. The Israeli authorities consider that their greatest challenge is the support I get from my Church and my nation.

Therefore, the Israeli authorities persist on humiliating my Church and my nation through me in retaliation. While I am alive, I will not be silent at this vicious, childish harassment. God, my conscience, my Arabism, my honor, and my manhood require me to resist, to the point of death, offense to the dignity of my Church and my nation. Hence, my hunger strike. My goal is not to demand my release, but to be imprisoned where my dignity, and therefore the dignity of whom I am honored to represent, is preserved and where I get opportunity for prayer, meditation, and reading.

My arrest, as I said, does not bother me. Rather, at the personal level, I consider my prison and its accompanying psychological and physical torment as God's greatest gift. How much I thank Him for this blessing! Through this, He granted me the honor of suffering for Him "who loved me and gave Himself for me." I am thankful because He gave me the grace of participating in His pain, so I may, in my flesh and spirit, for His same purposes, fill up what is still lacking regarding His afflictions. How sweet prison is as a way to atone for my sins. He is my Father who loves me. So, He chastises me to protect me and qualify me to bear His name and perform His mission faithfully and to participate in His spiritual bliss here and His heavenly kingdom there. "How

7 - Letters from Prison

many are Your works, Lord! In wisdom You made them all." I have never been happier than today, and in my lifetime, I have never been closer to Him than today. So, in my own heart, I feel joy overwhelming me and peace filling my heart. "Take My yoke... and you will find rest for your souls."

I have never truly known Christ as I know Him today. He is the life: "in Him we live and move and have our being." He is the water of life, the fountain of our lives, "Let anyone who is thirsty come to Me and drink." He is the resurrection: the symbol of our resurrection. As the path leading to resurrection was pain and death, mankind, if he does not die to himself, will have no life. "Whoever loses their life for Me will save it." "Unless a kernel of wheat falls to the ground and dies, it remains only a single seed. But if it dies, it produces many seeds." If the kernel is not hidden in the ground and if it does not turn into roots, it will not bear fruit or give life. How can I be like Christ in His resurrection if I do not participate in His afflictions? "Whoever does not take up their cross and follow Me is not worthy of Me." God established me as His ambassador and messenger. He mandated me to shepherd His flock. He entrusted all the people to me. "Take this deposit and keep it to the coming of our Lord Jesus Christ because He is willing to ask you about it." "My tongue is speechless to thank the Almighty for having qualified me, though unworthy, and granted me the grace of their love on His example to the end." Thus, I may compensate my shortcomings in my ministry for the duties I had missed towards His children. Is there anything more profitable, wonderful, or sublime than to dissolve gradually until we die for those whom we love and for what we love, so they may rise up after downfall and live with dignity?

The Almighty made me understand that what I had done in my life was little and that I am required not only for more, but for everything He is expecting from me, because He does not approve dispersed efforts. Finally, His light dispersed my darkness and guided my path. His grace overcame my weakness and my resistance, so I called out in surrender, "O God, behold, I come to do Your will which you had shown and commanded before Your suffering and resurrection: Love." "My command is this: Love each other as I have loved you." This means love without measure.

I chose the love of the neighbor as a path leading to Him, because it is equivalent to God's love. Our love to God without it is nothing but mockery and dodging. "Whoever claims to love God yet hates a brother or sister is a liar." I imagine that the Almighty on the Day of Judgment will hold us accountable for nothing but our love to our neighbor. "All the Law and the Prophets hang on these two commandments."

I took the path of love, because I heard from all corners the urgent screams of distress coming out from the hearts of the children of the occupied class: seeking help against injustice, oppression, suppression, defeat, and wrongdoing. I took it because I heeded the voice of my echoing conscience blaming me, "Is it not enough humiliation, deportation, and displacement for your Palestinian people? Is it not time yet for their return and stability? How much have they longed for their stolen homeland? If your people are forced to remain silent for fear of more abuse, is it not your duty as a shepherd appointed to serve them and entrusted with their interests and as a clergyman who underwent hardships, to protect them from the ferocious wolves?"

Through inspiration from my Lord, prison was the answer to the question, freedom, and reproof of my conscience. I accepted prison as a platform to raise the awareness of the world public opinion, so the world may become aware of our incurable tragedy, torment, humiliation, and the extent of our misery under the yoke of the occupation, and so it may act! I sought to be imprisoned as a sign of my love for all my people, every one of them, and my love for all people without exception, because God "causes His sun to rise on the evil and the good." "Who is suffering while I am not suffering?"

7 - Letters from Prison

In the service of our neighbor, our love for God, His pleasure, resembling Him in love and resurrection, are our sustenance for the kingdom. In love there is life. It is the pleasure of the world. It is happiness. Away from it, there is mirage, pain, loss, and death! From this conviction of mine came my insistence on the construction of the Patriarchate, the refectory, and the renovation of the Church. Prior to starting the work, I realized that the growing emigration of citizens is our future obstacle, because it represents the greatest danger to our steadfastness. What liberation could be done after the departure of the population? Liberation is for humans not for stones!

With emigration, we grant the enemy a golden opportunity. We allow them to carry out their plans and consider their occupation as a right: a possession. Therefore, I resorted to construction as a way to prove to my fellow citizens that emigration, as a result of our questioning of the future of the West Bank being Arab, and thus our fear for our tomorrow, is a grave mistake! The country is ours, and we are its people. They are only departing invaders. The future is for us with the power of God. Without my firm conviction and my strong belief, I would not have built what was costing me strenuous weariness and much money.

Construction was also an urgent necessity to secure a steady income: not only to guarantee the continuation of the Patriarchate's projects, but also for its prosperity and development. Our deteriorating financial situation had become alarming. The foreign supplies decreased and almost stopped! What should be done? How do we secure our people, priests, and nuns? Should we close our schools, hospitals, and institutions? A bleak picture haunted me for a long time like my shadow. It worried me and troubled my life! Today, as I have ensured our future, dignity, and economic independence through the help of God, I am happy and reassured.

This hard work required three consecutive years of hardships that exhausted me. Every stone cost me a tear! As the Patriarchate and the refectory became an enviable center in Jerusalem and the Church became an artistic innovation with unparalleled splendor in our Arab world, and before I could pick any fruit, what was expected from the moment I obeyed His commands and followed His inspirations took place. The Lord allowed me to go to prison. Let it be! "One sows and another reaps." While a mother is cooking, she is only thinking of her husband and children. Her happiness is to see them enjoying what she made. She may not eat it – it is sufficient for her to see them enjoying the food she made. This is her food, and in this her power. Why should I worry then as long as I attained my construction goal? The steadfastness of my people is in securing the future of my children. In this lies the perfection of my happiness. "What is more, I consider everything a loss because of the surpassing worth of knowing Christ Jesus my Lord, for whose sake I have lost all things. I consider them garbage, that I may gain Christ," by serving His people, my brethren.

After my deep thanks to God for His grace and favor, I express my gratitude, appreciation, and love to all the loyal friends who contributed to these projects. There are two types of donors: those who gave money as a grant (their names and the amounts of money they donated are listed in our records), and those who lent money without interest to be repaid, gradually and according to our ability, after the completion of the construction work. They unanimously agree that, in the event of my death, their loan will be a gift to the Patriarchate, because each is a personal friend of mine and all of them are careful that I may not leave any debts behind. It will not be said about me, "Yes, he built, but on debts!" Their names are written in the Book of Life in my heart, because they insist that they remain anonymous according to the advice of Jesus Christ, "So when you give to the needy, do not announce it with trumpets... do not let your left hand know what your right hand is doing." The amount of their contributions is listed in our records under the title "Payments from His Grace."

I am speechless before all the donors. I will not forget their favors. I remember them daily in the Divine Sacrifice, asking God to

7 - Letters from Prison

compensate them a thousand-fold in blessings, happiness, and accomplishment. I wish we could observe a yearly Mass for them permanently.

I paid millions for construction. The money that I personally received was spent to buy some furniture for the Patriarchate, and in the last period, to secure our daily expenses and the salaries of the priests and staff as our income became scarce. Today, I do not have a single penny. Even the garment that I wear is owned by the prison. I do not feel sorry, because I take pride in my poverty. "Do not store up for yourselves treasures on earth." But I have one wish: that you take care of my beloved mother. While I was in the monastery, my two dear brothers served her. However, since my Episcopal ordinance, I have seized this privilege from them and made it my right and duty. I hope you may persevere whatever the future the Lord has for me. Her favors to me are countless. I tried to write to her many times, but every time the pen would refuse to write under the weight of my filial feelings, and it would fall from my hand. I will try again. Perhaps a message from me would refresh her.

I have another request. Though my health is deteriorating, I will continue the hunger strike as long as the dignity of the Church and my nation is unpreserved. So, in the event of my death, I hope to be buried in Jerusalem, in our Church, under the Holy Temple. I put myself in the hands of the Almighty. May His name be blessed and His will be done.

May the Lord be glorified. In the midst of my pain, he refreshed my soul with sweet comforting news that brought strength to myself, comfort to my heart, and balm to my wounds. I am also happy for the reassuring news of the beloved Lebanon.

Thank God for the return of calm and stability to its territories! May God bless it and save it from its ordeal. It has come out of its tragedy with more determination to move forward in all fields. May love unite all hearts and bond all its people in one cohesive family so that it regains its pioneering role and returns as a beautiful oasis and an example of brotherly coexistence among its people of different doctrines and beliefs. Second, the wise steps towards unity between the two sisters Syria and Jordan heartened me and strengthened my resolve. Our people look forward to coordination and solidarity among the Arab brothers. May God achieve what our nation is dreaming of: an all-inclusive Arab unity.

Our strength is in our unity and especially in our common fateful historical circumstances. Our unity is our greatest and most important weapon. It is the sure guarantee of our renaissance, victory, restoration of our dignity, and return to our beloved Jerusalem: our homeland Palestine.

So I pray fervently that the gap between the beloved Egypt and Syria be bridged. I pray for unity among the various Palestinian organizations. I consider my life cheap for the sake of the unity of our ranks. This is my most precious wish. I hope that you convey, as you deem fit, my deep gratitude and appreciation to each of the Arab countries represented by its Minister of Information at the Cairo Conference for their attention to my cause. May God extend the lives of our Arab presidents, kings, and all their assistants. May God hold their hands and guide their paths to the prosperity of their countries and to the mobilization of their forces to our single national fight. Would you please convey my love, thanks, and gratitude to the beloved combatant, Yasser Arafat, for his efforts and brotherly affection towards me? Would you also convey my appreciation to the respected warriors: Zuhair Mohsen, George Habash, Nayef Hawatmeh, and Ahmed Jibril? They confirmed to everyone that I consider as a heavy debt the lives of the dozens of martyrs who sacrificed their lives trying to release me. Please convey to them that I, whether alive or dead, will remain for them, with them: continuing my supplication for each of them, to help them, and to protect their heroic soldiers. May God let them attain their aspirations: to fight the injustice suffered by the oppressed by restoring rights.

7 - Letters from Prison

Convey to His Holiness the Pope my highest respect with my deep filial love and gratitude to his favor. Emphasize to him that I got into prison only to protect the slogan of the Church, my mother, which I consecrate: justice and love.

As for you, Your Beatitude, my father, brother, and friend, how can I express my love, appreciation, and thanks for the hardship you suffered for me? May the Lord reward you abundantly with His blessings and consecrations. May He extend your days and keep you joyful and sound: "correctly handling the word of truth."

The distinguished bishops are always in my prayers and heart. For their respected priests, I offer my fervent prayers. I always pray for our monastic order, so it may grow in perfection and multitude before God and people. I will not forget that I am a monk.

Finally, my dear elder brother, please pray for my wish. Ask everyone to plead with the Lord so He may grant me His mercy. The prison, despite its torment, gave me opportunity to meditate and pray, cleared my conscience, and purified my heart. So, I am not afraid to appear before the Lord because I love Him. "Into His hands I commit my spirit." To remain for God, with God, either alive or dead is my destiny. May His will be done. From Him comes strength, and He is always worthy of thankfulness and glory.

*****

Letter to my Beloved Mother
Ramleh Prison, 28/2/1976

Dear Mother,

I kiss your hands and your cheeks, my beloved, and I ask for your blessings and prayers and that you be pleased with me. Do you blame me for not writing to you? Believe me, Mum, I tried to write, but I failed. I have a strong desire to write and to enclose in my letter my overflowing feelings: knowing well that they would alleviate the sharpness of your pain and revive you. Was it not said that correspondence is half of meeting? Therefore, I tried many times, but my pen failed to express on paper the feelings overflowing in my heart because of the heavy load of love and longing in my heart.

In light of my feeble pen and its deficiency in expressing my feelings, I had no choice but to surrender to that which accompanies me like my own shadow: the angelic vision of you that overflows with tenderness and makes me anxious and weak. I joyfully press it to my bosom, kissing, praying, and conversing, with the ardent yearning of the son thirsty for the affection and experience of his estranged mother, in body but not in soul. Now, will I be able to reach the end of this letter? O Lord, make my wish come true. Grant us this consolation.

This knowledge is my biggest concern in prison: I know the heaviness of the burden that I have cast on your back since my arrest. I feel its pressure and its painful impact on your tender motherly heart. I know how many tears you shed, the extent of anxiety, grief, and pain that I have brought to your heart, and your long sleepless nights spent imploring God for my sake. O Mum, I am sorry. Please forgive and understand me!

I will not ask you to rid yourself of your motherhood, kind and compassionate as you are. Rather, please let me explain what happened. Perhaps this explanation will relieve your distress a little.

My father, God rest his soul, passed away when we were young. I did not have the pleasure of knowing him. You were not past 25 years of age, but you turned away from the world and everything in it and focused your attention on us. You dedicated your whole life to raising us. We, your sons, became your religion, your world, and your joy. You loved us to the point of worship. How many were the times that relatives proudly repeated your reply to those

7 - Letters from Prison

who tried, after my father's death, to propose marriage to you given your unique qualities of intrinsic intelligence and beauty? You used to say, "I do not need a man to protect me as long as I have three men in my charge."

You were a mother and a father to us. Like a seasoned capable man, you tirelessly worked to collect the debts people owed to my father. Despite the wealth he left us, your vigor motivated you to work so that we would live at the highest standard. You enrolled us in the most refined institutes and never deprived us of any luxury.

You raised us with the firmness and expertise of a father, and you cared for us with the kindness and compassion and love of a mother. You taught us by example to be serious in life, do our duties, sacrifice, and give. Like a candle, you burned day and night to light our life, guide us, and teach us the noblest and most sublime principles of religion and life. You wanted us to be men, and manhood, Mum, is measured by productivity. The one who does not work is not a man. The one who does little work is only half a man. The true man - and you belong to this category, you counterpart of men - is he who musters all his energies for service: the service of his Lord, his country, his peers, and his family. I ask you by your life: are you surprised then that I am in prison? Aren't you the reason since you, through your actions, were the first one to teach me lessons in sacrifice and manhood!

I have worked all my life to follow in your footsteps as an expression of my gratitude for your favor and my appreciation of your merits. I have always tried to be a real man, so as not to disappoint you, to comfort your heart, and to make you forget all the distress of the sacrifices you made for us. I did not let you down. I never shamed you! Today, as well, perhaps more than ever, you can be proud of me. I am not in prison for a disgraceful matter. I am in prison by invitation from my Lord, in answer to the call of my conscience, and because of the lessons you taught me about duty and love.

In the Name of God

What is my duty as the messenger of the Lord, sent as the shepherd in charge of Jerusalem? By virtue of this divine messengerhood, the people of Palestine have become a precious trust in my keeping. Each Palestinian is a brother, like my dear brothers Antoine and Razeq; no, rather, like a beloved son, just as I am fully your son. My duty entails that I share with them their joys and pains, because by virtue of my bishophood, I have become detached from my own self and I belong to everyone except myself. What makes any individual happy delights me, and what pains them makes me weep. An Archbishop is a servant. On the Day of Judgment, the Lord will bring me to strict account regarding the extent to which I fulfilled my duty.

In line with this logical creedal concept of duty, can I not love them? How then can I not share their pains when I see them tormented, persecuted, and homeless: their rights usurped and their dignity crushed?! Did you not spend your life and sacrifice all things precious in love of your children so that we have a dignified life? And I, do I not love my brothers? Am I not zealous in matters concerning them? If I only stand and watch my Palestinian children and brethren, would you not blame me, chivalrous as you are? What then would be the extent of blame I would receive from my God, my conscience, my honor, my sense of belonging to the Arab world, and my manhood?

I have always regarded you as an ideal mother, a symbol of honor and pride, ever-giving, and universally praised for your intelligence and perception of matters. Therefore, kissing your hands, I beg you to stop worrying and weeping. You are a believer, Mum. No, rather, your faith is the source of your life. Patience is part of faith, and together they are the paradise of the oppressed. They are the balm for wounds. Let us walk together on the Via Dolorosa with patience and faith behind the Lord Jesus and his Virgin mother. The Savior, when carrying his cross and when crucified on it, suffered excruciating intolerable pain. His mother, walking behind him and standing at his cross, felt the sword of pain piercing her heart. Nevertheless, despite this physically and psychologically melting pain, and despite drinking

7 - Letters from Prison

a cup as bitter as wormwood, their hearts were brimming with peace, consolation, and reassurance, because they fulfilled the will of God. Their belief in the benefit of their torment for the salvation of mankind swiftly turned that torment to joy.

No doubt, both of us, my beloved, are in torment. My torment is doubled because I caused yours. But pain is very beneficial. Gold, if not passed in a crucible of fire, is useless. Is there anything more valuable than torment? It is the highest currency. With pain we can buy everything. For this reason, Christ chose it as a means to buy us, so that we believe like Christ in the value of torment; to find therein the will of God and the sign of His love for us. "For whom the Lord loves, He chastens."

Like Christ, let us offer our torment a price for peace in the entire world, especially in beloved Lebanon and Palestine, so that the Lord brings together the hearts of people through love and His name is hallowed and His kingdom come; so that I return with you, with my children, to my homeland, to my beloved Jerusalem; and so that we follow the example of Christ who believed in the value of his torment and our torment. Thus, let us be patient. Let us suffer like the Redeemer with a heart overflowing with hope: hope in the joy of resurrection and its fruits after the torment of the cross. Let us find consolation and tranquility.

However harsh winter is, however long its nights, and whatever it brings of lightning strikes and thunders, winter has an end! Spring after winter is an inevitable fact! Spring must come with its beautiful nature, soft weather, golden sun, bright hope, and delicious fruits. Our arduous night must then have an end. Injustice and its darkness must have limits. God, the Truth, is greater than them. There is no distress except that relief and joy follow it. The Lord who tested us will find a way out for us: He will give us joy. The signs of our spring are visible on the horizon. Soon you will see me in your arms: pressing you to my bosom and kissing you without ever quenching my longing for you. My eyes will not get enough of gazing at you.

In the Name of God

How sweet it is to be together after the separation: when the nightmare has passed, leaving behind gains and lessons. Exalted is the Almighty whose mills grind slowly, yet they grind exceeding small. He is the Truth who will reward us. There is a price to our torment. He is just. The soil I planted in the days of humiliation with faith, prayer, pain, and hope shall bear fruit... with dignity. The earth that I watered in my exile with my tears shall be fertile, and my return is its harvest. Yes, my estrangement will end soon... I will return to my land, to my country... dignified. I will return by the power of God. You, my partner in torment, will be with me, with happiness overwhelming us.

On the road of our return to Jerusalem, we will meet the returning caravans ecstatic with the return of rights to their rightful owners and the homeland to its sons after the long banishment and humiliation. You would thus join the procession of the mothers of detainees and share their exultation for the liberation of their sons. Do you know, Mum, that Israeli prisons are filled with peaceful prisoners like myself? They are no less than 2500, including doctors, lawyers, engineers, professors... etc. They all sacrificed life and what is in it as a price for their dignity and in love and defense of their country. Imagine their happiness at a reunion, their meeting after deprivation with their parents, children, wives, siblings, friends, and relatives. Imagine the joy all of us would feel.

This scene alone is sufficient to erase from our memories all the suffering we have been through. What a beautiful bright day it would be! Our hearts imagine it and they dance in glee. How would we feel then when we actually live that day? Yes, we will live it. It will not be a dream. We will return.

Nothing is impossible for the believer. He can move even mountains. Our living faith in the power of God the Just, in the fairness of our cause, and in the triumph of truth are the advance on our happiness, the source of our strength, and our route of return... to our land ... to our loved ones. Let us live this faith to

7 - Letters from Prison

rejoice and find tranquility and peace. O Lord, grant my mother, the mothers of all prisoners, and all of us more faith: "The Lord works righteousness and justice for all who are oppressed."

Do I need to tell you how much I miss you and how many nights and days I dream of you? Ask your heart: it is the best guide. In all my prayers, especially in Holy Mass, I ask God every day to give you a long life and to dress you in the garb of wellness so that our eyes would be comforted by the anticipated joyful meeting. How are my dear brothers Antoine and his family and Razeq and our dear friends and relatives? I mention them all incessantly in my prayers. They are in my heart. Kiss each of them on my behalf and give them, as usual, a lesson in faith and patience.

I want you to have complete peace of mind regarding me. As long as God is with me, who could be against me? Feeling that the Lord is pleased, that the conscience is clear, and that one's duty is fulfilled generates profound consolation, peace and happiness deep within, despite all irritations and grievances. "Where there is God, there is bliss." If you want me to be perfectly happy, do as I have begged you.

My kind mother, my beloved, I press you again to my bosom. I kiss your hands: asking for your blessing and prayers and that you be pleased with me. My brothers and sons in prison send you their deep love and ask you to be to their mothers and to all of us a force of patience and a role model of firm faith in the justice of God, in a dignified future, in sweeter days, in the definiteness of our return, and in the imminence of our meeting. Everyone wants you to be a symbol of hope: a bright hope.

Your loving son,
Hilarion

*****

In the Name of God

His Beatitude Maximos V Hakim, the Honored, Patriarch of Antioch and All the East, of Alexandria and Jerusalem
Ramleh Prison, 16/03/1976

Your Beatitude,

Complaining is not a habit of mine, and neither is grumbling, "Always give thanks to God for everything." I also hate to arouse pity! It is the weapon of the weak, and I am strong; not my own strength of course, but it is Christ who gives me strength. Pity breeds humiliation, but I hold my head high, "You, Lord, are a shield around me, my glory, the One who lifts my head high." However, it is my duty to inform you, as my superior and as a father, brother, and friend, of what is happening to me so that you are aware of my situation and know the whole truth.

Hunger Strike

I clarified to Your Beatitude in my last letter that I had started a hunger strike on Wednesday, January 28th, to demand that I be detained where my dignity is preserved (preserving thus the dignity of the entities I represent: my nation and the Church) and where I would find an appropriate atmosphere to meditate, pray, and read. I have spent the first 28 days of my hunger strike consuming only water.

On February 25th, after a long argument with the prison warden and his assistants about my strike, I yielded to their pressure and started consuming milk in a painful way through a tube they insert in my nose or my mouth extending to my stomach. I stipulated that this process would not last more than two weeks. My health was in critical condition because of my total abstention from food. Then the visits ceased...

When they saved my life with the milk, their worries were put to rest, not out of love for me, but rather, to protect their reputation and interests. Ever since then, they stopped coming, and I did not

7 - Letters from Prison

see the face of any one of them after that. In contrast, their visits to me before that were incessant when my health was in constant deterioration.

In the face of this intentional neglect, and in reaction to this manifest proof that they only seek their interest of avoiding a scandal by preventing my death in prison, and their total indifference to my demands, I have stopped again this morning, March 16, to consume milk: 20 days after my ultimatum.

Threat!

Around noon, the deputy warden came, surrounded by five soldiers, and demanded that I consume the milk or else he would resort to force!! I answered, "Forty-eight days have passed since I started my hunger strike and you have not given it any attention... Why wait? I am not begging! I am demanding rights established by conscience, ecclesiastical law, international law, our age-old Arab traditions, and common sense. No human being will oppress me. I will not accept the saying that 'the argument of the strongest is always the best.' Strength is ultimately for the truth, and truth is on my side. Your neglect is but proof of your intentional disrespect of me."

Another hunger strike...

"What is the purpose of your indifference except to persistently humiliate me!! Therefore, in condemnation of your shameful attitude, I will not continue to take milk. Enough disregard for my just humane demands! Enough of your obstinacy and humiliating treatment!"

Brutality...

While speaking, I saw them gnash their teeth and I detected fury in their eyes. When I finished, they pounced on me like beasts of prey: bruising my entire body. They almost strangled me, crushed my feet with their boots, and tore up my clerical robe. When I collapsed and my features were distorted, they backed up: leaving my body filled with blue patches from their punches and bleeding from their nails digging into my flesh.

This morning, out of precaution, I had put on my clerical robe, unlike other days. I wore the icon thinking that, during the expected argument consequent to my escalation of the hunger strike, they would be awed by the sacredness of my robe or they would respect the gloriousness of Christ that I carry on my chest. But the result was the opposite. My religious appearance provoked them even more, and they lost their senses and poured out all that their hearts had for me of grudge, abhorrence, and hatred. They executed their superiors' instructions with extreme brutality.

Serving my people and my homeland

"A disciple is not above his teacher… If they persecuted me, they will persecute you also." Persecutions are the gift of Christ to his servants, to his followers, out of his certainty of the infinite value of torment and its effectiveness in making us his partners in his death and resurrection, in his weakness and strength, and in his humbleness and glory. "And everyone who has left father or mother or houses for my name's sake, will receive, along with persecutions in this life, a hundredfold", and this is my share of his legacy! Pain is the tax that he imposed on me so that I receive the honor of being his disciple; "And whoever does not carry their cross and follow me cannot be my disciple." My cross is this, and it is my share in serving the people of Palestine, my people, my children, my brethren, and my congregation. In defense of my homeland, I carry it with all gratitude as perhaps "the kingdom of heaven has been subjected to violence…"

Rights are never granted: rather, they are taken by force. Therefore, I personally forgive them with content: "and forgive us our sins, as we forgive those who sin against us." But I will speak out as long as there is pulse in my veins against their defiance of what

7 - Letters from Prison

I represent: my nation and the Church. The clear goal of their blatant treatment of me is to undermine, through me, the dignity of my nation and the Church, to disrespect them, and to retaliate against them for supporting me. I will not make a truce no matter the results! This is what God and my conscience impose on me... This is what my honor and my Arabism entail.

"God chose the weak things of the world to shame the strong." Today's violent tempest has left me with a body drained of strength. As to my soul, praise be to God, it completely regained its tranquility after I recited the Great Compline. Therein, my soul found nourishment for its strength, consolation for its pains, and balm for its wounds. Is there anything sweeter than these hymns: "Lord of the Powers, be with us; for other helper have we not, in tribulations but you. Lord of the Powers, have mercy on us"? And "God is with us, know it you nations and be submissive, For God is with us."

"You mighty shall be defeated. For God is with us. Even if you should prevail, again you will be defeated; For God is with us... If God is on my side, can anyone be against me?" The language of force and violence is proof of bankruptcy and weakness. It is the weapon of the weak and their argument. It is evasion of the truth, of light, whereas the language of God is the power of God.

Your Beatitude, I find myself compelled to conclude because of excruciating pains. Include me in your blessings, pray abundantly for me because "the spirit is willing but the flesh is weak." "Lord, do not forsake me; do not be far from me, my God. Come quickly to help me, my Lord and my Savior."

Sincerely,
Hilarion Capucci
Titular Archbishop of Caesarea, Palestine
Patriarchal Vicar of the Greek Catholics in Jerusalem

*****

In the Name of God

Brother Yasser Arafat
Chairman of the Executive Committee of the Palestine Liberation Organization
Ramleh Prison, 2/5/1976

Dear Most Respected Brother, Mr. Yasser Arafat,

One year ago, I addressed to you with the most comprehensive words that I was able to produce from my detention. You were a fragrant start and today you are the fragrant end, since smuggling out my letters afterwards will be difficult.

How could I not think of you: praying for your triumph sincerely when you are living through hard days and a bitter crisis because of the appalling events in Lebanon that must definitely be hurting you and depriving you of sleep? I know what you hold in your big heart of sincerity and genuine brotherly love and appreciation for the noble Lebanese people. I know the love you have for this beloved disaster-stricken country and the extent of your concern for its safety and your keenness that it continues to rise and flourish to present a role model in brotherly coexistence: a living example of the coherent family and a guide for us in building our anticipated democratic Palestinian state. The role of mediator that you are undertaking to reconcile between its dissenting sons is manifest proof of the nobility of your sentiments. But its catastrophe did not just draw your attention and burden your shoulders: rather, it has plunged you into a delicate perplexing situation... God help you!

Lebanon's dire need to development; nay, rather to transformation in spirit and ways, is indisputable. My question is: does its medicine lie in its destruction? Or is the civil war our way to achieve the reform we wish for it? I wonder, when was chaos, ruin, and blood the goals of a true revolution? Revolution is spirit: the strength of spirit to build, advance, renovate, break the yoke of social discrimination, exploitation, and oppression, so that with justice, love would shine and prosperity and hope would prevail.

7 - Letters from Prison

Revolution is the determination of people for the flow of life. It is not destruction, grudge, or hate. It is a war on death, on what kills revolution, for resurrection.

The ongoing manslaughter in Lebanon is not condoned by logic. It is denounced by both God and human conscience. We will drag for long, in Lebanon and all over the Arab world, its disgraceful ramifications, its destructive setbacks, and its painful consequences. The only ones who will profit are the Zionists who schemed it to achieve their expansionist ambitions to reach the Litani River and to frustrate our plans for a secular Palestinian state, etc. The fruits of the destruction of Lebanon will not be reaped except by covetous invaders.

The escalating fierce fighting in the Lebanese arena is not Lebanese. It is, rather, a grinding conflict among major global powers who took advantage of the state of affairs in Lebanon and its favorable terrain to wreak havoc and secure their interests. Those conflicting parties that are competing to devour Lebanon and divide it shielded themselves behind the quarrels of the Lebanese people about the constitution regarding its political, social, sectarian, and tribal system. They hid behind the conflicting attitudes and opinions of the Lebanese regarding the presence of Palestinian organizations. They exploited these and other disagreements of the Lebanese as a screen behind which they hid to ignite the fire of sedition in their land and add fuel to it to make it an easy palatable bite for the gluttonous criminal. They sought to make it a gateway through which the tyrannical intruder would penetrate into our highly strategic region coveted by global powers since the Ottoman Empire started disintegrating in order to join it to his fleet and serve his interests while subservient to him. The Lebanese family is but a victim of the criminal invader who kills and destroys to build his glory on top of its ruins.

Shall we not learn from our tragedy to settle our differences radically by cutting the roots of the crisis? We would thus put an end to the sedition and destroy the criminal conspirators. The afflicted Lebanon is but a victim to the division among its sons. It was primarily the conflict among the Lebanese that gave the chance to their covetous enemy to creep in, and he seized that chance. Unless we sincerely hasten to remove the contradiction between the disputing brothers so that they come together integrating each other and overcoming their selfishness for the sake of the unified Lebanese front, the events in Lebanon would be but a link in a series that is not finished. Its ultimate end would be a catastrophe similar to that of Palestine.

Destroying Lebanon is a conspiracy against our nation to crush the call for a democratic Palestinian state. What efforts have neighboring countries made to prevent the suicide of Lebanon, preserve its independence, and abort the conspiracy in order to protect their own sovereignty and the national cause that they advocate? Why did the pleas of the Arab League reverberate in a far-off valley? The calls of its Secretary General went unheard because our nation is distracted by differences. Nay, rather, our Arab conflicts contributed to the division in Lebanon and made it bleed even more. Lebanon is the victim of those near and far. Its abysmal descent is a disgrace to the Arabs. Our divisions destroy us and are our fatal disease.

The divisions that infiltrated the rows of the organizations pain me deeply. Our disunity paralyzes our revolutionary movement. It hinders our advance and promises failure. The true picture of the naked truth, of our bitter tragedy, that the PLO publicly disclosed has turned all concepts upside down. It convinced the big countries of the extent of oppression and injustice afflicting the Palestinian people, and the legitimacy of their demands. The global public opinion's understanding of our wretched situation and our just national aspirations has awakened consciences after a long deep sleep. It won us a distinguished place in the international arena. A unified stand of the organizations, while enhancing such convictions and such sympathy and support, would urge the now conscious nations to rise to our help, to strive to give us justice, and to not suffice with talks and resolutions. A

7 - Letters from Prison

unified voice would turn our media wins into practical triumphs. But, unfortunately, our division prevents us from reaping the fruits of our strenuous efforts. We destroy with one hand what we build with the other. There is no alternative but unity in order for us to move forward with our achievements and to soar high. The rational person is he who heeds lessons and seeks guidance in them. In the Ramadan War, our weapon with which we defied the impossible was the weapon of unity. If we resume our march of unity, we would spare our nation a fifth war, because Israel today is up for grabs. The inferiority complex that "Israel" suffers from in the wake of its defeat has crushed it and spread confusion in its ranks. It has reflected on its internal conditions and led to the collapse of its economy. It has lost its international status and now lives in isolation. Tightening the rope around its neck through our unified voice is sufficient to melt it gradually, suffocate it, and force it to surrender. Israel's power is not absolute: its potential is relative. Its strength is drawn from the weakness of our ranks. If the decay of division continues to gnaw at us, we will never stand tall. No good is hoped for until we change. "Israel" is safe so long as the Arabs are disunited.

Our Arab peoples have long lived dispossessed of their rights and of their dignity. They have been persecuted in a struggle with evil powers that insisted on expelling them from history in order to live on their ruins. Our Arab peoples' chests are constricted and their patience is wearing thin because of the backwardness, deprivation, and displacement. They have had enough of challenges, degradation, humiliation, and extortion. Today, they aspire to come back to life at any cost: to assume their proper status and restore their past glory. This volcanic fire burning in our peoples: what would fan it and turn it into creative energies except the unity of Arab countries and the unified voice in the ranks of our Palestinian leaders.

How splendid is the anticipated union despite the different systems in the sister states Syria and Jordan. How it evokes hope and reinvigorates the soul! I was heartened by the warming of relations between you and the respected brother: George Habash.

If only the steps toward unification that are laden with lessons, informed, measured, and firm were wide enough to fuse us in one big homeland over which the flag of our one nation waves! If this wish – the dream of our peoples – materialized, we would do miracles. With precious unity, nothing would be impossible for us. Strength lies in selflessness.

If the tendency toward unification infiltrated the soul of the Arab citizen and conditioned him, it would shape him, encourage him, and give him distinction. Otherwise, he would live alone, backward and sterile, and he would die insignificant. The ego that does not have the capacity to transcend beyond itself within the group for fear of perishing is the one that perishes because it is isolated, whereas the ego that fuses itself into the group becomes happier, more successful, and more radiant, and it survives. Unless a kernel of wheat falls to the ground and dies, it remains only a single seed. But if it dies, it produces many seeds.

Any group, whether it is a party or an organization or a nation, if it does not break out of its narrow horizons and shatter its fetters to enter a broader world, will not realize its worth because it revolves in an empty circle and wilts in its narrow confines. Its vigor is in transcending itself. Its life is in renouncing itself to join the masses: living for the masses and by them.

While this reasoning liberates the individual and the leader from the worship of the "ego" and subjects egocentrism and selfishness to the general good and common interest, it generates a more perfect life that is more fertile, more mature, and more joyful. If we live by this creed, it will remove contradictions. It is the key to dialogue. With the removal of barriers, we run with time and civilization, manifest ourselves, and revitalize. In the citizen's interaction with his group and the melting of the group into the masses is life filled with the achievements and sublimity that we seek. Without it, they would all suffer paralysis and weakness.

7 - Letters from Prison

Qualified people would become mummified. In killing the "ego," there is fertility and abundance: there is life.

We all boast of our patriotism, but is patriotism a mere word that we sing in lyrics?! It is a responsible accountable word born of our faith in God. Faith is life and work rather than dreams and visions. Patriotism is selflessness and giving. It is not sentiments. We have voided patriotism of sacredness, concepts, and genuine momentum. Opportunists took advantage of it to serve their interests. Frequent use disfigured it, so its resonance was lost. Patriotism demands martyrdom, not just testimony. What sacrifice have I made for my nation? What have I achieved and would reap for my country? I will not recover from my stumble, and my nation will not rise unless I am prepared to taste death for the sake of my cause and my Arabism. Patriotism is an incessant disbelief in the self: not a fire ignited in a haystack only to die out quickly and turn into ashes. Serving one's country is a blessing only worthy of him who has prepared for it with his life, in every major and minor behavior; him who nourished it with deprivation to fix it firmly in the depths of his soul: thus getting his fill of it and growing up with it until he turns grey.

The love of God and love of country summon one another. Nay, rather, each of them is part of the other. Whoever dies in defense of his country, perishing for the sake of his Lord, is a martyr because he gave testimony to his faith in God. I am an Arab by the blessing and will of God, not randomly. My nationalist identity is the foundation of my Christian anointment. My Christianity is weak and sterile if I am not Arab to the core until the end. The weakness of my Arabism is ingratitude and betrayal of my religion. My efficiency as a Christian is measured by the extent of my interactiveness as an Arab. My martyrdom out of love for my compatriots is my testimony to the Savior and to redemption.

I learned how to be a fedayee in the school of Christ the Redeemer. I am a graduate of the institute of the Cross. There is no greater love than to sacrifice oneself for the sake of his loved ones. Christ sacrificed himself out of love for his sons and fellow humans, until blood, until death, through the secret of redemption, and the secret of his salvation of mankind. He became the role model of conquest. He opened for us the gates of heavenly Jerusalem... the leader of liberation who liberated us from worshiping the evil one... the ideal warrior in the broadest and noblest battle field, that of man fighting his desires and the forces of evil in order to live free and dignified. He was the very first fedayee, because by death, he trampled death. By death, he rolled away the stone that covered the tomb where they buried him, and he rose: defeating darkness and oppression and resurrecting light and life.

Thus, fedayee work is my work: it concerns me as a Christian. The world of sacrifice is familiar territory to me and a science wherein I was raised. I am not an intruder or a meddler. Every Arab must make the history of his nation and build its glory. My happiness is in reaping the sacrifices I had planted with the sweat of my own brow: not in picking the fruits watered with the blood of my brothers. I will not be dependent! On the paths of Arabism and of the wounded Palestine, I will accompany my leader, my teacher the Redeemer, in alleviating the pains of my sons and liberating my homeland to contribute to the realization of my nation's aspirations.

My bishophood, dear Brother, has anointed me a legitimate representative of God the Just, a messenger of the love of Christ, and a shepherd to his sons. On the Day of Judgment, God will take me to strict account regarding my faithfulness to his teachings, his values, and his charge, and about my sincerity to my Arab nation (my family, Palestine, my homeland and home) and its people, my brethren. My love of Palestine and the Arabs stems from my obedience to God and from my faith. My struggle for their sake is but an embodiment of my identity, of the voice of my conscience, to what I represent: justice and love. Therefore, the stolen homeland is my cross. How could it not be when each and every house in the land of Christ and the land of the Holy Sanctuary has turned into a Calvary! Defending my children

7 - Letters from Prison

and their cause is the deed of my bishophood and the certificate of learning from the Redeemer. I am not a "destroyer" as the enemies of God claim: rather, the fedayee is a savior!

On account of my detention, I carry out my duties relentlessly from prison! Are there temporal or spatial borders for struggle? Would I not continue to struggle while they hellishly escalate their attempts to crush me and deprive me of my dignity?! Their baseness did not deter them from beating me. I started a hunger strike on January 28 - which I will continue - to express my dismay with the maltreatment I am receiving and in denunciation of the disgraceful and unethical conditions stipulated for my imprisonment. In the first 20 days, I refused to consume food. Currently, I am consuming milk by force through a tube that they insert into my stomach: once through my mouth and once through my nose. Since the day I started my hunger strike, I have been sitting in a dark humid cell that resembles a grave. I do not see any ray of light. Diseases plague me. My weight has decreased from 89 to 64 kg. But never mind: a rocket is not launched except by a countdown to zero! On the ruins of the body, the spirit grows and soars. Pain is the ladder of the soul to God. Therefore, no matter the cost and regardless of the consequences, I will not acquiesce. I will not reconcile so long as their purpose is to degrade my nation and my people and to dishonor my Church.

In my estrangement, I do not waste my time. Rather, I find myself more efficient. When prayer and torment join forces, they purify the heart and bring us closer to God and also make miracles through their infinite value. From my hermitage, I daily raise to the Most High my sincerest implorations and I offer him my torment as a sacrifice for the sake of my nation: to unite its voice and support its rulers with victory, to protect the PLO who are my family, and its members and heroic leaders, to guide them to establish justice for those who are estranged and displaced from among my Palestinian children and for their martyrs, and to bring peace to our land and to the whole world. I am hoping that as you receive my letter, the Lebanese civil war would be over and the beloved Lebanon would be enjoying lasting stability with love prevailing in all its parts. O Lord, accept my torment and answer my prayers.

I swear, dear Brother, that what consoles me is that I profoundly feel your love and support for me. How could my tongue express my thankfulness and appreciation of the brotherly sentiment you expressed for me on different occasions and the efforts you exerted for my release from prison. Please convey to the respected brothers (George Habash, Nayef Hawatmeh, Ahmed Jibril, Zuheir Mohsen, and Abdulwahab al-Kayyali) my sincere affection and respect and my deep gratitude for the serious concern they gave to my case and the compassion they showed towards me. The specter of the righteous martyrs that you have sent to attempt to release me is always with me. I have vowed to their fragrant blood to follow in their footsteps in devotion to my nation, my country, and my people, and to increase my services in the ranks of the organizations until my last breath to make up for the work they missed and fill the void they left.

Now that I have poured out to you, dear Brother, what heartens me, and laid my pains on your wide shoulders, placing in your big heart my hopes, I feel overwhelmingly tranquil. My imprisonment does not exhaust me! My arrest has brought me closer to God, and living with God is happiness. But it is our schisms, the events in Lebanon and their ramifications and consequences, that make my heart bleed. Hence my lengthy talk about it. It is a nightmare perching on my chest and a heavy dark cloud that has added to the darkness and loneliness of my cell. The enemy cheered for it and blew it up over my own head, in their media and behavior, and in the form of an outpouring of mockery and gloating!!! How needy we are, in these fateful historical circumstances, to stand together. Our solid roar is the invincible barrier to stop the conspiracy woven against Lebanon to invade our nation. It is our major weapon in the battle of truth and dignity. If only my Lord accepts my life as a sacrifice at the altar of our unity, I would offer it wholeheartedly.

7 - Letters from Prison

This sincere wish of mine and my anguish that stems from my faith, please convey them to their Excellencies (the beloved presidents Sadat and Assad) coupled with my deepest love and respect. The sweet taste of our eternal victory in the Ramadan War, as a result of their union, we can still feel on our tongues. The Arab masses ask them for more.

I wish to express my affection and appreciation to His Excellency President Assad in return for his radio greetings to me. I follow with sincere prayers his strenuous efforts to bring peace to Lebanon and to spread brotherhood and love among the members of the Lebanese family. May God bless him and reward his relentless endeavors with success.

I offer daily prayers for our honorable monarchs and presidents, their peoples, their armies and helpers, and for you, courageous warrior brother, the brave leaders of our organizations, and the beloved PLO family. May the Almighty protect you with His watchful eye and preserve you with abundant blessings and favors. May He grant you success and unify your voice to achieve prosperity for our countries, happiness for our peoples, and victory and pride for our nation.

Lastly, my sincere loving heart that accompanies you with its prayers day and night and follows your enormous and incessant efforts to restore justice by the return of our Palestinian people to their stolen land and their dignity feels the extent of your concerns and the seriousness of your burdens regarding the unfortunate fighting in Lebanon. However, since the pleasure of life and its bliss lie in giving, and since rights are not granted except if fought for, I congratulate you for being the embodiment of giving and struggle. The edifice of dignity that you strive to build with your faith and heart's blood and with the help of our Arab rulers and your brothers (leaders of organizations) for your nation and for your brethren will undoubtably rise high and mighty, because God, the Grand Architect, is illuminating your way and guiding you. He shares with you in building, my dear brother Abu Ammar.

In the Name of God

Unless the Lord builds the house, they labor in vain who build it.

May God Almighty bless you and watch over you, my honored big brother Yasser, and may He make easy your historic national mission and fulfill it so that peace and justice will prevail in our land.

May He reward you abundantly for carrying the gravest burdens and facing the toughest hardships. May the Lord bless you with long life. May He comfort you with watching the processions of Arab caravans, reveling in victory and dignity, and singing in the midst of their praises of God for reuniting them after a long bitter separation on their way back to the beloved homeland: to family and friends, to their eternal Jerusalem, to Palestine ... By your favor and justice and by your power, O God, we are returning.

Hilarion Capucci
Honorary Archbishop of Caesarea, Palestine
Patriarchal Vicar for the Roman Catholics in Jerusalem

*****

Brother Yasser Arafat
Chairman of the Executive Committee of the Palestine Liberation Organization
Ramleh Prison, 01/09/1976

Dear Most Respected Brother Yasser Arafat,

I send you my sincere brotherly love and my best wishes: praying that you will be granted abundant blessings. I ask God to extend His high hand to you while you undertake grave responsibilities and to illuminate your path and inspire you with what serves the interests of Arabs and of Palestine and preserves their honor.

Four months ago on May 2nd (before we Palestinians were thrust into the ongoing Lebanese conflict and before our situation became complicated), when you were still undertaking the

7 - Letters from Prison

role of mediator between the disputing Lebanese brothers in complete harmony with all the disputing factions and with total coordination with the sister Syria, I managed to send a long letter addressed to you. You have not received it until now for reasons that the carrier of this letter will explain to you.

In the midst of the developments in our painful Arab events and their complications, and given that I - as a clergyman who brings people together not drives them apart - avoid interfering in conflicts and in what does not concern me of laying blame after the assignment of responsibilities... in the midst of all this, I would have loved to express my feelings as the son and servant in my large Arab homeland and as the prisoner of my love to Palestine which I worship next to God. I would have loved to translate my impressions regarding our Arab disunity and the Lebanese civil war so that you would realize the extent of my pain and grief. But how can I do that? My mere reflection on our current drastic divisions, this decay that gnaws at our unity, weakening us and sending us backwards, would ultimately destroy us if we do not hasten to treat it radically....

I think repeatedly about the disgraceful bitter status quo in Lebanon which has become more like fiction and about its ramifications at the Arab level (the innocent lives lost on its land, the pure blood that is spilled, the tragedies unfolding on its arena, the resultant moral and material destruction, the grudges and sediments that this fighting leaves behind at the national, Lebanese, and Palestinian levels). I realize the extent of our failure to find the remedy for our crises that have continued too long and have become extremely critical: melting our national gains, vaporizing our hopes, and taking us down to the lowest depths... to rock bottom. This bleak Arab picture makes my heart bleed and my eyes flow with tears. It disheartens me, paralyzes my hand, and prevents me from writing!

When was war, especially among brothers, ever a path to harmony and a road to reform and construction? When the victor himself

In the Name of God

who conquered the enemy and scored a manifest victory comes out of battle a loser, what triumph is that which one scores over his brother? What is it worth? What is its benefit? It is but a mirage in the middle of the desert. It is sterile and destructive. Therefore, the Arab conflicting parties and the factions fighting on Lebanese land will not reap of their disputes except losses and disappointment. Our common enemy who cheers for our bloodshed is the sole victor.

Our tragedies are beyond imagination! The consequences of our Arab deterioration are something that no eye has ever seen, no ear has heard, and no mind has imagined. Even "Israel" that feigns weeping and sheds crocodile tears (the mastermind of the bloody events who fans its fire) has never dreamt of this deterioration of ours and the gains it has given her. I ask you by your Lord... have we conscripted our sons, who are our hope and our most precious possession, to fight in the field of honor, side by side, dignified, in defense of their homelands... or to fight and crush each other and turn their homes into graves wherein they are buried in humiliation!!! The weapons that we acquired in return for "the morsel of bread," for what have we dedicated them? Is it to direct them at our chests for our suicide? Have we sacrificed all that is dear and precious only to subject ourselves at the end to serve Israel so that it would build its glories on our ruins, on our dismembered bodies, and on our graves? Have we insisted on dying only to make it live?!

This wretched situation undoubtedly hurts you much more than it hurts me: you who have spent your entire life a living example of sacrifice and giving in the service of your Arabism and in striving to defend your stolen homeland and your displaced people. The escalation of the conflict in our lands and the cracking of the Palestinian edifice that you have built with your heart's blood and for which you have worked incessantly must be keeping you awake at night and causing you pain and grief.

Therefore, as I share your agony and long for what you aspire to

7 - Letters from Prison

of unity, love, prosperity, and dignity, I beseech you, by the name of the Lord, from my heart (joining my voice to the whispers of your live conscience and to the call of your heart that beats with the love of its nation and its interests and that overflows with zeal regarding its stolen land and its children) and by the blood of all martyrs, to resume your constructive honorable mediation which you have undertaken at the outset of the events in order to reconcile between our disputing countries. I beseech you to put an end through cooperation and coordination to the bloody fighting in Lebanon and the massive destruction it has wrought. Enough grudges, enough losses, and enough humiliation! Our disgraceful conflicts that cost us dearly without any benefit are only profitable to our gloating enemy. He alone is the winner! Is it not time for us to have one voice, to bandage our wounds, and spread joy and evoke hope! Let us rise to build what we have destroyed ... to restore to our nation its honor and might through the unity of its ranks... and to restore to the tattered Lebanon its unity and its pioneering role through reuniting its family. There is no alternative to this path to fulfill our nationalist wishes. This is the greatest guarantee of our return to our homes. How strong we are as Arabs determines how dignified and triumphant we are as Palestinians.

As I send again to you my heartfelt greetings and respect, I ask God to bless you and protect you by His favor. May He answer my prayers and accept my torment, watch over you and guide your steps, and fulfil your wishes and what the children of your nation and country aspire to of love, solidarity, peace, honor, and prosperity. He the Almighty is competent over all things.

Sincerely,
Hilarion Capucci
Titular Archbishop of Caesarea, Palestine
Patriarchal Vicar of the Greek Catholics in Jerusalem

*****

In the Name of God

Respected Members of the Palestinian National Council[3]
Ramleh Prison, 25/12/1976

Dear Brothers,

Our sincere love and respect to you and our loyalty to our wise revolutionary leadership are what motivated me and my sons detained in Israeli prisons to address our statement to your noble council. We declare in public that we, more than ever, honor the covenant and pledge our lives to Palestine until our last breath.

We want to prove that we dwell in prison only in body whereas our spirits are ever present among you. We follow the steps of your struggle with our thoughts, and we pray for your protection by abundant grace and for the success of your endeavors.

Our arrest for doing our duty, for defending the holiest of holy sanctities, our beloved land, in defense of the truth and in preservation of our dignity, is a favor that gives us pride and consolation. We are thankful to God for it. All happiness is in exerting oneself. Our beloved Palestine will only rise through sacrifice. Rams must be presented for the burnt offering. Our fort will not rise high and strong except by the contribution of each Palestinian in building our homeland: least of which is to add one stone to the structure. This is what we aspire to. We live to realize this hope and this is our creed. Our conduct in prison is but a reflection of this conviction, of this persistence: a live translation of our felicity and pride. Consequently, the enemy conducts relentless psychological warfare against us and tries grudgingly and vengefully to humiliate us, belittle us, and crush our resolve and morale. However, his failed attempts only increase our faith, steadfastness, and persistence.

---

3 Archbishop Hilarion Capucci, while in the Zionist Ramleh Prison, addressed a letter of solidarity on behalf of all the Palestinian freedom fighters detained in the prisons of the Zionist enemy to the Palestinian National Council in its 13th session held in Cairo. The letter was dated 25/12/1976 and was supposed to be read while the Council was in session. However, the situation in prison did not allow the Archbishop to deliver the letter on time.

7 - Letters from Prison

Rights are never granted; rather, they are taken by force. What we suffer of torment and of insult, we consider a sacrifice to the Almighty Lord to bring about truth and justice and to spread love. While you hold your honorable conference, our hearts will soar over each of you and raise their implorations to God. Unless the Lord builds the house, they labor in vain who build it. May the Lord guide you to issue historic resolutions that bring glory to God in the highest, peace on earth, and goodwill towards men. May they give us glad tidings that send joy and consolation to the hearts of our Arab peoples and give us tranquility and hope.

Is it not time for this darkness to fade away, for these chains to be broken, and for this humiliation to end? We will not fulfill our national ambitions except through solidarity with our Arab brothers. We will not achieve our goals in Palestine except through joining our forces and coordinating among ourselves. Would we forget the extent of support that our beloved Arab countries showed to our cause, what they have sacrificed, and what they exert to protect our dignity and impose our existence? Are we not the children of one family? Our goals and our interests are common, and our destiny is one.

No weapon is stronger than our Arab unity in the battle of liberation: a means to regain our full rights and to determine our fate. Our Palestinian ranks are the guarantee of our present and future success. Our prosperity, dignity, and triumph are contingent on our unity. There is power in unity. Our Lord, guide us to the straight path.

Go forward, leaders of our caravans. May the Almighty watch over you and engulf you with His lights. O God, bless this assembly so that it may bear the tastiest fruits. Guide the steps of our beloved assembled brothers and support them to open wide the gates of return for our yearning peoples.

Our Lord... by your might we shall return.

In the Name of God

Sincerely,
Your brothers detained in Israeli prisons
On their behalf: Archbishop Hilarion Capucci
Titular Archbishop of Caesarea, Palestine
Patriarchal Vicar of the Greek Catholics in Jerusalem

*****

Brother Yasser Arafat
Chairman of the Executive Committee of the Palestine Liberation Organization
Ramleh Prison, 27/12/1976

Dear Respected Brother Yasser Arafat,

I write to you words motivated by a true profound brotherly affection. It is my heart writing them not my pen. God alone knows how much I remembered you during the hard, bitter days you lived during the Lebanese crisis. Like your shadow, I was with you night and day!

In your support, I have deployed all that I possessed in prison (prayer and my agony), so that the Almighty would help you with His power, strengthen you as you carry the gravest duties on your shoulder, make easy your paths, and grant you light, resolve, and patience until you emerge, and us with you, safe from the crisis.

How relieved I am now that things are normal again. Praise be to God that you do not hate an evil, for perhaps it is good for you. Deducing lessons from events, regardless of the consequences, is leadership! Realistic treatment of problems is proof of intelligence; rather, it is proof of genius. Therefore, from the bottom of my heart, I congratulate you on your realistic initiative to settle differences. It is manifest proof of your complete selflessness and your infinite devotion to your cause, your people, and your nation... You present conduct is true evidence of wisdom and knowledge. This is where your greatness lies. I am proud of the devoted wise leader that you are.

7 - Letters from Prison

Please forgive the delay of my letters, as I find great difficulty in getting them out. Their carrier will explain this to you. Months have passed since I wrote them and thus they have lost their subjectivity. Therefore, I hesitated much in sending them.

My matter, apparently, is still complicated. Patience and faith are the paradise of the oppressed. Blessed is the name of the Lord regardless. The conditions imposed on me in prison are harsh and inhumane! But since I find in them the best platform from which to make known our cause, the extent of injustice and oppression inflicted on our people, I find myself happy. This is what consoles me – after God. In the future, if God wills, I will dedicate what is left of my life to the service of my Palestinian brethren and my nation. God gives respite but He does not neglect.

In mind and heart, I am always with you and with the beloved brothers George Habash, Nayef Hawatmeh, Ahmed Jibril, Zuhair Mohsen, and Abdulwahab al-Kayyali. I ask God to grant you success, to unite and unify our ranks, and to grant us a near return and peace for our land and for the world. Convey to each of them, your assistants and their helpers, my brotherly greetings coupled with my love and appreciation. May God bless you all with His light and guide your steps in the service of our beloved Palestine and our beloved nation.

Often I ask Him to give comfort to the souls of our righteous martyrs and shelter to the displaced of our children and brothers. I ask Him to heal their wounds and compensate what our revolution has lost of men. Lastly, I send you my warmest sentiments of affection and respect, and I greet you for the New Year 1977. May God make true the wishes of your big heart, grant you wellbeing, and take your hand to achieve what you relentlessly seek: serving Palestine, which is the pride of the Arabs.

Sincerely,

Your Brother

In the Name of God

Archbishop Hilarion Capucci
Titular Archbishop of Caesarea, Palestine
Patriarchal Vicar of the Greek Catholics in Jerusalem

*****

Brother Yasser Arafat
Chairman of the Executive Committee of the Palestine Liberation Organization

Ramleh Prison, 17/03/1977

Dear Most Respected Brother, Yasser Arafat,

The murder of Mr. Kamal Jumblatt is a tragedy denounced by every noble person regardless of his ideology or principles. It is a shameful detestable crime. I was shocked by the horrible news! His assassination is a stark attack on the morals, values, and ideals for which he lived and for the sake of which he died.

I have known him, God rest his soul, to be devoted to his Lord and his conscience, steadfast in his beliefs, and faithful to his Arabism and cause. Like a candle, his life melted in the service of his homeland. He spent his life as an ascetic hermit dedicated to Lebanon, which he loved and held sacred and which he defended until his death.

May the sinful hands that extinguished this candle be paralyzed. Woe to the grudge that blinds the vision and turns human beings into ferocious wolves! Since when was violence a means to solve problems and settle disputes? It is the weapon of the weak and cowardly. Assassination is an embodiment of baseness and degradation. Only the ignorant riffraff resort to it... only those with sick inferior souls undertake it.

A true brother never stoops so low, regardless how heated the quarrel with his brother becomes and the difference between their viewpoints. That is a band that has sold its soul to the devil

7 - Letters from Prison

and used it to serve the goals and interests of the enemies of our nation, expose bandaged wounds, harm both the Lebanese and their Palestinian brothers, and destroy what is left of Lebanon and the new hopes and safety built with the fire of a civil war. I wonder, has the thirst of those murderers for blood and destruction not been quenched yet?

Verily, until the sinful identity of those criminal agents is revealed so that they receive their punishment, I am certain that you, with the help of the wise and with the wisdom and experience you possess, will foil the hellish schemes of those hired conspirers: thus cutting off the roots of the sectarianism for which they had planned and which they desire.

Would you, dear Brother, be kind enough to convey to the deceased's son, dear Mr. Waleed, and to the honorable Jumblatt family, my profound sadness and pain? Please tell them how sorry I am for the calamity and terrible loss that has afflicted not only them but also every person of dignity in Lebanon and the Arab World.

Kamal has gone out of sight to live in hearts and to lay near his Lord with the chosen ones, the strivers who have paid their dues to life, and the defenders who have done well by their religion and their worldly life.

O Lord, bless us with many men like him. How needy we are for them! May God grant our dear beloved deceased an abode in His vast paradise and give us patience and consolation.

Verily, to You we belong and to You we shall return.

Sincerely,

Hilarion Capucci
Titular Archbishop of Caesarea, Palestine
Patriarchal Vicar of the Greek Catholics in Jerusalem

In the Name of God

*****

To His Majesty
King Khaled bin Abdulaziz Al-Saud
Ramleh Prison, 11/07/1977

Your Majesty,

In my heart, there is a beautiful portrait of you painted by your glorious services. The portrait is an ideal manifestation of your belief in your Arabism and your love for your nation in response to the call of your live conscience and corresponding to your characteristic attributes. Therefore, it is surrounded by an aura of reverence. "The ear may find delight before the eye sometimes". This old dictum is true.

Your Majesty, your devotion to defending our common Arab cause; your relentless struggle for the sake of our beloved Jerusalem (an Arab Jerusalem); the tremendous efforts you exerted to hold the Arab League Summit in Riyadh in October 1976; the brotherly atmosphere it gave rise to, the clouds it dissipated, the firm bonds it renewed among the convening parties, and the decisive resolutions it issued to end the bloodshed between the brothers in the beloved Lebanon and the honorable powerful stance of the Kingdom of Saudi Arabia during the Ramadan War by imposing the oil embargo and participating in the battle for liberation are inscribed in the memory and deep in the hearts.

Therefore, when you were indisposed, I raised my eyes to heaven imploring God Almighty to grant you perfect recovery and wellbeing, so that you would return safely to your nation, your people, and your children, and that you would resume your march laden with efforts and struggle.

But today, motivated by that same love and my faith in your devotion to your people and your zeal regarding their interests, I turn to Your Majesty to pour out my concerns to you: hoping to

7 - Letters from Prison

receive your help in the name of God.

Your Majesty, I am an Arab. This is the source of my pride. The Arab nation is my family: in its prosperity is my honor and in its status is my dignity. To shed my blood in its service is my wish.

I am a man of religion. My Arabism and my Christianity are twins. The love of God and the service of country summon one another. Whoever does not love his nation betrays his Lord.

*****

His Excellency
Ahmed Hassan al-Bakr, President of Iraq
Ramleh Prison, 18/08/1977

His Excellency, Most Respected, President Ahmed Hassan al-Bakr,

Your Excellency,

On the occasion of the second anniversary of my arrest, you have kindly ordered the issuance of a postal stamp that carries my picture: me, the prisoner who expresses through tears running down with blood the injustice we are suffering, the misery we are enduring, and the persecution we are undergoing ever since the Zionists' state was built on our ruins.

Is there any justice or correctness or wisdom in forcing the Palestinian citizens out of their homes and turning them, after stealing them, into a home for forsaken homeless people?! To solve a problem by creating a more grievous and chronic problem is gross injustice. It is sheer stupidity. Our plight, for as long as it continues, will remain a disgrace to its plotters.

Since admitting a mistake and redressing it is a virtue, perhaps the major powers would take the initiative to open their blind

In the Name of God

eyes to the light and protect truth and justice: realizing their heinous crime of imposing "Israel" on the global family. Perhaps they would sense their guilt, heed the lesson, and refrain in the future from supporting a group that is a burden on mankind and a constant threat to global peace.

Mr. President,

As you issue this stamp of great media value, I seize this opportunity, while buried in the darkness of my prison, to make my resonating voice reach public opinion through my picture, proclaiming to the world what burns my heart and makes every Arab shed tears of blood. I wish to convey this to the noble Iraqi people, represented in yourself, as a debt that warrants gratitude.

Please forgive me for my failure to repay this debt until this day. Regrettably, I am deprived of means. What I am suffering in isolation, surveillance, and inhumane terms and conditions prevented me. But Your Excellency, Mr. President, has bestowed upon me an honor that I do not deserve and that had never crossed my mind.

I am a man of religion, representing God, and God is love. Love is nothing but life, work, exertion, and giving. Love is a sacrifice, not just a hollow sentiment. Who deserves my love in times of distress more than my family, my brethren, and my children? Is not the friend in need the friend indeed?

By virtue of my bishophood, I have dedicated myself to God by serving people's interests. Authority is service. My greatness is in my humbleness, and the master of the people is their servant.

I am an Arab. I believe in my Arabism just as I believe in God, and I worship it after worshipping Him. I love my nation as I love my religion. My failure to defend my country is betrayal to my Lord. Is not love of country part of faith?

7 - Letters from Prison

Since these principles imposed my humble role on my conscience, there is no need to thank me for what I did. I only did my duty, and this duty is more deserving of honoring than me. So, I dedicate this appreciation to the spirits of our righteous martyrs and to the thousands of imprisoned rebels from among my brothers and sons who are patiently enduring their torment. In their name, I send Your Excellency the most profound gratitude.

From the stolen land and from our den, our prayers along with our hearts are with you. Our eyes look up to you in this critical fateful stage in the history of our nation, wherein conspiracies are woven to liquidate our cause as the powers of evil join forces to support "Israel" to serve their interests and their expansionist goals.

May the Almighty grant you His support and fill you with His lights: guiding your steps towards more solidarity and coordination so that we march forward as one solid row until we achieve victory through unity, which equals power. It is an invincible barrier and a destructive weapon. With unity, we fix the flag of victory in place.

I pray that your noble people live their national slogan which I have painted on my symbolic gift to Your Excellency, in admiration of its profound meaning. As the beloved Iraq embodies the sublime meanings of its slogan, it gives the world a beautiful sun and a guiding light glowing with love and solidarity towards strength, honor, and victory. God bless our beloved President and grant him long life. O God, shower him in favors and supply him with your resolve, pleasure, and light so that his eye would be comforted with honor and prosperity for his sons, triumph for his cause, and dignity for his nation.

Lastly, Mr. President, I send you sincere affection and respect. I, along with my fellow freedom fighters, thank you again for honoring us. It motivates us to harbor even greater love for our grand Arab homeland, our eternal nation, and all its children. This honoring will push us towards further belief in the justice of our sacred cause and the authenticity of our Arabism.

In the Name of God

We are full of hope that God will bestow upon your struggle a near future illuminated with triumph and crowned with a victory that breaks our chains and frees our captives.

By your might, O God, we shall return to our people and our eternal Jerusalem.

Sincerely,
Your brother Hilarion Capucci
Archbishop of Jerusalem in exile

*****

8 - Freedom

"Capucci embodied the activist church - spiritual leaders who were prepared to translate their principles into action and struggle against injustice." — Hanan Ashrawi, Palestinian legislator, activist, and scholar.

I

How Archbishop Capucci's Release was Conducted

On October 30, 1977, the office of Ephraim Katzir, President of the State of "Israel," issued a press release announcing that he had received this message from Pope Paul VI:

> We are extremely concerned about the health condition of Archbishop Hilarion Capucci in prison, which has reached a very serious life-threatening stage ... We have received many requests petitioning us to seek a solution for this dilemma. Henceforth, we ask that Your Excellency use your constitutional right of "pardoning and release of prisoners" in the case of Archbishop Capucci... We assure you that releasing the prisoner Archbishop will not bring any harm to the state of "Israel." We regard your decision, when it materializes, as an initiative of friendship and an amicable gesture towards us, and it will be met with sincere appreciation on our part...

On Sunday evening, November 6, 1977, the Israeli authorities released Archbishop Capucci. He was transferred from Ramleh Prison to Lod Airport in a heavily-guarded convoy of four military vehicles. At 8 p.m., he was the last passenger to board Alitalia Airways on a direct flight to Rome.

In the Name of God

The exhausted Archbishop stood at the airplane boarding stairs surrounded by a group of Israeli soldiers. He bowed towards the ground. Two soldiers tried to grab his arms thinking that he tripped and was falling down because of his feeble health. But he straightened up with vigor and dismissed them with a spontaneous gesture. Then he knelt down on his knees and kissed the soil of Palestine for the last time. After this, he climbed the stairs with his head held high.

When the plane landed in Rome later that night, a large crowd was waiting. At the head of the crowd was the Patriarch of the Melkite Greek Catholic Church, Maximus V Hakim; the Apostolic Delegate to Jerusalem, Monsignor William Carew; and Archbishop Maximus Salloum. A crowd of citizens from various Arab countries and a large number of journalists and correspondents from Arab, local, and international broadcast media were also present.

II

An Emotional Reception in Rome

When we asked His Grace Archbishop Capucci how he felt at the historical moment when he descended from the plane in Rome and embraced his greeters, he reached inside a drawer and removed a leather suitcase. He drew out a bundle of documents, pictures, and newspaper clippings that chronicled everything about him since his arrest and until his release from prison. He removed an article published on the front page of the Lebanese newspaper An-Nahar, on November 7, 1977, by Mr. Rafik Shalala who accompanied Patriarch Hakim to the plane to receive the freed Archbishop. The Archbishop said, "The writer of this article was an eyewitness to that moment. Publish the article as it is."

8 - Freedom

Mr. Rafik Shalala's account in An-Nahar

Groups of Palestinians occupied the arrival halls at the airport since morning to receive their Archbishop who was returning from prison... Photojournalists were also waiting, and so were heavily-armed policemen.

The airport director explained to the Patriarch and the Vatican representative the measures that were taken in preparation for Archbishop Capucci's arrival, including that his plane would land on an exclusive runway commonly used for hijacked planes or those experiencing malfunction in order to keep inquisitive eyes away. While police officers dressed in civilian clothes or military uniforms were hurriedly entering and exiting, Palestinian chants in support of Fatah resounded throughout the main airport hall. It was chanted by Arab young men wearing keffiyehs.[4] Prevented from approaching the landing area, they threatened to block the road before the car that would transport Capucci to his hospital in order to receive blessing from the Archbishop.

At 10:10 p.m., the procession of the Patriarch and the Papal Envoy moved amid heavy guard to the northern runway while the Alitalia plane was landing and approaching its designated spot.

Twelve small and large police cars and trucks surrounded the spot where the plane parked. Policemen cordoned the area and subjected everyone, even airport staff, to inspection.

He emerged with tearful eyes

At 10:15 p.m., the plane came to a stop and stairs were brought to the front door. Patriarch Hakim went up to receive the Archbishop, but Capucci was tired and preferred to wait until all the other passengers had disembarked.

---

[4] A chequered black and white scarf that is usually worn around the neck or head. The Palestinian keffiyeh has become a symbol of Palestinian nationalism dating back to the 1936-1939 Arab revolt in Palestine.

In the Name of God

A few minutes later, the Archbishop of Jerusalem emerged from the plane. He was holding his crozier (pastoral staff), the Virgin Mary icon was on his chest, and he was dressed in full clerical garb. The pastoral ring glittered on his right hand. He looked thin in loose clothes and had a long beard.

He paused for a few seconds and then looked tearfully at Patriarch Hakim, his superior. Both crying, they locked in a long embrace. Standing a few steps away was Msgr. William Carew, the Apostolic Delegate to Jerusalem, who, along with Archbishop Maximos Salloum, accompanied Archbishop Capucci. The four of them descended the stairs with firm footsteps. Capucci greeted the policemen receiving him and the police officers saluted him. In the flashlights of Italian TV cameras, he walked to the Vatican car and sat in the back seat next to Patriarch Hakim. Archimandrite Laham sat in the front seat. Before the car left, the Archbishop blessed his "greeters" with his hands clasped around his crozier.

At 11 p.m., the car started moving with police cars ahead and behind it. Msgrs. Carew and Monterezzi and Archbishop Salloum stayed behind to claim the baggage. During the car ride, Archbishop Capucci recounted to the Patriarch some of his suffering in prison and how he insisted on wearing his clerical robe despite the Israelis' demand that he wear civilian clothes. Capucci said that the passengers on the plane recognized him and jostled towards the first class where he was sitting to greet him. He expressed during the conversation his sadness at leaving Jerusalem.

His first appeal

The Archbishop addressed his first appeal to the Lebanese people and the Arabs in An-Nahar. It was his first public announcement since December 1974. He wrote:

> My meeting tonight with His Eminence the Patriarch, who to me is a father, brother, and friend, made me forget some

8 - Freedom

of my grief and alleviated my pain. It is like a balm to my wounds. However, despite my joy to meet you, I feel some bitterness deep inside, and along with Christ I say: 'My soul is crushed with grief,' because when I learnt of the harsh conditions stipulated for my release, I felt that I was leaving one prison only to enter another that is bigger, more cruel, and more bitter.

What is prison? Prison is locked iron doors: it is suppression of freedom. If what I was told is true (that from now on high fortified walls will be between me and my nation, my sons, my compatriots, my brethren, and my Levant; the doors of Arab states will be locked in my face; and my hands and legs and even my tongue will be enchained), then I am in a big prison. I am a captive. I am a prisoner.

Thus, deep down I feel bitterness, pain, and much grief.

He added:

Words cannot express my gratitude. What the Patriarch has done for me is more than what one would do for his own brother. I am indebted to His Beatitude and to His Holiness the Pope for their love and compassion and relentless efforts to release me. His Beatitude the Patriarch and His Holiness the Pope are fathers to me, and a father thinks with his heart. When they felt the extent of my agony and suppression in prison, they reluctantly accepted harsh conditions. But these conditions to me, despite my wholehearted appreciation, are like a death sentence. How sweet death would be, because one dies once, but in my case, I will die a hundred times a day when I am away from my sons, my people, Palestine, the Arab states, and my Eastern Church. Every year in August, my brethren, the archbishops, convene in Lebanon. What will it be like when I am unable to see them and inquire about them?

I have great hope in God, and I thank Him for this blessing. I thank His Holiness the Pope and the Arab countries for their noble stance, their support, and their many attempts to release me. I will not forget the martyrs who died for the sake of my release, and I appreciate the Arab states and their stances. My ordeal has fused me into the greater Arab world. I feel that I belong to every Arab state and that I am a son and servant... every Arab country is my country.

Archbishop Capucci concluded his appeal, saying:

I thank An-Nahar newspaper for the efforts it exerted to investigate my news and disseminate it to the world. It has always been "An-Nahar" (lit. daylight), and it will always remain a bright daylight.

Hakim: "I am proud of his sacrifice."

Patriarch Hakim said to An-Nahar:

Today, I feel joy and pride. Joy because, after the three long years that I consider to be three generations, we see Archbishop Capucci despite his feebleness and exhaustion. We hope that he regains his health, resolve, and vigor to continue his efforts for his church, homeland, and denomination.

I cannot but be proud of what the Archbishop has done and of his sacrifices that history will never forget. He has given us an example of sacrifice, patriotism, and self-surrender for the sake of the general welfare. That is the Archbishop that we are receiving today. Therefore, I ask God to grant him success and bless him with a long life. We thank His Holiness the Pope who was keen in every meeting I had with him – the most recent was three months ago – to say to me: "Capucci is my brother and we must do for his sake whatever is possible." We express the same gratitude to the

8 - Freedom

Arab states that appreciated Archbishop Capucci, loved him, and respected him. It is sufficient that they spread his picture worldwide on their postal stamps.

We now feel that a nightmare is over. By the grace of God, from now on, there will be nothing but good for the general welfare and for the homeland and the church.

First mass in Rome with Arab ambassadors

At 11:30 on November 8, the ambassadors of Arab countries started arriving at the small chapel where Patriarch Hakim was holding a "Prayer of Thanks for the divine blessing upon Archbishop Capucci." The Patriarch and the Archbishop then moved to the second level, and the Archbishop donned his liturgical vestment for the first time since August 1974. The voices of nuns started flowing with hymns in Arabic.

Seated inside the chapel were the Ambassador of Egypt to the Vatican, Mr. Al-Shafei Abdel-Hamid; the Ambassador of Syria to Rome, Mr. Farouk Al-Sharaa; the Ambassador of Iraq to Rome, Dr. Ismail Mirza; the Ambassador of Libya, Mr. Qadri Al-Atrash; Head of the Arab League Office in Roma, Ambassador Mohammad Sabra; Mr. Shafiq Al-Hout, representative of Mr. Yasser Arafat; a delegation from the PLO office in Rome headed by Mr. Nimr Hammad; and others. The Lebanese Ambassador to the Vatican, Dr. Antoine Fattal, apologized for not attending because of prior diplomatic engagements.

Everyone was waiting for the Archbishop to emerge in his new-old look. He came into the chapel giving blessing with all eyes focused on his face and following his every move. The prayer of thanks started, headed by the Patriarch and assisted by Archbishops Capucci and Salloum, Archimandrite Lahham, and Father Elias Garwan. This was Archbishop Capucci's first open mass after years of holding daily mass alone in his prison cell.

In the Name of God

Badges from the olive trees of Jerusalem

Thereafter, Archbishop Capucci expressed his gratitude to the ambassadors of the Arab countries that honored him by printing his picture on their postal stamps. He recounted how he made badges from the olive trees of Jerusalem in the Ramleh Prison. He engraved on each the flag of an Arab country, the date he made it, his name, and the name of the prison he was in. He said that he had sent some of these badges to the heads of the respective Arab states and revealed that he had made them in cooperation with a British engineer called David Kelly. Kelly was his prisonmate and had designed the "Kfir" combat aircraft for the Israelis. After accusing him of dealing with "hostile states," the Israelis put him in prison lest he expose the secrets of the aircraft.

Capucci narrated how, one day, the prison warden seized the Libya badge from the engineer's hands. When the Archbishop objected, he said, "Were the badge for other than Libya, I would've returned it to you. But Libya, that's impossible."

Archbishop Capucci then handed the attendees thank you letters from himself to the heads of states for issuing postal stamps carrying his picture. He then presented to each ambassador the badge that symbolized his country. He announced that he had sent the badge of Palestine to Mr. Yasser Arafat earlier and he was keeping a replica of it.

Afterwards, Capucci met privately with Messrs. Al-Hout and Hammad. He expressed hope that they would meet with him again today when Mr. Farouk Kaddoumi, Chairman of the PLO Political Department, has returned to Rome after his trip to Moscow.

I finally heard my mother's voice

Nine minutes was the duration of the first telephone conversation

8 - Freedom

Archbishop Capucci had with his mother and brother. He called them from his residence in Rome, two days after his release from prison. His mother did not believe that it was him on the line, and they had the following conversation:

> Mum, I'm the Archbishop...
> I miss you so much my dear. I hope you're in good health.
> I'm fine by the grace of God. With your prayers, I will be better.
> I want to see you, to kiss you, to receive your blessing.
> On Wednesday we will meet.
> I'm waiting for the day I see you, my dear. I have no one left in this world but you.
> You were always with me in prison; always on my mind. You encouraged me and I was patient because you taught me patience... What's wrong with your eyes? I read in the newspapers that you cannot see because you cried so much... As soon as I see you and smell your scent I will become better and I will see you better...
> And when I see you, my life will start again.

Then his mother started crying. The Archbishop could not stand it and cried as well. Their voices choked with crying and tears.

9 - In Exile

"Monsignor Capucci's personal witness to the cause of Palestine has won him high standing in the Arab and Muslim world. At least five countries – Iraq, Egypt, Libya, Sudan and his native Syria – have issued stamps in his honor. The highest and eternal reward will, of course, be awarded to him in Heaven." — Revd. Frank Julian Gelli, *Islam Today*

I

Homeless ... in Latin America

Archbishop Capucci's stay at the German Sisters monastery in Rome only lasted a few weeks. After this, a decision was issued by the Congregation for the Oriental Churches in the Vatican to appoint him Apostolic Delegate to South America. The Archbishop complied reluctantly with the Vatican's decision and headed to Venezuela. With much bitterness and anger, he described his move from Rome to Latin America:

> After my release from prison, the Israelis demanded that I be transferred immediately to Latin America, but the Vatican asked for some time to execute the commitment to appoint me Apostolic Delegate in those distant lands because of my poor health condition and the feebleness I was suffering after the hunger strikes.
>
> On December 16, 1977, 40 days after my arrival in Rome, His Holiness Pope Paul VI received me for the first time. I was accompanied by His Beatitude Patriarch Hakim. On the same day, only one hour after the meeting was over, the official spokesperson announced the decision to appoint me Apostolic Nuncio in Latin America. I obediently complied

with the papal orders and left Rome for Venezuela on January 21, 1978. Upon arrival at Caracas Airport, I was greeted by an official reception and large crowds of people from various Arab countries. We left the airport for the Lebanese Club in Caracas where a reception was held in my honor, during which I explained the circumstances of my arrest and the torture I suffered in prison for three and a half years. The next day, the President of Venezuela, Carlos Andres Perez, received me, and I thanked him for his noble stances in support of the Palestinian cause.

After one month in Caracas, I left Venezuela for Brazil and then went to Argentina. From there, I moved around the countries of Latin America. Although I was honored and appreciated in all those stops, my heart was still stuck in the streets of old Jerusalem. After each stop, I persistently asked the Vatican to allow me to return, but my request was in vain. Two months into my stay in Argentina, I received an order from Rome to remain in exile until further notice. I was obliged to wait. What would I do? Where would I go? How would I live?

I moved from one country to another, dragging around my misery and sadness. For a whole year, I lived as a "lost bishop" ... estranged wherever I went. I ultimately returned to Argentina for a few months.

I suffered much in that stage, wishing repeatedly to return to prison, and I announced this in the newspapers despite the ban that the Argentinean authorities imposed on me against engaging in any political activity or taking part in any public discussion about the Palestinian cause. None of the countries I visited treated me the way the Venezuelan government did, whose stances in support of the Arab causes stood apart from the others. Mexico, on the other hand, rejected my visa application when I decided to visit the country in May 1978. The Mexican embassy in Buenos

Aires refused to provide any justification for this rejection. Thereupon, I made a statement to the press, stating: "The decision of the Mexican government is the result of Zionist pressure, because Mexico and 'Israel' are the only two countries that I cannot visit."

With much bitterness, Archbishop Capucci summarized his memories of that time:

> It was a year and a few months since I had left prison and I still felt that I was living behind the cell bars. I could not visit any Arab country. The Israelis monitored my every move and exerted constant pressure on the Vatican, which made matters worse in restricting my freedom and preventing me from undertaking any activity.

II

Return to my Beloved Homeland, Syria

More than a year into this enforced estrangement, I ran out of patience waiting for new instructions. Thus, I sent a letter to the President of Syria, Hafez al-Assad, asking him permission to return to my birthplace, Syria. His Excellency welcomed my return and said, "You are Syrian, and you can return to Syria whenever you wish."

Before writing the letter to President Assad, I received an invitation to participate in the conference of the Palestinian National Council in Damascus. Brother Abu Ammar (Yassir Arafat) invited me personally in a phone call. Although his invitation made me happy and I considered it a wonderful way out of the suffering I was enduring in Latin America, I found myself obliged to turn down the invitation.

My answer to the PLO was:

In the Name of God

I thank you from the bottom of my heart, and I consider your invitation a grace from heaven. It is the best thing that has happened to me since my release from prison... but I wish I could accept it. There are Vatican restraints that cripple me and prevent me from any activity related to the Palestinian cause. I cannot leave Latin America without Vatican permission! How would they permit me to go to the National Council upon an invitation from the head of the PLO?

A few days later, I received an invitation from President Hafez al-Assad filled with sentiment and tenderness. He said: "We cannot wait to see you in Syria... Strange that you want me to invite you to your home while Syria is your homeland! You must visit your homeland to meet your brothers and family. You can come at any time. The invitation will remain open until you are able to answer it. We will be quite pleased to see you."

After reading President Assad's letter, I called Brother Abu Ammar and said to him, "As long as President Assad emphasized my Syrian nationality in his letter, now I have a justification to go to Syria with which I can face the Vatican." I asked him to renew his invitation for me to attend the National Council meeting, which he did. I then received an invitation from President Assad through the Syrian embassy in Argentina. Thus, I went to Syria invited by the Palestinian National Council on the one hand and by the President of Syria on the other. Consequently, any measures taken against me in this case would be indirectly targeting the Syrian President who had invited me. The Vatican was keen on avoiding any dispute with Syria, especially now that I was a Syrian national answering the invitation of the President to a short visit. On these grounds, I packed my bags and left Venezuela for Syria.

I later returned from Syria to Rome to live in the hospitality of the Lebanese Order of the Sisters of the Cross. Had the Syrian President not saved me back then, I would have remained stranded in Latin America.

9 - In Exile

The Archbishop answered President Hafez al-Assad's invitation with this letter:

Your Excellency President Hafez al-Assad,

Most Respected, President of the Syrian Arab Republic,

Your kind letter overflowing with love and generosity had the most profound effect on me. I am most thankful to Your Excellency for kindly inviting me to visit my beloved homeland, Syria. I am eager to meet your noble person whom I have loved before meeting him. Does the ear not love before the eye sometimes?

Meeting my beloved Syrian brethren and staying amongst you would fill my heart with serenity, joy, and hope. My exile far from my homeland and my nation torments me and hurts me deep inside. Therefore, being on Arab soil in an atmosphere of love, brotherhood, and solidarity would alleviate my grief and diminish the sharpness of my pains: pouring balm on my deep wounds.

Mr. President, as I impatiently, look forward to that joyful day, I extend to Your Excellency again my deepest gratitude and my utmost respect and affection: praying that you be granted abundant grace, blessings, good health, and success in your arduous national tasks. For the noble Syrian people, I pray for perpetual honor and prosperity under your wise leadership.

Sincerely,
Hilarion Capucci
Archbishop of Jerusalem in exile

In the Name of God

III

A Hero's Welcome in Damascus

Among the documents that Archbishop Capucci asked us to publish in the book is a detailed report on his first visit to Damascus after his release from prison, and his participation in the Palestinian National conference. The report read:

> Archbishop Capucci arrived in Damascus at dawn on Saturday 20/01/1979 at the invitation of President Hafez al-Assad and Mr. Yasser Arafat, Chairman of the Executive Committee of the PLO. Receiving Archbishop Capucci at the airport were Mr. Adib Melhem, Minister of Presidential Affairs; Mr. Abdel Muhsin Abu Mizar, Official PLO Spokesman, a large number of the Palestinian National Council members, and a huge crowd of citizens.
>
> Also receiving him were the Palestinian freedom fighter Fatima Bernawy, the renowned Palestinian poet Mahmoud Darwish, a group of freedom fighters from the Occupied Territories, and a host of journalists and correspondents of international broadcast and television networks.

The Archbishop descended from the plane with tearful eyes and prostrated himself on the ground: kissing it three times. He said to his greeters, "The first kiss is for the beloved soil of Syria; the freedom-fighting, persevering, Arab Syria." He praised the role that Syria played, under the leadership of President Hafez al-Assad, in the causes of our Arab nation in general, and he thanked the President for inviting him to visit his homeland.

He also praised the historical meeting between the sister countries Syria and Iraq, saying, "This meeting embodies all our wishes and what Arabs everywhere aspire to." He stressed that the prospective union between Syria and Iraq would be the nucleus for a comprehensive Arab union, which is the ultimate hope of all Arabs.

9 - In Exile

Archbishop Capucci expressed his joy in meeting his Palestinian brethren, saying, "My feelings today are those of a captive soldier who was released from captivity and returned to the battlefield. I will not rest or find peace of mind until we return to every inch in Palestine and every inch in our beloved Jerusalem."

The Archbishop saluted the Palestinian freedom fighters suffering in the prisons of the Zionist enemy. He also saluted the steadfast Arab people in the Occupied territories, saying, "We die to live with honor."

Capucci, the freedom fighter, concluded with the words: "We will attain our rights because we are not begging for something; rather, we are entitled to those rights and we must return to our homes and our sacred places in the Aqsa Mosque and the Church of the Holy Sepulcher."

Archbishop Hilarion Capucci expressed his joy at visiting Syria, saying: "I am indebted to Syria, who taught me to love all the Arab states without exception. And I am indebted to Syria because it taught me to love Palestine and to love the Arabs."

He added: "The lessons in Arab patriotism which I received in Syria at an early age inspired me to conscript myself for the service of Palestine."

Archbishop Capucci referred to the national initiative of the Syrian Arab State in Lebanon, saying: "Syria considers Lebanon an inseparable part of the Arab homeland. Hence, it considers defending Lebanon a patriotic duty against all those who harbor evil for Lebanon. Syria's defense of Lebanon is driven by its patriotism, steadfastness, and its history of fighting for freedom."

He stressed again his joy and happiness to be in Syria, saying: "I am happy to be in Syria, not only emotionally but also patriotically, because Syria is indeed the fortress of steadfastness, and it is the throbbing heart of Arabism. This is not mere sentiments and slogans; rather, the glorious history of Syria is filled with struggle."

In a television interview that Damascus TV aired on the evening of Saturday, January 20, 1979, Archbishop Capucci said: "I kissed the Syrian ground involuntarily the minute I stepped on Syrian land, in praise of its struggle, steadfastness, and Arabism. In my kiss for the land of Syria, I included a kiss for every Arab land and for every Arab person in any Arab state, and for every Syrian citizen on the beloved land of Syria . . My joy to visit Syria today is the joys of the thirsty when he quenches his thirst with sweet cool water. In the Syria of struggle, the Syria of steadfastness, the Syria of sacrifice, I have found all compassion, affection, and praise. This indeed filled my heart with joy."

The Archbishop expressed his appreciation for the warm welcome he has received since his arrival in Damascus.

> I would like to thank His Excellency President Hafez al-Assad who sent me, immediately after my release from the prison of the Zionists, a most splendid message in which he said, "We are eagerly looking forward to seeing you and to your presence among us" . . . Two days ago, His Excellency renewed the invitation to me to visit my homeland Syria on the occasion of the convening of the Palestinian National Council in Damascus. I was thus able to combine pleasure with duty: the pleasure is my presence on this good land among my Syrian brothers. I particularly love Damascus, and of course I love Aleppo because it is from where I come. I love Damascus because I lived in it ten successive years. I have said it many times that I am extremely happy to be on this good land of generosity, grace, and struggle. . . I am indebted to His Excellency President Hafez al-Assad for inviting me to visit Syria. I am grateful for his hospitality from the bottom of my heart. I would also like to thank my Syrian brothers for the love and care they surrounded me with at the time of my arrest and after my arrest and in the present time. I pray that the Lord watches over His

9 - In Exile

Excellency the President with His watchful eyes and that He guides him towards what serves the Arabs and the Palestinian cause and what achieves prosperity and success for the beloved Syria. And I wish happiness and success to every Syrian."

IV

Archbishop Capucci at the Syrian People's Council

The People's Council of Syria (Parliament) held a session at 6:00 p.m. on Wednesday, January 24, 1979, under the chairmanship of Mahmoud Hadid, Chairman of the Council, and in the presence of Prime Minister Mohammed Ali al-Halabi and several ministers. Archbishop Hilarion Capucci and Khaled al-Fahoum, head of the Palestinian National Council attended, as well as guests of honor.

Upon his entrance into the Council hall, the Council members met Archbishop Capucci with a roaring round of applause. Then Mahmoud Hadid gave a speech wherein he welcomed the Arab freedom-fighter and Archbishop, the man of religion and revolution, who employed his clerical potential in the service of the causes of his nation and people, his leadership skills to serve the cause of the Palestinian people and the Arab people, and who furthermore employed these skills to wage war against Zionism, imperialism, and occupation. Neither Zionist terrorism nor the terror of his Zionist jailors, who wanted to undermine his leadership and revolutionary skills, could dissuade him from his national duty.

In his speech, Hadid said: "I am pleased to welcome him here among his family, among his people, and I am also pleased to invite him to speak on this occasion; the occasion of meeting their excellencies the members of the People's Council; the representatives of our people in the Syrian Arab Republic under the leadership of President Hafez al-Assad who leads it towards liberation and victory now and forever."

Archbishop Capucci then spoke:

> His Excellency, Chairman of the People's Council; His Excellency, the Prime Minister; Excellencies, ministers and members of the People's Council,
>
> Am I dreaming, or is it heavenly grace that made me stand amongst you this minute, to greet through you and to embrace through you the people of Syria; and through the people of Syria each and every Arab people.
>
> Am I dreaming, I, the one who constructed with faith his Arab homeland in exile, or was it that particular faith – faith in God and in Arabism – that returned me today to the heart of Arabism and the fortress of steadfastness, to the lion's den, to Syria.
>
> Brothers and Sisters, when I heard on the plane that carried me back from my distant exile the voice of the steward saying: "The Syrian Airlines welcomes you onboard its flight to Damascus," I felt a quiver under my skin and the tears of joy burning my eyes. I felt that it was only at that moment that I was released from prison.
>
> At the Damascus Airport, I found myself spontaneously getting down on my knees and kissing the ground. When I left Palestine, I got down on my knees and kissed the ground of Jerusalem. I planted my heart there just as a kernel of wheat is planted. If it remains under the sun, it dries and perishes, and when it is buried, it survives. The stipulation for its survival and resurrection is its death and burial.
>
> But here, I kissed the ground because I was lost for words. My sentiments were greater than any words. Therefore, I

9 - In Exile

wanted to put in the ground all my yearning, belonging, and thirst.

When I kissed the land of Syria, I was kissing every Arab land. I was kissing the land of Palestine. Isn't Syria the beginning of the road of return?

Brothers and Sisters, I was once asked about my identity and I said: "Record that I am Arab." I said: "Record that I am Syrian." I said: "Record that I am Christian." As to being Arab, we are Arabs first and foremost, and we all submit to God. If it is a beautiful thing that nationalism brings together brothers and brings together the Christian and the Muslim, then what is more beautiful is that the crescent and the cross melt together in the crucible of Arabism, nationalism, and the one nation; rather, in the one God.

As to being Syrian, it is because Syria is my country. If I love it, it is not only because it is my country, but also because it is our bridge to Jerusalem.

Syria is a role and a mission. It is the true state of the Arab existence, and it carries the banner of Arabism. It has adopted the Palestinian cause; rather, it has made the Palestinian cause its own cause and placed all its potentials at its service. It has exerted and continues to exert all that is within its capacity for the sake of defending the dear stolen land and restoring the usurped rights at any cost.

His Excellency President Assad, in his wonderful national speech before the Palestinian National Council, embodied Syria's commitment to Palestine; to its cause, its people, its rights, and the Liberation Organization.

Yes, I am Syrian. If I love Syria, then I should love it twice, once because I am its son, and once because she is worthy of it.

In the Name of God

As to my being Christian, it is because I am Christian and I am a clergyman, and I am certain that my effectiveness at the Arab and national levels are contingent on my interaction at the religious and Christian levels.

The Christian is the student of Christ. Christ is love incarnate. Therefore, the Christian must embody love in his life. Love is not a mere passion; it is life, it is work, it is exertion, sacrifice, and giving.

Christ says: "A new commandment I give unto you, that ye love one another as I have loved you;" meaning, unto sacrifice, unto death, unto redemption.

When I took the road of redemption, I was only following the first Redeemer, the son of Nazareth and the son of Palestine, Christ.

Ladies and Gentlemen, if the Palestinian cause belongs to politics, I am not a politician. As I have said, I am a cleric, and the cause to me is a humanitarian national cause. It is the cause of a people, my people, who were unjustly persecuted and humiliated. The cause then is one of truth and justice.

Who is more entitled than a clergyman to fight for truth, justice, and humanity? Since God is truth and justice and love, and since a clergyman is a servant ... the clergyman is a father, brother, friend, and, in particular, a servant, because he is a pupil of Christ. Christ came not to be served but to serve and offer himself to redeem the oppressed.

It is Syria that taught me that we, Arabs, are but one closely-knit family. We are parts of one body. What affects one part affects the whole body. Hence my love for Palestine. It is because Palestine is an inseparable part of the Arab nation. And hence is my love for you Lebanon; yes, hence

9 - In Exile

is my love for Lebanon. Rather, it is because of my love for Lebanon that I love Palestine, and it is because of my love for Palestine that I love Lebanon.

My torment in the enemy's prison was multiple. I was tormented for the sake of Palestine and I was tormented for the sake of Lebanon. From there, from prison, I wrote to the Lebanese, entreating them to return to dialogue, to mutual understanding, and to love, because Lebanon is love.

Because the Lebanese Christians, inside and outside Lebanon, have always been free Arabs, defending the homeland with their blood and souls in the face of the Zionist invasion from its outset, any tarnishing of this image of my Lebanese brothers is but a conspiracy against true Christianity and against Lebanon itself.

Lebanon is always in my heart in its greatness and its misery, its glory and its injury, but none would save Lebanon but the Lebanese themselves.

I pray to God that all the groups would overcome their grudges and come together in the midst of this conflict of multiple motives and purposes; this conflict of multiple internal and external sources. I pray that they would come together upon a unified concept of victory and all meet at a round table to study the situation of their Lebanese home. I pray that they do not exit this meeting except in solidarity in terms of land and people, in order to block the Zionist attack that covets Lebanon: that they exit with one single concept of victory (an independent sovereign free unified Lebanon).

I would like to stress that whoever calls for colonial settlement in the South of Lebanon, that is the severance of a part Lebanon, is a traitor, because this constitutes an implementation of the Zionist conspiracy that wishes to partition Lebanon and plant the Palestinians in Arab countries so that they would forget their identity and so that the name of Palestine would be obliterated.

If we were given the choice between the whole world with everything and everyone in it on one side of the scale and an inch of the land of Palestine on the other side, we would relinquish the world and everything in it. To this inch, we hold on, and to it we shall return.

My people! My brothers! What gives me most joy and fills my heart with consolation is my presence amongst you in this particular time that witnesses the embodiment of the dream of every Arab who believes in his Arabism and his just cause; rather, every Arab who believes in his might; in these historic days that witness the reunification of the siblings, the Syrian and the Iraqi peoples.

This brotherly meeting between Damascus and Baghdad is the outcome of fervent prayers and flowing tears shed by millions of sincere Arabs faithful to their Arab identity and cause. It is the correct response to the defeatist resolutions in Camp David.

My dear friends, the "I" is frail and weak and destined to perish; whereas the "I" that melts into the "We" is the only one destined to success and victory, since in union there is strength.

Christ said that a house divided cannot stand. Hence are the joy and comfort that I find in the steps towards a union between Syria and Iraq: the twin states. We have now begun to walk on the correct straight path towards honor and dignity, towards realizing our national goals in return and liberation.

I ask God to make this solidarity and coordination the

9 - In Exile

beginning of full union and the seed of a comprehensive Arab union, such that no flag rises above the Arab flag save the unified flag of the unified Arab nation.

Mr. Chairman of the People's Council, you have given me great honor by inviting me to your respected Council. I am immensely grateful to you for this kind initiative that gave me this joyous opportunity to meet through my brothers, the respected Council members, all the beloved Syrian people to whom I belong.

Lastly, with all my heart, I extend a greeting of love and respect to the Honorable Brother, the freedom fighter, the beloved of the Syrians and the Arabs, the good son of Syria, its protector and its lion, His Excellency President Hafez al-Assad.

A greeting filled with sincerity and devotion, in expression of my gratitude for his favor, for the care, compassion, and love that he engulfed me with at the time of my arrest and following my release, and for kindly inviting me to my homeland, Syria, to enjoy the bliss of living with you and to find the comfort of my eye in seeing you. This is all imprinted, not on the pages of my heart; but rather, in the depths of my conscience.

O Lord, protect him for us, watch over him with Your eyes, and guide him to success to achieve what he aspires to: the prosperity of Syria and the embodiment of our national hopes in dignity and liberation.

Peace be upon you.

After Archbishop Capucci delivered his speech, which was interrupted repeatedly by applause, the Chairman of the People's Council again welcomed the freedom-fighting Archbishop as a dear guest of the Syrian Arab people and of the leader of the

In the Name of God

procession, President Hafez al-Assad. He saluted all Arab freedom fighters on the Arab arena, especially those in the occupied Arab territories.

10 - Political Stances

His participation in the Mavi Marmara showed that he was ready - much like the Palestinians - to adapt to new ways of resistance. — Ilan Pappe, Israeli historian.

I

My Relation with the Iranian Revolution

Regarding his relation with the Iranian revolution, which was in its initial stage, Archbishop Capucci stated:

> My love for Iran and my respect for its revolution stem from the fact that I see the finger of God in it. If we wield logic and try to explain how this revolution triumphed and survived to this day, it is incomprehensible. It overturned all standards, because it sprang out of faith. The embodiment of religion in actions generated popular momentum that changed all equations.
>
> The people faced the Shah's tanks with their bare chests. They raced to march in the front lines where they confronted, with steel fists, an army ranked fifth in the world. The bodies of martyrs were falling before enemy fire, yet they continued their march. With religious persistence emanating from the depths of the heart, and with faith, the revolution triumphed. It remains ongoing despite the difficulties it is facing because it possesses a faithful popular momentum that is capable of sacrifice and giving.
>
> The Iranian revolution defied the United States of America despite the U.S.'s power and might, and it forced her to give up and retreat based on the power of faith, not by

virtue of atomic bombs. I see the fingers of God in it. I only understand the success of the Iranian revolution if faith is its main stimulus, because you cannot explain this success except through faith and the role of providence that watches over mankind.

How needy we Arabs are to learn a lesson from the Iranian revolution. We have a sea of people and natural resources. If we did the right thing, used our human and material potentials, and achieved our unity, we would impose ourselves on the world and liberate our land and our people.

Instead of being a mighty power, we are undergoing the most difficult and most adverse circumstances.

II

The goal is to partition Syria and bring the arabs to their knees

At the time of the interviews with His Eminence Archbishop Capucci in April 1979, Egypt and Israel had signed the Camp David Accords on July 17, 1978 under the auspices of US President Jimmy Carter. The agreement followed 12 days of secret negotiations that took place at the summer residence of the US Presidency in Camp David, Maryland. President Anwar Sadat represented the Egyptian side while Prime Minister Menachem Begin represented Tel Aviv. At the center of the accords was the execution of UN resolutions 242 and 338, which clearly stated the return of "Israel" to the 1967 borders. Archbishop Capucci spoke about that phase and declared his perspective regarding what was being planned in Camp David and the extent of its serious implications on Lebanon, Syria, and the Palestinian cause. It seemed like he was foretelling the future. Everything that he warned against that day has happened with serious repercussions. Today, almost 40 years after they were signed, the Camp David

Accords did not achieve their major goal: the normalization of Israeli relations with Egypt. In this respect, it remains only ink on paper. This is what Capucci said:

> Camp David is a legitimization of oppression. It is a perpetuation of the occupation. What is the meaning of autonomous rule under occupation? As long as the Israeli flag is raised everywhere, and it is the Israeli army that has control, and security is in the grip of "Israel," then there is no real value to autonomous rule, which is limited to installing sewage pipes and lamp poles.
>
> This is the work of municipal authorities, and they are doing it now without the favor of autonomous rule. Regarding the Palestinians abroad, Camp David plants them in the Arab countries they are in and deprives them of the right to return to their lands. Thus, it creates a crack in the Arab body and puts a definite end to the Palestinian cause.
>
> If we go back in time a little we find that the Balfour Declaration went hand in hand with the Sykes-Picot Agreement that divided our region between the two colonial powers: the French and the British. The Balfour Declaration would not have been realized except after dividing Syria. So long as Syria remains united, this declaration, even if it was passed, could not have endured. The practical means to realize the declaration in reality is by dividing Syria. This scheme is still active and awaits the chance to be executed. The Camp David talks are the American political bridge to that goal.
>
> The Lebanese tragedy was created for this purpose as well. While the war was raging in Lebanon, the Camp David Accords were underway and the Washington resolutions were issued, drawing the execution plan. Now is chapter two of the conspiracy, which is to transfer the disease that has become endemic in Lebanon to Syria. This is what we have

started to witness on the Syrian stage. They have planted the epidemic (a reference to the activities of the Muslim Brotherhood and their terrorist acts in Aleppo, Homs, and Hamah) and they are trying to secure a conducive climate for it to grow and spread in order to divide Syria further. The moment Syria divides, it will fall to its knees. The moment Syria falls to its knees, the Arabs will be brought to their knees, and the Camp David resolutions will be executed.

No sincere Arab would accept Camp David, because its resolutions are contrary to every international standard and to all the resolutions issued by the United Nations.

I would like to ask President Anwar Sadat: "When you went to Jerusalem and gave a speech at the Israeli Knesset, you said to them that you had crossed all lines and standards and came for a just peace. Is just peace the return to the borders of 67? How could you accept what is less than that? Where do you stand today from your statement of yesterday? Where is the pioneering role of Egypt? What have you done to the Palestinian cause with this decision? What dear prices the Arabs would pay in the coming years because of a hasty decision that you made? What would Egypt and the Egyptian people pay in the coming decades?"

I also ask President Jimmy Carter: "Where does Camp David stand in relation to the first statement you made after you were elected President of the United States when you talked about a homeland for the Palestinians and about the establishment of two states? What project do you present to Palestine today? How much blood would be shed for the sake of an illusionary peace that would never see the light?"

I consider even the return to the borders of 1967 a feeble demand. When the Tunisian President Habib Bourguiba spoke in Jericho in 1965 about division and called upon the Palestinian refugees to be realistic and accept the 1947

10 - Political Stances

division, his project included regions that were much farther than the borders of 67. Nevertheless, the Palestinian people rejected his suggestion, and the Arabs unanimously supported the Palestinian stance.

If the main demand today is to return to the West Bank, Gaza, and Jerusalem, we were there before the defeat of June 5, 1967. The '67 war turned the Jewish dream into an established reality. What was rejected and unacceptable to Arabs two decades ago has now become an open and public demand.

Accepting the 1967 borders means relinquishing almost half of Palestine to Israel, which is what international Zionism has been dreaming of since the Basel Conference in 1897 and until this day. The Arabs accepted this situation while "Israel" did not accept it, and its expansion is in continuous growth.

The solution for the Palestinian cause that calls for the establishment of a state in the West Bank and Gaza is a monstrosity, because it resolves the problem of the people of Jerusalem, Naples, and Ramallah, but it leaves out the rest. What do we do with the people of Haifa, Jaffa, and Nazareth? Do they continue to live under the yoke of occupation or do they remain homeless abroad?

It is impermissible that all Palestinians return to a "homeland" called the West Bank on the grounds that it is part of Palestine. Nay! Each person must return to his home, his land, and his possessions in all parts of a complete Palestine. Such is the "right to return" as I understand it. The son of Haifa wants to return to the house that his father built in Haifa with sweat and hard work one stone at a time... and whose cost he saved one piastre at a time.

As a person, I do not have the right to make political

decisions that affect people's lives, but, as a citizen, I have the right to express my opinion. I do not like half solutions: it is either all or nothing. Half solutions always reflect defeat. I want to take my rights in full.

The Palestinian cause is not just the political borders that "Israel" accepts or that a certain Arab regime demands. Rather, it is a humanitarian cause before subjecting it to political solutions and bargains. It is the cause of a people who were expelled from their lands, pulled off their fields, and evicted from their homes. Now they wish to return to the entire soil of their homeland.

Therefore, I do not participate in negotiations that aim at the establishment of a Palestinian state in part of the land of Palestine at the expense of the other parts. I will not participate in the government of a state of that kind. Neither do I accept an international committee whose purpose is to internationalize Jerusalem. Jerusalem is Arab, and it will remain Arab.

But if I were offered the chance to join a government whose goal is to liberate the entire soil of Palestine, then I would accept without any hesitation.

I say it loud and clear: I do not believe in the so-called good intentions of "Israel." I do not imagine, for a single moment, that "Israel" would accept something called peace. Peace means the end of "Israel." "Israel" is a state founded on war, and perpetuated by the power of war. The strategy of its existence is based on creating an unstable and highly hostile environment around it to preserve its internal unity and cohesion and to mobilize all the powers supporting it abroad.

Despite the major compromises that the Egyptian President Anwar Sadat offered it, we see it today obstructing the

10 - Political Stances

ongoing negotiations for autonomous rule. It has defied UN resolutions more than once.

It currently continues the policy of encouraging settlements despite objection from the USA and the UN and despite its contradiction to the Camp David resolutions, which it had agreed to and signed under American auspices and on American land.

If one day the Arabs accepted to relinquish the West Bank and Gaza and said to Israel "take all that you have gained so far and give us peace..." then I am certain that "Israel" would refuse! Its dream is not to suffice with what it has taken; rather, it is to take more. Its dream state extends from the Nile to the Euphrates, and it is still at the beginning of the road.

The Arab situation has never been worse than it is now. We were never as divided and conflicting as we are now. Unfortunately, the state of division and fragmentation is escalating.

III

We are on a downslide towards demise

The Arabs lost all the wars they have fought against "Israel." In the war of 1973, we lost some territories, but we won as far as morale is concerned.

If the frontline states, joined together and supported by the Arabs, could not defeat "Israel," then the defeat of the Arab states is bound to be much worse when they are scattered and warring among each other. Could any Arab state fight "Israel" individually and triumph over it? No! Each Arab state sings the praises of liberation in its own way and promises refugees the right of return. But is this the reality? Are we logical and practical?

Today, no one is a fool. Even the simple unlettered person listens to radio broadcasts and follows the news. What I am saying is on every tongue in the Arab and Palestinian street. We are heading in a terrifying downslide towards catastrophe. Our current situation will ultimately lead us, if it continues, to destruction, degeneration, and total melt.

The only healing medicine that gives us some hope and restores our momentum is ending Arab disputes and uniting our ranks. As long as "Israel" does not want peace, it would not accept it unless it is imposed on it. Peace is only achieved by the power of weapons and unity. The optimum weapon in the face of "Israel" is unity. Therefore, it is working on destroying this lethal weapon with all it possesses of material, human, and intelligence capabilities, international relations, and media efforts for which it has dedicated unlimited amounts of money.

But, in my opinion, achieving unity to confront "Israel" is possible. This goal is not impossible if we purify our intentions and if each of us looks through the perspective of public interest and acknowledges that the destiny of each Arab state is ultimately entwined with the destiny of Palestine and the Palestinians. The scheme of "Israel" is not restricted to Palestine: rather, it extends from the Nile to the Euphrates. Israel has drawn a comprehensive long-term plan that might take decades before it reaches its projected targets. This plan includes all the Arab states without exception. "Israel" follows the knots policy: it creates one knot after another, and moves from destroying one country to destroying another, or at least crippling it and eliminating it from the equation, as it did with Egypt after Camp David. "Israel" is not in a hurry, because it does not want peace. It is quite comfortable with the state of no war no peace it has imposed on its surroundings through international resolutions.

I visited the town of Quneitra after the 1973 war, and I saw the destruction and ruin that befell it. The houses of Quneitra were not destroyed as a result of military action and air bombardment; rather, it was the result of an organized planned action that serves the schemes of "Israel." They destroyed the city after occupying it. They blew up its houses with explosives: leaving no stone on top of another. They pulled down all the houses and buildings and rebuilt them according to their methods of Judaization. What happened in Quneitra is a small-scale example of what is intended for all Arabs.

What happened in Palestine is an introduction to what is intended for Lebanon, Syria, Iraq, Jordan, and the whole Arab world. We cannot achieve anything unless we become aware that the danger threatens every Arab country. Today it is the turn of Palestine and the Palestinians: tomorrow, it will be the turn of all the Arab countries surrounding "Israel."

IV

The events in Syria are an external conspiracy

The target of the events in Syria is not the Syrian regime: it is Syria, which is known for its history as a fighter for freedom. The people of Syria are a people of freedom fighters, whether we like it or not. They are a strong people and a steadfast people. The saying that Syria is the "heart of Arabism" is true. The ultimate target of what happened in Lebanon is not Lebanon: rather, it is to make Lebanon a terrorist bridge into Syria with the intention of destroying it. They set Lebanon on fire so that the fire would extend to Syria because the ultimate purpose is to implement the Camp David scheme.

Some factions from the Syrian opposition have joined the pariahs, which is unfortunate. When the events in Syria broke out, a conspiratorial faction launched them. The faction was working for external interests that wish to destroy the homeland. Then another faction from the opposition joined the conspirators because it resented the regime. The opposition is made up of two factions: (1) one that hates the regime and wishes to change it and (2) another that is against Syria and has waged war to destroy and divide it.

I, as a Syrian citizen, believe that this conspiracy must be stopped and the citizen informed of it. Mistakes were made, and the President fixed them and announced them in newspapers and seminars.

Some reforms must be introduced in many fields, but this is one thing and the Syrian entity is another. The Syrian people must be aware. So long as the Syrian citizen loves Syria, he must be wary of the conspiracy planned against him as a Syrian and as a citizen, and not against the regime.

The people must be wary for their moral and national good before their material interest. They must realize the danger of those conspiring against Syria as a whole. What matters above all is that the homeland survives. After that, the opposition settles its score with the rulers and demands what it needs, because the basis of the political scheme is to seize opportune chances to strike Syria.

They created the tragedy in Lebanon, or we can say they set fire to Lebanon so that the flames would reach Syria and burn it. The ultimate goal of the conspiracy is not Lebanon: rather, it is Syria. This is clear. While the Lebanese tragedy was underway, Camp David was held and the Washington resolution was issued. The question now is: how will the Camp David resolutions be applied? How will Begin, Carter, and Sadat execute what they agreed upon? The only way is that the disease that started in Lebanon be transferred to Syria where we have started to see the precursors of a sectarian civil war. What matters is that this situation does not escalate so that Syria does not get divided. As I said before, the moment it is divided, it will be brought down to its knees; and the moment that happens, the Arabs will be brought down to

10 - Political Stances

their knees with her.

What do they want practically? Forfeiting the borders of 1967 is forfeiting half of Palestine. When you forfeit half of your right and you accept the existence of "Israel" on the other half, what do you achieve? The goal of "Israel"? We accepted death and death did not accept us!

They want self-rule?

What the PLO is temporarily proposing is a Palestinian state on any inch of liberated land and the acceptance of a state in the West Bank and Gaza.

Honestly, one cannot say everything on his mind! In my opinion, when I accept a solution for the Palestinian cause that is based on a state within the pre-1967 borders, I would be ridding the sons of Jerusalem, Naples, and Ramallah of the occupation nightmare. But what about the sons of Haifa, Jaffa, and Nazareth who live in refugee camps? Would we have solved their problem in this way? Is the German in East Berlin different from the German in West Berlin?

A complete solution is the establishment of a Palestinian state on the entire land of Palestine. As a Palestinian, I cannot return to the West Bank because it is part of Palestine and consider that I have received my rights. Nay! I want to return to my house, to my land, to my possessions... I want to regain my private rights. Would returning to the West Bank and Gaza solve all the problems of the Palestinian people? Of course not! Hence, this is not a just solution to the Palestinian cause.

Also, a group of landowners from 1948 are residents of the occupied territory that is called "Israel." It is my duty to preserve their rights. We cannot solve the problem of one group of people and turn our back on the other groups.

I can never believe that "Israel" has any intention of peacemaking. It does not accept something called peace: peace means the end of the state of "Israel." Why? Because "Israel" is a state founded on war, and it cannot survive except in a climate of war. The cornerstone of all its wars is its hostility to Arabs. For that reason, the day peace prevails between it and the Arabs and it becomes similar to any of the surrounding states, its end begins, because it loses the justification for international protection and support. At the time of peace, there is no need for anyone to protect it. But at the time of war, protecting it is more than necessary because it is a military base for imperialism.

Internal wrangles will set it as the big fish eat the small fish. It will wind up and disappear on its own.

It is in the interest of "Israel" to maintain its disputes and wars with the Arabs in order to preserve the war community that creates its unity. The Arab pursuit of peace puts "Israel" in an international dilemma because it does not want peace. It has defied the United Nations and its resolutions even in respect to the issue of settlements, which in essence is a breach of the Camp David Accords. It continues to establish settlements, and it will not stop.

V

Reconciliation in Lebanon ... quite unlikely

The only way I comprehend what happened in Lebanon and what is happening in Syria is in the context of the Camp David orchestra. The bloody events in the two beloved countries pave the way for the execution of the Camp David resolutions.

The war in Lebanon is into its fifth year, and there are no signs of any real solution. Destruction takes an hour but rebuilding requires years of reconstruction. What happened is beyond belief.

10 - Political Stances

Who could have expected this amount of moral deterioration and programmed barbarism?

I wish for reconciliation and understanding among the Lebanese, because there will be no winner in this war. The Lebanese people and Lebanese officials must be realistic and start to ascend the staircase one ring at a time. Coming out of the bottom of the abyss and reaching the top or returning to it is not easy. I wish and pray that Lebanon returns to what it was. This is what I truly want and what every person sincere to the beloved Lebanon wants. However, I must be realistic and understand the reality of the situation, just as it is. Honest realism says it needs time, and I believe in the effectiveness of time. Time is the real problem solver. I always say that time is the best element to face some crises. What you cannot do, time can do.

I do not wish to discourage people: the solution in Lebanon needs time. I support reconciliation, but I know that it will not transpire by a magic wand.

This is the age of a race between conspiracy and steadfastness, and this struggle aggravates division and partition in the Arab world. One must admit that, truly, the Arabs have never seen worse days than these. We have never been so divided. Let us be realistic: all the wars we have fought against Israel to date, we have lost. Even the October 1973 war we only won morally, but territorially we lost. The Israelis occupied Quneitra and reached the gates of Damascus. If the frontline states jointly failed in defeating Israel, how can these states overcome it while they are divided, quarreling, and fighting amongst themselves??

All the signs indicate that the Arab-Arab wars will escalate in the coming years, and we are heading downhill. Why do I show such pessimism about the Arab future? Let us take a look at the status quo of the Arab situation: a so-called unified Arab strategy does not exist, no Arab state coordinates with another Arab state, and each state lives for itself as if it is a remote island in a distant

In the Name of God

ocean. Can any Arab state go to war with "Israel" and win single-handedly without its neighbors? Impossible!

In contrast, every Arab state sings the praises of liberation, promotes it, and promises the people an imminent return to Palestine and the recapturing of Jerusalem. What do we call such a claim? A reality? Are we logical or realistic? It is an illusion that expands like a mirage and annihilates the Arab peoples in a desert of ignorance.

They want us to believe otherwise! Or to convince our people and ourselves that it is otherwise? Is this possible? Today, no one is a fool. The street peddler listens to the radio while pushing his cart. No one is simple anymore: everyone is "savvy." The things I am saying even the youngest of the young knows them and is capable of analyzing. Our present situation will lead us to destruction, decline, the waning of the Palestinian cause, and the Camp David Accords.

In my opinion, no good medicine gives us hope, restores our momentum, or fulfils our expectations except settling our differences, unifying our ranks, and facing the world together rather than as scattered parts. This is the only solution to our problems.

So long as "Israel" does not accept peace except if it were imposed on it by force, and since peace is not imposed save by weapons, then the best weapon for the Arab world is unity.

Is there any hope that such unity would be achieved? When the intentions are sincere and when each one regards the other from the viewpoint of the general interest, unity becomes possible. When every Arab state realizes that its ultimate destiny would be like that of Palestine, because the Israeli scheme is a replica of the Biblical project "from the Nile to the Euphrates," unity becomes possible.

10 - Political Stances

I mentioned previously that I saw all the houses blown up in Quneitra. They were not destroyed by war and aerial bombardment: rather, "Israel" destroyed them by bulldozers. The destruction of Quneitra is a miniature of what is intended for the Arabs and the Arab nation as a whole.

What happened in Palestine is an introduction to what is intended for Lebanon, Syria, Iraq, and the whole Arab world. When every Arab state realizes that, in defending Palestine and the Palestinian cause, it is ultimately defending itself, only then its attitude would change and it would take a different stance towards the cause. When it understands that Palestine has fallen at the forefront and its turn would come, it would then change.

No one in the West Bank can sign an individual agreement with "Israel." Even if someone wants to do that, they cannot do it because they would not dare!

Resistance is active in the West Bank, and it will remain active, because the Palestinian people no longer fear "Israel." The mounting spirit of resistance is intensifying daily and it will not die regardless how offensive the enemy becomes.

Is the future of the West Bank with Jordan? In light of the circumstances, everything is subject to tidal changes. Ultimately, cooperation is needed between the two banks, and no doubt remains regarding the benefit of that.

VI

Frankness with the Vatican: enough exile!

I did not know the conditions that "Israel" imposed on the Vatican for my release. I did not see any written text or pledge. I complied with the Vatican's decision as a bishop subject to the authority of the Church. They asked me not to go to Arab countries at this stage, not to talk about any issue related to Palestine and the Palestinians, and not to attack "Israel" in the press or on public platforms. But now I feel that I am tied up, paralyzed, and losing energy.

In this context, I once said to a Vatican official:

> Have you ever driven a sports car? A fast car that can reach a speed of 200 km/h on the highway, and if you drive it for a long distance at 5 km/h, its engine might burn out. It must run at its full capacity in order to achieve its purpose. I resemble a sports car. I want to take off at the speed of 400 km/h on the road to return to Jerusalem and you are restraining me and forcing me to walk like a turtle at less than 5 km/h. This attitude burns me psychologically and morally... I can no longer continue on this road. This bitter reality that was imposed on me in exile must change. I do not see any political aspect to the Palestinian cause. To me, it is a humanitarian cause: a cause of truth and justice. If there is one person in the world obliged to defend it, it is me...

I started explaining to the official the many reasons that oblige me to defend Palestine. First and foremost, I am the Archbishop of Jerusalem and I believe in its Arab identity and that it is the cradle of Christianity. I reject its Judaization, and I am prepared to sacrifice my life for its sake.

In that long interview, I added:

> At the behest of the Holy See, I do not engage in any political activity or present political solutions for this cause. I do not have any plans like the return to the 1967 borders or the re-division of the Arab territory. Political issues are not my concern and I do not seek any political role. I am clarifying my right to return to Jerusalem. I do not wish to live in exile like a feather in the wind. I do not know today

what my tomorrow will be like. I feel that my hands and feet are shackled. I do not know what to do.

I need to live like all other people: to be a human being having all the components of a human being. The first of these are dignity and freedom. I am without freedom. I am here in prison. What is prison? Prison is wires, walls, and locked doors that come between the person and his freedom! As long as I am in exile, walls and locked doors prevent me not just from going to Palestine, but to any Arab country including my birthplace in Syria. In exile, I am a prisoner. I am not free.

The epitome of dignity is the homeland, and I live in Italy away from my homeland. My homeland is the Arab countries and Palestine… hence; I am not a human being because I have neither dignity nor freedom.

In the absence of any convincing answer from the Vatican official, I continued:

If you insist that these restrictions remain imposed on my movement and my statements because you have an agreement with "Israel" and you are forced to implement it because you vowed in writing to do so, and you are currently avoiding any crisis with "Israel"; as long as the situation is as I have mentioned and there is not any intention to change it, I will return to "Israel" without your approval…You are forced to accept the terms of "Israel", so I will return now without your approval!!

Why don't I just board a plane tomorrow from Italy to Amman after I call His Majesty the King… and I hold a press conference there wherein I connect the dots, then I head to the bridge and turn myself in at the borders to the Israeli authorities? I would make them face a new "fait accompli" whose result would liberate me in all cases:

Either they say to me: "Go back to where you came. Your presence is not welcomed here." I would thus be liberating myself by myself, because I returned to them and they released me. The first time around, they released me by virtue of an agreement with the Vatican. When I return to the borders and I get arrested then released, I absolve the Vatican of responsibility.

As a bishop and a committed person, I do not wish to start a dispute with the Church. Let me turn myself in, and if they refuse to let me enter and say to me "Go back home," I would have freed myself by myself.

The first time, you freed me upon conditions. I can no longer abide by those conditions. I can no longer endure the prison of exile. You are asking me to bear what is beyond my capacity. If my maximum load is 20 kg, how do you expect me to carry 100 kg for a long distance? I have reached a point where I can no longer carry this heavy burden. Then again, I do not wish to tarnish the Vatican's reputation and the credibility of the Catholic Church. I hold the Church sacred. Were it not for it, I would not have been an archbishop or a Christian. I owe everything to the Church, and I cannot offend my Church in any way whatsoever. When I arrive in "Israel" suddenly, I free my Church, I free myself, and I get rid of my heavy burden.

There is the second probability; that they put me in prison, which is better because I believe that being in prison serves my cause better than being outside prison away from my land and bound by these conditions.

With a sad choking voice, Archbishop Capucci went on to say:

This is my plan for 1980. This situation cannot go on the way it is now. It must change. Either I regain the freedom to go wherever I wish and to say whatever I wish or I confront

10 - Political Stances

the Israelis right in their midst in the manner I described to the Vatican official. No more and no less. Either I become free or I return to prison and my soul rests... I would then feel total satisfaction, return to struggle anew, and start planning again when I would get out... I might even start a hunger strike from day one.

VII

Would the Vatican appoint an Archbishop to replace me in Jerusalem?

Until now, all the Arab states oppose such a step and form a strong barrier against appointing a substitute for me in Jerusalem. They consider that taking me away from my congregation and my home is the best gift that could be presented to "Israel." Keeping me away from my congregation is a blow to the spirit of resistance inside the occupied territories. Nothing would make "Israel" rejoice more. Why would the Vatican give a gift to Israel? When I die, a successor would be appointed. This is natural. But to appoint an Archbishop for Jerusalem now would be an admission of the legitimacy of the occupation, because, naturally, "Israel" would approve the new Archbishop. Its approval is in itself an implied acknowledgement on part of the Vatican of the new situation of Jerusalem. The annexation of Jerusalem is absolutely unacceptable!

International conventions dictate that diplomatic representation be at the same level of relations. When relations are good, a state is represented by an ambassador; and when they are bad, representation is limited to a chargé d'affaires or less... a secretary. What is the extent of our excellent relations with Israel? What is the reason we have to appreciate it to the extent of appointing an archbishop for it? It deserves no more than a priest or a deacon!

In the Name of God

VIII

Earth is not a Stage but a Site of Struggle

In my exile are two oases. The first is a spiritual heavenly oasis, and the other, I sincerely say it, is you, sons of the Arab land, my hope in return to my homeland, to my eparchy, my Church, my Palestinian family...

In my estrangement, I live with my memories, and memories generate nostalgia. Nostalgia is filled with agony: it is death because, practically, death is separation ... from children, friends, home, etc. The drink forced upon me in exile, as long as it is separation, is moral death. Physically, a person dies once, but morally he dies many times daily. Therefore, exile is a lasting torment. But, my children, the kernel of wheat that is left exposed to the sun and light dies, but the one that is buried in the soil survives. We must die in order to live. Either we live with dignity in our homeland, which is the epitome of honor, or we die with dignity in defense of our right to our homeland. I am Arab... the Arab lands are my homeland. Since I went to prison for the sake of the cause, I feel deeply that I am an Arab citizen and a servant of the Arab nation.

We, wherever we are and to whichever ideology we belong, we make up one family... Our God is one, our blood is one, our language is one, our hopes are one, our destiny is one...

Our principles, values, and ideals, which we learned from our two religions, Islam and Christianity, are also one. Hence, beautiful is the entwinement of the cross and the crescent to fuse us into one crucible: the crucible of the one God, the one nation, and the one cause. No matter how much some people wish to bury it in the ground, it remains our sacred cause for which we are fighting until the last breath regardless of how long that takes. The Arab cause is the cause of Palestine that has cost wealth, casualties, and martyrs. So how could dignity and torment be sold for a handful of dust that measures 325 km²?

When the partition was announced in 1948, it gave Israel 55% and the Arabs 45%. When the Arabs rejected the partition, "Israel" occupied Upper Galilee: thus occupying 77% of the lands of Palestine. As to the remaining 23%, which is 6000 km², it occupied them in 1967. Now we sign the treaty to regain Gaza 325 km² and Jericho 325 km², with Jewish settlements inside them over an area of 325 km². So, what are we regaining? A mere 325 km²!

IX

The Danger in separating Jerusalem from its Holy Sites

I am Syrian by birth and Palestinian in terms of identity. My heart is in Lebanon, and I belong to the Arab world. I was keen not to settle in an Arab country despite being invited to stay in several countries, because I committed myself to exile until the liberation of Jerusalem in order to be included within the right of return to the whole Palestinian people.

But, unfortunately, the treaties that were signed have forfeited the national rights of the Palestinian Arab people, for which their struggle continues.

The partition decision plundered half of Palestine, but the Jews plundered three quarters of it in 1948. Then they expanded and divided the people and the land into three divisions. I was hoping that the Arab reaction would be much stronger to the Judaization of Jerusalem, and that the reaction of the Christian and Muslim worlds would be strong and loud to the offensive posters against the Messenger and our Mother Mary. We need a fighting spirit to spread throughout the nation and more action to create awareness in the foreign populations that are waiting to move along with us.

In the Name of God

Currently, the most dangerous proposal regarding Jerusalem is the separation of the future of the holy sites from that of the city and its people: considering that what is required of the Arabs is to hold on to the Arab identity of Jerusalem and to work towards preserving it through practical means.

11 - The Indefatigable Archbishop

"Age cannot be measured by years, as long as we can give, we are young." — Archbishop Capucci

Though restricted to an ecclesiastical life outside Palestine, Capucci remained a vigilant force in Palestinian resistance efforts. He disobeyed Israeli orders to stay out of the Middle East and continued to garner international support for the Palestinian cause wherever he turned up. His dynamic and engaged faith took him around the world and into a myriad of social, religious, and political engagements. Both Israel and the Vatican tried to restrict his freedom of movement, but the indefatigable Archbishop circumvented the restrictions by placing himself at the centre of international humanitarian efforts.

I

No Limit to Struggle

Capucci fearlessly maintained his activism throughout his life. His dedication to assisting others in achieving sovereign, dignified lives in the face of persecution and occupation made him a revolutionary hero and an icon of the Palestinian liberation struggle. Once he broke through the curfew imposed by Israel by attending a meeting of the National Council of the Palestine Liberation Organization in Damascus in 1979, Capucci exploded on the world stage. He became politically active across the Middle East and elsewhere: offering advice and assistance on various levels.

Capucci travelled to the hotspots of the world offering his services. On November 4, 1979, Iranian students seized the

US embassy in Tehran and detained more than 50 Americans ranging from the Chargé d'Affaires to the most junior members of the staff. They held the American diplomats hostage for 444 days. During the crisis, Capucci visited the American hostages several times and negotiated an agreement for their release that only collapsed at the last minute because of a leak in the French press. He did, however, succeed in securing the release of the bodies of American soldiers who had died in the failed rescue attempt. He later received a letter from President Ronald Reagan thanking him for his efforts.

Capucci's good relations with Arab leaders gave him a clear edge over other mediators. In 1985, with the help of the Syrians, he secured the release of a French hostage held in Tripoli, Lebanon. A year later, he turned up in Paris to offer his help after a series of bombing attacks by an ultra leftist group called the Committee for Solidarity with Arab and Middle Eastern Political Prisoners. The suspected Lebanese guerrilla leader, Georges Ibrahim Abdallah, was among the prisoners sought by the group. Capucci was allowed to visit Abdallah in prison as part of an effort to press the terrorist group to stop its violent campaign for Abdallah's release. He was the only person allowed by the French authorities to visit Abdallah.

In 1990, he travelled to Baghdad to help secure freedom for 68 Italians. The Italians were among hundreds of Westerners Saddam Hussein's government had prevented from leaving Iraq following its invasion of Kuwait that year. The Archbishop was among the few politicians, prominent public figures, and peacemakers allowed entry into the country by Saddam. Capucci's close contacts with senior officials in beleaguered Iraq paid off in 2000 when he led an anti-sanctions delegation to Iraq. Flanked by a group of Italy-based clerics and intellectuals, he flew to Baghdad from Syria on a humanitarian flight authorized by the U.N. sanctions committee. While in Iraq, he visited a shelter that was struck by a U.S. missile during the 1991 Gulf War. The U.S. military believed the building was an intelligence-gathering

11 - The Indefatigable Archbishop

facility. More than 400 civilians were killed, and Capucci called the bombing victims "Iraqi martyrs." Later, he told reporters that two nations were suffering in the Middle East, "the Iraqis because of sanctions and the Palestinian people, who are fighting for their dignity."

Capucci deplored the sanctions against the Iraqi people. It was galling for him to see Iraq devastated and reduced to the brink. During the second war on the country in 2003, he came out strongly against the invasion and derided President George Bush for putting war ahead of humanity. He later wrote:

> To send bombers to destroy an entire country and to sow death amidst a people already in agony, in the name of God, is the greatest offense committed against Jesus Christ, and the most terrible curse laid against the Peace and Love of Christ. This is because Peace, for us Christians, is a Person: the Person of Christ. Jesus Christ is the Victory of Peace and Love. The unbearable sight of the suffering Iraqi people is Christ on the Cross. It goes beyond that: the youth raised under sanctions in a country destroyed by bombs have minds suffocated with hatred, have nothing more to lose, and are ready for every kind of vengeance. In an Arab country where mutual harmony between Christians and Muslims was a model, bombs are placed in churches and tens of thousands of Christians are fleeing abroad. Even the children of Iraqi Christians are being kidnapped. Before the invasion of Iraq, the peaceful coexistence between Christians and Muslims was a model. Now it has been replaced by a nightmare. The war against Iraq has destroyed years of dialogue with Islam, has given new pretexts to Islamic extremists, and has fed discord between the Arab world and the West.

Capucci's prognostication that the destruction of Iraq would open up too large a can of worms came true in Syria. Fearing the worse for his homeland, he dismissed Western claims against Bashar al-Assad as baseless and counterproductive and made every effort to expose them to informed opinions. The impact of the war on the country's unity and delicate social fabric and its repercussions on Muslim-Christian relations and the fate of Christianity in the region came back to haunt him. His response was typical Capuccian. He shuffled between Rome and Damascus to lend his moral support, participated in public demonstrations against the war, appeared on television and other media outlets to explain the fallouts, and met heads of states to ward off war or to lobby for a resolution to the conflict. In 2014, he participated in the first international conference on the war on Syria in the city of Montreux. The UN-sponsored international peace conference on the future of Syria brought the Syrian government and the Syrian opposition together with the aim of ending the Syrian Civil War. Capucci's attendance took everyone by surprise (especially the official delegation of the Syrian government). Some years later, the Presidential Political and Media Advisor, Bouthaina Shaaban, recalled Capucci's exact words to her: "How could I not be here with you and with our beloved Syria?"

The Syrian regime reciprocated with the same care and attention. On February 7, 2017, it honored Capucci with a memorial mass at the Patriarchate of "Dormition of Our Lady" Melkite Catholic in Damascus. State Minister of Presidential Affairs, Mansour Azzam, attended the mass upon the directive of President Bashar al-Assad.

Capucci's record of activism is too long to display completely. He visited almost every Arab country and many non-Arab countries unmoved by official rhetoric. In 1999, he led a team of Italian environmental experts to Libya and met Gaddafi. In 2001, he travelled to Jordan and was received by King Abdullah. In 2005, he issued a statement from Beirut condemning the Mehlis Report into the Rafiq Hariri assassination as a "programmed defamation campaign" against Syria. In 2016, he turned up in Algeria flaunting the Algerian flag alongside that of Palestine. Capucci could not be stopped. In true activist fashion, he moved around constantly matching his words with deeds and reminding those

11 - The Indefatigable Archbishop

in his presence of the scope of the mission he was shouldering.

Along the way, Capucci faced bans, criticisms, and other distractions. Naturally, the most vociferous opposition came from Israel, which continually expressed to the Vatican its displeasure over what it considered continuing anti-Israeli activities by the archbishop. The Israeli complaint reached its peak in a long series of approaches to the Vatican in 1983 following Capucci's appearance on Italian national television during which he stated at length his support for the PLO. Israel viewed the television interview as a breach of the 1977 Vatican undertaking that Capucci would not be allowed to make political statements against Israel and also as a defiance of that undertaking in Rome itself. The Vatican's reply was short and sharp: "attempts to restrain the 60-year-old prelate had proved fruitless."

Capucci was occasionally barred from entering certain countries due to his anti-Israel stances. For example, Canada refused to grant him an entry visa to participate in a series of symposiums, sponsored in part by Le Mouvement Quebecois pour Combattre le Racisme, on colonized peoples and national rights. When quizzed about the ban, a spokesman for the External Affairs Department in Ottawa replied:

> Canada has consistently supported the free expression of views pertaining to major political issues, such as the Israeli-Arab dispute. We have not, however, permitted the entry into Canada of individuals, whatever their political viewpoints, who have been associated with acts which are directly related to the perpetration of violence."

Paradoxically, the Canadian government had no qualms about admitting Israeli individuals such as Ariel Sharon, whose perpetration of violence was thorough and well-documented. Also, just as certainly as there was wide support for the prelate in the press, so, too, there was strong opposition from certain corners. The pro-Israel press was particularly vocal and slanderous.

It tried to belittle Capucci by resorting to character assassination or downplaying the scope of his exploits. One example is an extract from a 1996 CIA Publication entitled "A First Tour Like No Other" by the CIA operative William J. Daugherty:

> Easter Sunday [1980] passed quietly, but long after midnight that night I was awakened and taken upstairs to meet Archbishop Hilarion Capucci, the former Archbishop of Jerusalem, who had once been imprisoned by the Israelis for gunrunning. This occurred in the ambassadorial office, which was crammed full with our captors, some of whom I had not seen in months. It was a non-event for me, however, and to this day I do not understand the purpose. My picture was not taken, and I was not given anything. The Archbishop, the first non-Iranian I had seen in months, said nothing memorable. After a few minutes, I was taken back to my room, befuddled as to why my sleep had been interrupted for something that was apparently meaningless.

Regrettably, Daugherty missed the whole point of this exercise, which was that Capucci had wanted to see that he was still alive and in good health. He was not there to entertain him.

Mostly, the press tried to undermine Capucci by focusing on the nature of his "gunrunning" escapade rather than the causes. Any reference to the prelate was often made in the context of "terrorism" rather than "resistance." Accordingly, aspects such as "occupation," "Judaization," "self-defense," and the "right of resistance" under international law were often blotted out in order to caricature Capucci as a renegade cleric with no social weight or coherent ideological role. The Archbishop was aware of this prejudice against him in the Western press, but paid little attention to it. He preferred not to be drawn into protracted polemics that could distract him from his primary tasks.

11 - The Indefatigable Archbishop

II

Priority Palestine

Ultimately, it was Palestine for which Capucci had a special passion. Jerusalem, specifically, was always on his mind. On one of his humanitarian visits to Iraq as head of a delegation of 24 men of religion and intellectuals, he told the waiting press:

> I pray to God to unite the Arabs to achieve our goals of dignity and pride and lift the sanctions on the Iraqi people, liberate the Golan Heights, and liberate the whole territories in southern Lebanon and Jerusalem that do not belong to the Palestinians only, but to the Arab world and the Christian world as well. We all have to struggle to liberate Jerusalem.

Capucci did not let an opportunity pass to express his dissatisfaction with Israeli occupation. He travelled extensively, issued political statements, held high-level meetings, and attended almost every forum and conference on the Palestine issue. In 2001, he defied an international ban on Iran and attended the Bayt al-Maqdis Conference in Tehran in support of the popular Palestinian uprising (intifada). At that conference, he lobbied for economic assistance "in order to dissuade the Palestinians from helping the enemy's economy," broached the issue of Jerusalem, and called for a tougher stand against Israel: "What is taken by force must be retrieved through forceful means. The real basis of power is not arms but unity and cooperation."

Wherever he went, Capucci underlined the necessity of battling Israel until all the Israeli-occupied Arab territories are liberated and an independent Palestinian state is established with Jerusalem as its capital. He carried this message throughout his work and impressed it on his audience. Asked about his goal in 2010, during a television interview with al-Jareerah, the prelate replied: ""to establish a free, sovereign, independent state, with Jerusalem as its capital."

Indeed, Capucci was unrelenting when it came to Palestine and Jerusalem. He took his theology liberation very seriously: so much so that he was prepared to place himself in risky and life-threatening positions for Palestine's sake. Israeli remonstrations to the Vatican about his political involvement did not strike a chord with him. He continued to attend meetings of the PLO's National Council, meet with PLO leader Yasser Arafat, and participate in public shows of solidarity with Palestine and Jerusalem. His defiance of Israel reached a new level in December 2000 when he arrived on the Lebanese-Israeli border alongside Sheikh Nabil Qaouq, a Hezbollah leader. In front of reporters, Capucci picked up a stone and hurled it in the direction of occupied Palestine, noting: "I wish I had been with the heroes of the intifada to take part in their battle for the independence of Palestine."

Despite the burden of time, Capucci's visibility on the Palestine rostrum remained as strong as ever. In 2009, he was invited to the United States by the American-Arab Anti-Discrimination Committee (ADC) to deliver the keynote address at its Annual Convention. As usual, Capucci used the occasion to speak about the Palestine problem and to reflect on the plight of Jerusalem under the occupation: "Israel is erasing its Christian character, its sacred nature. Our Jerusalem has become obliterated and effaced. It is fading away." He closed his address with a "nationalist" prayer to God:

> Oh, it is so beautiful when you reunite and embrace a loved one after a long absence, a long torment," talking about his beloved Jerusalem – the City of Peace. "While the minarets recite Allahu Akbar in rhythm and synchrony with the church bell ringing joyfully calling us to return to our beautiful Jerusalem, to our Masjid el Aqsa and our Church of the Holy Sepulchre," he prayed to God. While his prayer to return to Jerusalem was not fulfilled, Allahu Akbar ringed loud last month when Churches in Palestine made the Muslim call for prayer in protest at Israel's ban of the Muslim call to prayer in Jerusalem. He concluded with

11 - The Indefatigable Archbishop

a verse from the Quran, "Accept this prayer from me for it is you – you who are all hearing and all knowing and you have power over all things."

That same year, Capucci participated in the Free Gaza Movement's aid flotilla. Subsequently, he was held by Israel at the Beersheba prison and later deported to Jordan. Asked to explain his experience and why he was attacked, Capucci replied: "[Although] the goal of the Freedom Flotilla, the second of its kind, was aimed at breaking the blockade imposed on the Gaza Strip ... [we also wanted] to meet the tortured, persecuted, and wronged kinfolk in the strip to assure them that we are with them morally and spiritually." He added: "We are with them all the time. We share with them their suffering and pain and take pride in their struggle, steadfastness, and heroism." The saga became an occasion for the aging archbishop to underline his message of theology: "Religion is not just a title, an institution, or a host of ideologies but a way of life. "What counts is what we do for God, for our relatives, for our nation, and for our homeland." Undaunted by danger, Capucci continued to partake in the second flotilla of 2010, which, however, did not sail. He later stated: "Age cannot be measured by years, as long as we can give, we are young."

In March 2012, the Global March to Jerusalem, an annual event held the first week of June to mark the anniversary of the start of the Israeli occupation of East Jerusalem following the Six Day War in 1967, issued a declaration:

1. We assert the importance of Jerusalem politically, culturally, and religiously to the Palestinian people and humanity as a whole. We call for the protection of the Holy Places and all archeological sites and consider all the efforts done to change its Arabic and cultural identity as a crime against humanity. We call on all international institutions to do their duties towards the city.

In the Name of God

2. The defense of Jerusalem and its liberation are a duty of all free people around the world, and we call on all institutions, organizations, and individuals to participate in this duty.

3. We condemn the Zionist campaign of ethnic cleansing in Jerusalem and the rest of Palestine including all ongoing policies intended to change the demographic and geographic situation in the city and aimed at its Judaization. We also condemn the continuation of the Zionist occupation forces in building the apartheid wall that aims to expropriate more Palestinian lands and convert the occupied areas into shrinking cantons isolated from each other.

4. We support the right of the Palestinian People to self-determination, to liberate their lands and to live on them in freedom and dignity like all other people on earth.

5. We support the non-negotiable and inalienable rights of the Palestinian People, including their families, to return to their homes and lands from which they were uprooted.

6. We reject all racist laws that distinguish between people based on ethnicity or religion and call for their cancellation and criminalization.

7. The Global March to Jerusalem does not represent any one faction or political party, but we call for participation of all social forces, political factions, and ideologies.

8. The Global March to Jerusalem is a global peaceful movement, which does not use violence to achieve its goals.

11 - The Indefatigable Archbishop

Sure enough, Capucci was among the signatories to the Declaration. He partook in its planned marches and advocated for the Movement alongside other notable religious dignitaries (both Christians and Muslims).

III

Interfaith Dialogue

Hans Küng, a Professor of Ecumenical Theology and President of the Global Ethic Foundation, said: "There will be no peace among the nations without peace among the religions. There will be no peace among the religions without dialogue among the religions." Capucci strongly believed in the wisdom of this phrase. He attended many conferences and symposiums on religion and peace-building and made several important contributions to interfaith dialogue at both the ecclesiastical and academic levels. His address to the Symposium on the Concept of Monotheism in Islam and Christianity, held in Rome in November 1981, is a clear case in point:

> How glorious is this atmosphere which covers us, full with faith and friendship. It is a heavenly atmosphere because of the presence of God with us and amongst us. Thus, it is His love joining us together. God is love and, therefore, we are all blissful, we, the members of one great family, being all brothers to all of us as we are the sons of One God.
>
> They will find that the nearest of all believers to them are those who said: "We are Christians and amongst us are priests and monks. And they are never behaving conceited."
>
> Every time the two heavenly religions Christianity and Islam are meeting, it is for the good and the joy of mankind, because their meeting creates warmth and light and life. Thus, while meeting today, we are all rejoicing because it is

a meeting between truth-loving brothers whose aim it is to spread - for the sake of goodness, righteousness, and peace - the principles, ethics, and good morals all over a world conquered by materialism and ruled by the forces of evil and atheism which are planting hatred where God wanted to grow love and beauty.

These meetings are but a result of cooperation between these two religions since the beginning of Islam. In the beginning of the Islamic mission, the early Muslims were exposed to the hatred and tyranny of the Quraish polytheists. So they took refuge in Ethiopia where the Christians opened their hearts to these Muhadjirin who were also worshipping just One God, were believing in the doomsday and in the resurrection, in the torments and just rewards of hell, in angels and in the holiness of Mary, the first among all women. The Quran even dedicated a whole Surah to her. They regarded Jesus as a Prophet emanated from the spirit of God, and he is mentioned many times in several Surahs, although they were not recognizing him as God Himself.

The Muhadjirin (those early Muslim refugees) stayed in Ethiopia until God granted them glorious victory. Then they returned to their homeland, but not without leaving behind their hearts because of the hospitality and care they were met with there. In the course of time, the connections to their former hosts grew and became stronger, and they shared happiness and sorrow with them. This finds its expression in the 30th Surah of the Quran which reads as:

> "Defeated are the Romans in the neighbor-country. But after their defeat they will soon be victorious in some years. God's is the determination prior (to their defeat) and afterwards (after their victory). On this day the believers will be glad about the help of God. He helps whom He is willing, and He is the All-powerful, the All-merciful." (Surah 30/1-4)

The days passed by and when the Calif Omar conquered

11 - The Indefatigable Archbishop

Jerusalem, he rewarded them (i.e. the Christians) for their good deeds (to the Muhadjirin) by sparing their churches and monasteries. He also refused to pray in the Resurrection-Dome: thus, emphasizing his respect for the Christian customs and saving their friendship and brotherhood as well.

In the course of time, this mutual respect, coexistence, and reciprocal assistance reached its summit and found its expression where Christians and Muslims worked together in building up the great empire. They were - for instance - the poets of the Ghassanids and Manadhira. During the Abbasid era, they were translators, authors, physicians and philosophers: thus, bringing forth a superior civilization to which the world bowed in respect and by which the West profited for many centuries.

From time to time, this blooming picture was shaken by wars and conquests arisen here and there between the two brothers. It resulted in separation from each other and turning their joys to grief. But, thank heavens, these bypassing storms left no traces behind because of the ever-existing goodwill and good intentions which constantly worked towards good, love, and peace in order to lead mankind back to the blooming beginnings experienced under the banners of Christianity and Islam when the two understood each other well and worked together.

My brothers, I beseech you in the name of God to further follow up this righteous path - thus realizing your hopes by completing a great building a new society more advanced and more beautiful, which is based on religion, good morals, principles, culture, and welfare.

Capucci's involvement in interfaith dialogue was central rather than ephemeral. For him, it was not just words or talk, but action and interaction. In keeping with his theology liberation, he cared and advocated for it not for its own sake but as a spiritual obligation to end the religious divisions and the senseless human suffering caused by them. Just as vital for Capucci was the political advantages that interfaith dialogue had the potential to deliver: (1) as a platform to address the pressing need for Muslim-Christian unity in Palestine and (2) as a panacea to the Judaization of Jerusalem and the restoration of the city as a centre for all monotheistic religions. Interfaith dialogue leads to unity, and unity, as far as Capucci was concerned, was the key to success. "Unity is my religion," he once declared. On another occasion, he said:

> You are meeting now under the banner of One God, and let thus unity be your aim! Please, do work for such a unity between all followers of the two heavenly religions wherever you find them, and especially in the Middle East, this very explosive region which can be set on fire every moment. Do so for the priority of justice to injustice, righteousness to tyranny and suppression, love to hatred, and peace to war. Striving for unifying your rows shall be your duty because there is no strength without unity.

Capucci often quoted from the Quran to underpin the need for unity and cooperation. One of his favorite verses was: "Oh mankind! We created you from a male and a female and made you into nations and tribes," which implied respect for each other's beliefs. Capucci went so far as to call for the merger of the Quran and the Bible into one, and he often prayed alongside Muslim clerics in a show of religious unity and tolerance. His words were:

> The embrace of Cross and Crescent is nice, but nicer by far and more efficient is the merger of Quran and Bible in the spirit of One God: better serving the higher ideals of mankind and further safeguarding our interests and common problems (amongst them the Palestinian problem headed by the problem of Jerusalem).

11 - The Indefatigable Archbishop

IV

Palestine and Jerusalem

Whether praying, preaching, touring, public speaking, or advocating, the specter of an occupied Jerusalem was a constant on Capucci's mind. Almost everything he did and worked for came back to Palestine and Jerusalem: the city he loved and served with all his heart. His closing statement to the Symposium on the Concept of Monotheism was:

> Jerusalem is the rose of all cities, the target of the whole world, whereupon our hearts are dwelling many a time each day. Our Jerusalem, this wonderful sacred city has lost its holy character, is deformed. Jerusalem, once the city of prayer and worship ... a pilgrims' city, has come to be a mere tourist-attraction. With the stretch of occupation, our sacred locations gradually lose their holy character because the believers are taking leave and staying away. If nothing happens to stop this, Jerusalem soon will end: all stones, museums, and mummies. Sow, sow ere it will be too late for the liberation of Palestine and for the rescue of our Jerusalem from occupation as well! Our Jerusalem is entrusted to us, it is our responsibility before God, before our own conscience and before mankind. Our peoples are hopefully looking your way: please prove worthy their hopes. Do not disappoint them!

Not only Jerusalem, but all of Palestine was important to Capucci. It meant the world to him:

> The Palestinian people are my flock. You see this ring on my finger; it is my ring of engagement to Palestine. All the children of Palestine are my children and extended family.

In a recall of his theology liberation, Capucci described himself as a "father" adding:

> ... and the sign of fatherhood is compassion. A father can't watch his children suffer and sit idle with his hands tied. He must stand up to defend his children. The people of Palestine are my children. They have been oppressed, they have suffered a great injustice, their rights have been denied, their dignity trampled upon, their daily companion is nothing but suffering.

Drawing on his teacher, Jesus, Capucci saw life as a divine gift sustained not only by food and drink, but also by honor and dignity epitomized in full nationhood:

> Palestinians will live in dignity, free and independent in our homeland, with Jerusalem as its capital. We will not capitulate, we will not give in, we will not submit, no matter how long it takes.

12 - Death

> *"In his farewell, we can only say that he was a strong man, determined and immutable, just like the Citadel of Aleppo that he so loved."* – Raymonda Al Tawil, Palestinian poet and journalist.

Shortly after Christmas 2016, the 94-year-old Capucci was taken to a Rome hospital suffering from a lung infection. He passed away on January 1, 2017. The Palestinian ambassador to Italy Mai Al-Akaila arranged the transfer of his body to Lebanon to a waiting crowd of Lebanese government officials and admirers. Political and religious officials flocked to his funeral at the Greek Melkite Catholic patriarchate in the north Mount Lebanon town of Rabweh, where he was bestowed a posthumous Cedar Medal of Honor. The Syrian archbishop was laid to rest at the St. Savior Basilian Order of Aleppo in Sarba, Kesrouan, next to his mother's grave in accordance with his wishes.

The mass was conducted under the patronage of Greek Melkite Patriarch Gregorius III Lahham helped by a group of bishops and priests from various Christian denominations. Patriarch Laham said:

> "We are gathered herein in this humble funerary prayer to bid our beloved deceased - God be merciful of him- goodbye, the late archbishop Hilarion Capucci, patriarchal vicar and bishop to Jerusalem. He is the late martyr of victorious Aleppo, the late monastic of blessed Aleppo, of the patriarchal church of the Melkite Catholics, of Jerusalem – capital of our faith, of Palestine, of the resistance, of freedom, and of dignity.

He was my brother. We have both been leading a fierce battle in Palestine since 1974. During his stay in prison, he grew full of magnanimity and pride, and I myself came under the spell of his faith and unwavering values. He even entrusted me with the task of completing the decoration of the cathedral in Jerusalem and with the rehabilitation and development of the patriarchy in Jerusalem. I used to attend his conferences on an almost daily basis, wherein I made the acquaintance of pilgrims from all four corners of the world. To those pilgrims I spoke of the archbishop Capucci, of the significance, the importance, and the unique character of global engagement in the Palestinian cause, and of the difficulties the latter had had to bear the cross of in the process. And so, I personally believe myself to be Mgr. Capucci's pupil.

The late archbishop was born in Aleppo, the cradle of resistance, on the 2nd of March 1922. He was ordained Aleppo's Basilian monastic monk. In 1947, he was ordained priest, and ultimately head of Aleppo's Basilian monastery (from 1962 to 1965); thus and so, he partook in the Vatican's second council. He was the last of the Patriarchal Church of the Melkite Catholics' bishops to participate in the Council. In 1965, he was ordained bishop by patriarch Maximos IV Sayegh; the episcopal ordainment was carried out with the assistance of Mgr. George Guargios Hakim, bishop to Haifa, Nazareth, and the whole of Galilee, who later became patriarch Maximos V. He was later on named General Patriarchal bishop to Jerusalem, as successor to the deceased Mgr. Gabriel Abu Saada in 1965.

In 1974, he was apprehended by the Israeli occupation authorities, and sentenced to twelve years, three of which he served in a narrow individual cell in Israeli prisons. It was only through the intervention of the late Pope Paul VI and the heads of the churches of Jerusalem in unison, that he was granted freedom in 1977 and I personally welcomed

12 - Death

him at the airport in Rome. The late patriarch Maximos V later on named him catholic apostolical visitor to western Europe until 1999. He remained in tenure as patriarchal vicar to Jerusalem until his dying day, as I deemed it wise not to abide by a system that coerces bishops into resigning at the age of seventy-five. I also asked the late patriarch Maximos V Hakim to postpone my ordainment as bishop out of respect for my brother and friend Mgr. Capucci. Following his banishment from Jerusalem, he remained in exile in Rome. He paid not a single visit to any Arab country prior to the expiration of his twelve-year sentence in 1986. His first visit was to Syria, where he was welcomed as a hero.

Mgr. Hilarion, monk of Aleppo, dedicated his life to the Lord with three wishes at heart, yet his greatest and most unique wish remained Palestine. Ever since his appointment as patriarchal vicar to Jerusalem in 1965, he grew into a symbol of the Palestinian cause. He dedicated his life to serving the Palestinian people in their homeland and wherever else they had been displaced to, across the Arab countries and the world. The Palestinian cause had become his very own. During his illustrious speech at the Greek Catholic school of Beit Hanania, he declared that Palestine was mother to all of his children. His words set the Palestinian people's sentiments ablaze, and in turn, a slew of maneuvers were launched with the purpose of arresting and incarcerating him. He was apprehended on the morning of August 8 and subsequently tried in Jerusalem and sentenced to twelve years in prison.

The deceased was really a champion of the Palestinian cause. He continued to defend it until the last breath of his life. He continued to give lectures, traveling to many Arab and European countries to keep abreast of the cause and the rights of the Palestinian people, both Muslims and Christians, persevering with courage, pride and his famous eloquence in Arabic and French.

In the Name of God

Capucci repeated his desire to return to Palestine to meet his Palestinian children, to be near them and share their pain and suffering. He put in a great effort to obtain all kinds of assistance to support Palestinian institutions, particularly social institutions in Jerusalem and the West Bank. He has become a symbol and a high mark of the Palestine cause. I tried during my service in Jerusalem to organize for him a visit to his beloved city, but in vain. Many activists were allowed to return to Jerusalem, but not him, because his return meant a great deal, both locally and globally.

The struggle of our beloved Archbishop Hilarion, his struggle and his sacrifices, are a source of pride for Palestine, Syria and the Arab homeland, as well as the Church of Melkite Catholics. As we say farewell to this great fighter, we remember other bishops who stood up in the defence of the Palestinian cause: Bishop Gregoire Hajjar (1901-1940) Bishop of Acre, Haifa, Nazareth and all the Galilee, who was killed under mysterious circumstances on his return from Jerusalem to Haifa after attending a conference in support of the Palestinian cause, and Bishop Gabriel Abu Saada, from Beit Sahour (near Bethlehem) vicar patriarchal general in Jerusalem (1946-1965). We even say that the defence of the Palestinian cause is the heritage of the Roman Catholic Church. It has been marked by a large number of bishops supporting the Palestinian question and Arab causes in general. The Catholic Church in particular, in the person of the Pope, offers the greatest support and dedication to the Palestinian cause. Pope Francis considered justice for the Palestinians as the key to peace (Amman - 24 May 2014).

Capucci was a fighter for freedom as well as an established man of prayer and spirituality. He entered an isolated cell on Sunday, January 26, 1975, with only a small table near the bed on which the Holy Bible, a cup and a tray were placed. He celebrated mass every day and always observed a precise daily agenda, with hours strictly regulated for the fulfilment

12 - Death

of his prayers and all the details of his life. And from that tiny cell, he used to communicate with the Arab heads of state in a hidden way from the director of the prison!

My semi-weekly visits to his cell lasted from two to three hours. His meetings and lessons were courses in evangelical spirituality, patriotism and piety, patience and submission to the will of Christ the Saviour, and trust in God. He repeated: "God is patient, but He does not neglect." He encouraged us and kept our morale high, and his local and international visitors, clerics and others, admired the strength of his faith and determination.

He got out of jail wearing all his episcopal clothes kissing the land of Palestine for the last time before boarding the plane for Rome on November 6, 1977. He was accompanied by Archbishop Maximos Saloum and the Apostolic Nuncio. I had preceded him with His Beatitude Patriarch Maximos V Hakim and we welcomed him with the Palestinian community at Rome airport.

Indeed, our late archbishop was a man of faith and prayer. He often described himself of Syrian origin and a Palestinian fighter with an Arab identity. Archbishop Capucci's weapon was prayer and high morale. It represents the dedication to the Palestinian cause. He was a Syrian Arab global figure. We must have a Capucci today as we did yesterday. We need people like him in any honest and sincere defence of the Palestinian cause or Arab issues, even global ones.

We bid farewell to this great man of Galilee with our holy prayers, and we ask our Saviour, Jesus Christ, to grant him glory like those who came before him, with faith, hope, love, righteousness of worship, impartially and with humility, apostolic zeal and pure life."

News of Capucci's death drew mixed reactions. His detractors, mainly Israelis, were gladdened by the news; others were more cautious and prudent. The Western press was particularly tactful. It maintained a neutral position by confining its obituaries to Capucci's adventurous life without calling him "terrorist" or eulogizing him as a "hero." A desire not to upset Israel or the Vatican probably influenced the framing of its reaction.

Elsewhere, the reaction was mostly positive. Capucci was hailed as a "freedom fighter" and a "revolutionary hero" who risked his life for his country and beliefs. Despite the onset of severe political and military instability in the Middle East, almost every government in the Arab and Islamic world paid tribute to Capucci's unwavering spirit and dedication to the Palestine cause. He was acclaimed as a courageous advocate for humanitarian causes: both local and international.

Yet, of all the tributes that flowed, one captured the quintessence of Capucci. The Italian journalist, Alberto Palladino, wrote:

> Capucci was a man with the force of a lion, framed by his full beard, and at the service of peace in his beloved Middle East and the entire world. He was a rare man, one of those who looks you in the eye because he knows he has nothing to hide, and much to teach. He taught above all with silence, and with the example of a life spent for the cause of the least, those least among us who won't give up in the face of either the powerful or the terrorist.

When Hilarion Capucci passed away, everyone said "rest in peace." This is unlikely to happen, even in Heaven, until the day that Jerusalem is declared as the undivided capital of a liberated Palestine. Anything short of this is a gross betrayal of Capucci.

Index

A
Abdallah, Georges Ibrahim 228
Abdel Nasser, Gamal 27
Abdel-Hamid, Al-Shafei 185
Abu Firas, Mustafa 37, 40, 43, 46-48, 50, 72
Abu Jihad 37-38, 72
Abu Mizar, Abdel Muhsin 194
Abu Saada, Gabriel 244, 246
Agence France-Presse 92
Al-Akaila, Mai 243
Al-Ashqar, Boulos 57-58, 101
Al-Assad, Bashar 229-230
Al-Assad, Hafez 101, 191-194, 196, 198, 203-204
Al-Atrash, Qadri 185
Al-Bakr, Ahmed Hassan 175
Al-Fahoum, Khaled 197
Al-Halabi, Mohammed Ali 197
Al-Hout, Shafiq 185
Al-Kayyali, Abdulwahab 162, 171
Al-Quwatli, Shukri 27
Al-Sarraj, Abdel Hamid 27-29
Al-Sharaa, Farouk 185
Alitalia Airways 179, 181
American-Arab Anti-Discrimination Committee (ADC) 234
Amwas 124
Aqsa Mosque 120-122, 195, 234
Arab Bar Association 50
Azzam, Mansour 230

B
Bach, Gabriel 67
Balfour Declaration 44, 207
Basel Conference 209
Basilian Aleppian Order 22, 30
Basilian Aleppian School 22-23
Bayt al-Maqdis Conference 233
Begin, Menachem 7, 24, 206
Beit Lid 62
Beit Nuba 124
Beit Shemesh Prison 55, 62

Ben-Gurion, David 26
Ben-Porat, Miriam 67
Bernawy, Fatima 194
Bethlehem Cave 91
Black September Organization 38
Bourget, Christian 50, 67-68
Bourguiba, Habib 208
Bush, George 229

C
Caesarea of Palestine 120, 135, 153, 164, 167, 170, 172-173
Camp David 202, 206-208, 211-214, 216, 218
Carew, William 55, 57, 99-101, 180, 182
Carter, Jimmy 206, 208, 214
Casaroli, Agostino 99
Cedar Medal of Honor 243
Church of the Holy Sepulcher 43, 121-122, 195
Church of the Nativity 121-122, 130
CIA 232
Cohen, Eli 100
Collège des Frères 20, 43, 60, 73-74
Committee for Solidarity with Arab and Middle Eastern Political Prisoners 228
Coussa, Gabriel 22

D
Darwish, Mahmoud 194
Daugherty, William J. 232
Deir al-Ahmar 71
Deir el-Chir Monastery 22, 26, 30
Deir Yassin 26, 74
Dormition of Our Lady 230
Dumas, Roland 50, 67-68

E
Eastern Orthodox Church 14
Entebbe Airport 96-97

F
Fairuz 105
Fatah 38, 67, 74, 181
Fattal, Antoine 185
Feast of St. Maximos 127
Free Gaza Movement 235
French Hospital 32

Index

G
Gaddafi 230
Garwan, Elias 185
Gate of Remission (Bab al-Huttah) 32
Gaza 11, 120, 209, 211, 215, 225, 235
Geneva Convention 70, 90
German Sisters monastery 189
Global Ethic Foundation 237
Global March to Jerusalem 235-236
Golan Heights 233
Gregory, Peter 41, 54
Gulf War 228

H
Habash, George 142, 158, 162, 171
Hadid , Mahmoud 197
Haganah 26
Hague Convention 11
Halawi, Ahmad 39
Hammad, Nimr 185
Haram al-Sharif 120
Hariri, Rafiq 230
Hawatmeh, Nayef 142, 162, 171
Hebron Gate 40
Helou, Charles 39
Hussein, Saddam 228

I
InterContinental Hotel 108
International Zionist Organization 26
Irgun 24, 26
Israeli Ministry of Religions 40
Iwan of Khosrow 79

J
Jesus Christ 13, 15, 17, 25, 67, 81–83, 91, 109, 120, 137, 140, 229, 238, 247
Jibril, Ahmed 142, 162, 171
Jordan River 36
Judaization 12-13, 18, 33, 70-71, 124, 213, 220, 225, 232, 236, 240
Jumblatt, Kamal 172-173
Jumblatt, Waleed 173

K
Kaddoumi, Farouk 186
Kafr Qasim 26, 74
Katzir, Ephraim 7, 179

Kelly, David 107, 186
Kfar Yuna 62-65, 85-87, 92-93, 108
King Abdullah 230
King David Hotel 23-24, 59, 72, 74
King Khaled bin Abdulaziz Al-Saud 174
Kissinger, Henry 44, 59, 73
Küng, Hans 237

L
Lahham, Patriarch Gregorius III 185, 243
Le Mouvement Quebecois pour Combattre le Racisme 231
Lebanese Order of the Sisters of the Cross 192
Litani River 155
Lod Airport 179

M
Malaabi, Suhail 60, 72-73
Mehlis Report 230
Melhem, Adib 194
Melkite Catholic Church 13
Middle East Airlines (MEA) 39
Mirza, Ismail 185
Mohsen, Zuhair 142, 162, 171
Monsignor Monterezzi 99, 182
Muslim Brotherhood 208

N
Nakbah 111
Naqoura 43-45
Nasrallah, Naqoula 41
National Nahda School 26

P
Palestine Liberation Organization (PLO) 12, 41, 154, 164, 170, 172, 227
Palestinian National Council 168, 191-199
Palladino, Alberto 117, 248
Pasha, Habib 57-58
Patriarch Maximus Hakim 95, 180
Pellegrini, Michele 32
Perez, Carlos Andres 190
Pontius Pilate 67
Pope Paul VI 99, 112, 126, 179, 189, 244

Q
Qaouq, Nabil 234
Quneitra 39, 212-213, 217, 219

Index

R
Rabin, Yitzhak 40
Ramadan War 134, 157, 163, 174 (Delete in 1973)
Ramleh prison 86-89, 93, 117-118, 127, 135, 143, 150, 154, 164, 168, 170-175, 179, 186
Reagan, Ronald 228
Red Sultan 28
Roman Catholic Patriarchate 50
Roman Catholic Synod 57
Rosary Sisters of Jordan 103

S
Sabra, Mohammad 185
Sadat, Anwar 30, 163, 206, 208, 210, 214
Safawi, Salim 77
Saint Anne's Seminary 23-24
Salloum, Maximus 180, 182, 185
Samaan, Bartholamus 57-58
Shaaban, Bouthaina 230
Shalala, Rafik 180-181
Sharon, Ariel 231
Shehadah, Aziz 50, 67-68, 79, 81
Six Day War 235l
Song of Songs 120
Spellman, Francis 17
St. Savior Basilian Order of Aleppo 243
Sykes-Picot Agreement 207
Symposium on the Concept of Monotheism 237-241

T
Talhouni, Bahjat 39
Tulkarm Governorate 62

U
United Arab Republic (UAR) 27-28
United Nations 124, 208, 216

V
Via Dolorosa 121-122, 146

W
Wailing Wall 59
Washington resolution 207, 214
Weber, Max 16
West Bank 7, 33, 35-36, 38-41, 45, 50, 54, 66, 70, 74, 76, 103, 120-124, 139, 209, 211, 215, 219, 246
Women's League 33

Y
Yalu 124

Z
Zahra Gate 40
Zarathustra 107

www.ingramcontent.com/pod-product-compliance
Lightning Source LLC
Chambersburg PA
CBHW050137170426
43197CB00011B/1865